A Cord of Light

A True Story
of Courage, Healing,
and Timeless Love.

Jane E. Bardon, Ph.D.

Cover design by Jane E. Bardon, Ph.D.

Printed in the United States of America

First printing: October, 1998

ISBN 0-966-7964-0-3
LCCN 98-93931

Printed and bound by Printing Images, Inc., Rockville, MD

Additional copies can be ordered by sending a check or
money order for $13.95 plus $2.00 for postage and handling
to the address below. Maryland residents please add $.70 sales tax.

Dr. Jane E. Bardon
P.O. Box 882
Silver Spring, MD 20918

To the soulmate who helped me remember that love is eternal.

ACKNOWLEDGMENTS

First and foremost, I would like to thank the officials of the U.S. Agency for International Development, who were responsible for eliminating my position during the Reduction in Force (RIF). Without the RIF, I would still be carrying this amazing story in my head and would be telling myself that I was too busy to write it down. Thanks are also due the U.S. government for providing funds and facilities for my career transition.

I am grateful to my family and friends, who kept me from getting distracted by frequently asking about the status of the book and assuring me that they wanted to read it. I am very grateful for the use of the National Library of Medicine in Bethesda, MD, where I spent many hours reading about personality development and disorders.

Dr. Janet Cunningham facilitated the explorations into my unconscious, provided excellent insights, and encouraged me to write this story. Dr. Anne Highland, a friend of many years, provided additional insights and assistance, and answered numerous questions. Dr. Brad Blanton taught me the basics of Gestalt therapy, pressured me to complete the book, and gave a free lecture on telling the truth at the U.S. State Department.

Dr. Walter Eubanks allowed me to use his laser printer during the initial drafts. John Lewis provided encouraging words and useful advice and got me in touch with Kay Garrett, who did an excellent editing job. Bill Myers took the time to read the final draft and to provide useful comments.

Last, but not least, I am grateful for the miracle of my life and of the lives of those who grace these pages. Their names have been changed to protect their privacy. As Chief Seattle said more than one hundred years ago, "We did not weave the web of life, we are merely a strand in it. Whatever we do to the web, we do to ourselves."

INTRODUCTION

If somebody had told me before August 3, 1992, that I would become a firm believer in love and God, I would have laughed in his/her face. I was a big Mr. Spock fan, i.e. I worshiped logic. I went to church once in a while and recited the Lord's prayer, but it did not resonate with me, partly because of the gender issue. Love was terra incognita. I cut off my feelings and got into my head at a young age in order to survive. At the same time, I declared that there was no God.

It took a long time and a few determined people for me to be able to enunciate the words "I love you," but there was no feeling attached to them. My secret opinion of men was that they were scum good for only one thing. I could see myself bowing to society's pressure and marrying one, but having children was inconceivable, primarily because of two reasons: 1) I did not want to repeat my painful childhood; and 2) I did not want a long-term bond with a man.

The irony in this was that I had always been popular with the male gender. As a tomboy who had easily passed the most important tests of boyhood, I was accepted by my peers as an honorary boy. Being a curvaceous blonde in a Mediterranean country, insured a slew of fans during adolescence. A possessive father, who threatened to do bodily harm to anyone who came near me, increased my desirability. By age nineteen, I had already turned down two marriage proposals. Three years later, a disappointed suitor declared to anyone who would listen that I had a steel pump instead of a heart. So, how did Ms. Steel Pump change to Dr. Warm Heart?

It was a lengthy process fueled by my determination to know myself, my life's purpose, and how it fit into a bigger whole. The process was aided by my insatiable curiosity and willingness to take risks. My experience has proven true the statement in the Bible, "Seek and ye shall find. Knock and it shall be opened unto you." My experience also proves that when one finds love, one is bound to find God. Love is uplifting, not something one falls into. Fear, however, is precisely what drags one down. Being in love, rather than in fear, is a choice. Whoever makes this choice is transformed. The butterfly on the cover symbolizes transformation.

Jane Elias Bardon
Silver Spring, MD
September 5, 1998

TABLE OF CONTENTS

CHAPTER ONE
Central Asia Beckons

Turkish Airlines Flight 630 touched down at Baku, Azerbaijan as scheduled. The pilot parked the plane on the tarmac close to a rundown building with the Azeri flag flying in front. Stairs were wheeled to the front door and the flight attendant opened it, letting in a blast of hot air. After the Baku passengers deplaned, my colleague Tim and I got up and stood by the open door for a better view. My excitement mounted at the thought of being in the former Soviet Union. It was Monday, August 3, 1992. The United States had established embassies in the New Independent States (NIS) the previous March. Our delegation was headed to Central Asia to start up technical assistance projects in the region.

A big yellow truck pulled up next to the plane and the luggage was loaded manually into it. Afterwards, the truck was driven and parked next to the building, where the truck bed was elevated, and the luggage was unloaded, piece by piece, onto a second story deck. Rumor had it that sometimes people arrived in Tashkent or Alma Ata to find out that their luggage had been unloaded in Baku. Tim's fancy suitcases were more of a theft target than mine. I had borrowed my boyfriend Gerry's twenty-year-old Samsonite suitcase with the combination lock and had a change of clothes and my valuables in the carry on.

Cleaning women wearing scarves came on board carrying plastic bags, looking more like peasants than airport employees. The Boeing 737 took off shortly after the cleaning ladies deplaned. Next stop was Tashkent, Uzbekistan, our delegation's first stop in Central Asia. Tim followed delegation head Sean Scaggville's example and started to snooze right after take off. Since most of the passengers had gotten off in Baku, Tim, Sean, and I had three seats each.

I stretched out thinking how welcome this break from the Washington grind was. Working for the NIS Task Force at the Agency for International Development (AID) was like being in the eye of a hurricane. The NIS Task Force, created by President Bush to deliver assistance to the Former Soviet Union, was housed in the State Department. The hours were grueling, but that was okay with me. Being in the eye of a storm was an environment in which I thrived. I badly wanted to be NIS Economic Restructuring chief, but the job had gone to Sean. This trip was part of his orientation. He was scheduled to come on board in September. I had six weeks to impress him and get the deputy job. Things had gotten off to a bad start, however. Sean had only agreed to come to Central Asia after his own trip to Russia and Ukraine had fallen through. Not yet officially on board, Sean had demonstrated a lack of political sense. The latter was crucial to survival in a highly visible and politically sensitive program like the NIS restructuring. Having spent five years as U.S. Treasury desk officer for Mexico at the height of the Latin debt crisis, I had developed strong political instincts. I did not pick fights I couldn't win and never floated lead balloons. Not yet officially on board, Sean had already done that, giving me a bad feeling.

1

My thoughts drifted to Gerry, my boyfriend of seven years. The parents on both sides were dropping hints about when we would tie the knot. My mother was especially impressed with the neat house Gerry kept. He could cook and was very handy around the house. My girlfriends thought Gerry was a hunk: tall, blond, blue eyed, really built. What was I waiting for? I was waiting for things to click and they hadn't. Every time I visualized being asked: "Do you take this man to be your lawful wedded husband?" My inner voice always answered with a resounding "No." It was totally irrational. Gerry was a kind, responsible, honest man. What more could I want? It was fish or cut bait time. I took out my pocket calendar and considered possible wedding days. I settled on June 27, 1993, but still had reservations. God, I thought, please send me a sign, if I'm doing the right thing.

The plane approached Tashkent, the capital of Uzbekistan. This was the heart of Central Asia. Indiana Jones territory. Images of ancient caravans traveling to and from China on the Silk Road flashed through my mind. I could not wait to see bazaars filled with exotic people, foods, and spices, and speaking exotic languages. The plane landed and taxied among several planes with Aeroflot markings parked on the tarmac. New airlines were formed by the new countries expropriating Aeroflot planes that happened to be parked in their territory at the time independence was declared. And from the look of things, Uzbekistan had done quite well in the expropriation business. But how good are those planes? We would find out in about seventy two hours when we flew to neighboring Bishkek, Kyrgyzstan.

It was over 100 degrees Fahrenheit when we stepped out onto the tarmac. Someone said the temperature was actually 120, as we boarded the bus for the short ride to the arrivals building. Inside, there was only one guy checking passports. Depending on how fussy he was, this could take hours. Fortunately, we already had visas and an embassy officer was waiting. A man with a graying mustache, receding hairline, and a button down shirt was looking at me from the other side of the passport line.

"Are you Paul Norris?" I asked.

He nodded yes.

"Janet Bradley. We're babes in the woods around here."

"Not to worry," Norris reassured me. "Everything is on track. We have two cars waiting to take you to your hotel."

While we were waiting for our luggage, Norris gave us our schedule. Some meetings had to be confirmed, but it was very full otherwise. He also said that Ivan Bergman, the consultant I had hired, was already at the hotel waiting for us. He had flown in from Moscow that morning. I glanced at the first activity on the schedule:

19:00 Dinner with Charge Marcus Metamarro and Emboffs.

The Charge was probably a boring old boozer; the last person on earth I wanted to spend time with. In my line of work, cocktail parties and dinners were part of the job. After a while, however, they were hard to take. The cars pulled up in front of the Hotel Uzbekistan (the only game in town for foreigners) and Norris helped us check in. It was almost 6:00 p.m. Barely time for a swim before dinner.

"How about a swim before dinner? I'm melting," Tim said.

2

"It's on the top of my list," I replied.

"See you in a few at the pool," Tim called out as he walked toward the elevator.

A few minutes later, Tim and I were standing, all suited up, at the edge of the pool looking skeptically at the water. It looked like the Chesapeake Bay, green and dark. Four Russian soldiers were playing cards by the pool, but nobody was swimming.

"What do you think, Tim?" I asked. "Should we chance it? It looks awfully dirty. I would hate to get sick on my first day in Central Asia."

"Let's see," Tim said. " If we keep your heads above water, we won't have to worry about germs getting into our eyes, ears, nose, and mouth. You have goggles besides. We don't have open wounds. This leaves the below the waist orifices. Our chances for infection are two out of six. I say pray and dive in."

"Okay. What the heck," I laughed. "My prayer response is great."

Needless to say, we did not keep our heads above water, so we had to pray twice as hard. Tim was not into doing laps and got out shortly.

"Don't forget. Dinner with the Charge in a few minutes," he called out, as he was leaving.

I was running a few minutes late as I stepped out of the elevator into the lobby. A tall, thin, dark-haired man talking to my travel companions caught my eye. He was wearing a light blue golf shirt and carrying a navy blue backpack. As soon as I saw him, the following thoughts went through my head in rapid succession: Kindred spirit. This is the man I'm going to marry. Oh, it's you. What took you so long to find me? This is nuts. I've never seen this man before in my life.

At that moment, two pictures from ancient times flashed through my mind. In the first one, two teenagers, a boy and a girl, dressed in white togas were riding a golden color chariot pulled by a white horse. In the second picture, a young, Asian couple was kneeling on a Chinese-style, mahogany poster bed. They were slightly built, barely past puberty. They were embracing, naked. The woman was tilting her head back and the man was kissing her neck. The room had dark brown walls and was illuminated by torches. My knees turned to rubber. Oh, my God, I thought. I'm cracking up. I've been working too hard.

I took a deep breath and walked to the other end of the lobby toward the group of Americans. As I approached the group, the dark-haired man looked at me and smiled. I felt the urge to put my arms around him and say: "I'm so glad you've finally come."

With almost superhuman effort, I controlled myself. I didn't want anyone to think I was around the bend.

"Well, here's Janet, finally," Tim exclaimed.

Ivan Bergman, ever the flatterer, remarked, "Boss, you look great."

"She brought along a cheerleader," Sean observed.

The dark-haired man laughed and said, "Hello. I'm Marcus Metamarro, the Charge d' Affaires here."

"You're the Charge?!! I...I expected someone more... ah more... mature," I stammered.

Everyone burst out laughing.

3

"We should write down the time and date," Tim commented. "It's not often that Janet is at a loss for words."

The other woman in the group introduced herself.

"Hi. I'm Diane Fein. I also work at the Embassy."

"Diane and I are old buddies," Tim explained. "We met the last time I was here."

"You know Paul Norris?" Marcus asked me.

"Yes, of course. We met at the airport."

"Shall we go then?" Marcus said. "We're going to the Korean restaurant on the top floor."

In the elevator, I was looking at Marcus thinking. OK, so he's not a traveling student. Maybe he's here temporarily like Norris. Better check.

"Are you stationed here, or are you here on TDY (temporary duty) like Paul?"

"Oh, no. I'll be here for two years. I just arrived last month," Marcus replied with a smile.

I got goose bumps. I knew beyond the shadow of a doubt that this was no chance encounter. But what did it all mean? My analytical mind got into gear and started observing Marcus. He was in his thirties, thirty seven tops. Athletic, runner for sure, maybe skier. He talked and walked fast like me. We got to the top floor and entered the restaurant passing the bar on our right. Some guys were sitting at the bar smoking.

"What a filthy habit," Marcus remarked. "Unfortunately, there's a lot of this going on around here, partly courtesy of U.S. tobacco companies."

Non-smoker, I thought approvingly.

We asked for a table for seven and the waiter put two tables together.

"May we order for you?" Diane asked. "They don't speak English around here."

"Ivan is a native Russian speaker. Janet also speaks Russian," Sean announced.

"Oh, go ahead. You know what's good around here," I said.

"How about kapamaki?" Marcus suggested.

"Good idea. I love Japanese food," I said.

"Marcus is vegetarian," Diane announced to the group.

"Really?" I exclaimed. "I'm quasi-vegetarian. I eat seafood and on Thanksgiving I have a bite of turkey."

"Anything to drink?" asked Diane. "There's imported beer."

"I'm a terrible drinker," Marcus said. "One beer is my limit."

"This must be a horrible disadvantage in the Foreign Service," I remarked.

Bradley, I thought, you were wrong on all counts on this one. He's certainly not old and certainly not a boozer. And sure as hell not boring. Nobody else has turned your knees to rubber before.

The beers came first, then the food. Marcus started wolfing down his food at the same speed I was. I was getting the eerie feeling of seeing myself in him. I was shaky before and the beer made things worse. How could this be? No other human being had ever had this effect on me before. Something about him seemed so familiar. And yet, it wasn't his body. In a flash of insight, I knew. It was his

4

energy. That's what was familiar about him. For the first time in my life, I felt I was on the same wave length with someone. And this happened in Tashkent, of all places. I could barely follow the conversation. They were talking shop. I interjected a mundane observation here and there, but my mind was drifting.

"Janet, are you OK?" Tim asked.

"Yes, fine. The jet lag is getting to me, I guess. I don't do west to east travel well, although the stop in Istanbul helped."

"We'd better go soon," Marcus said. "We have a big day tomorrow. Meetings all day, then a dinner hosted by the Foreign Ministry. You all better get a good night's sleep."

It was 9:30 when we got up to leave. The restaurant had live entertainment that started at 9:00. A woman dressed in a tiger suit was cracking a whip. Was she the tiger, or the tiger tamer? Strange show. We started walking out, as the band was playing Hello Dolly. Marcus grabbed Diane and did a few dance steps with her. I watched, feeling a twinge of jealousy.

Norris, who lived in the hotel, and our delegation agreed to meet for breakfast in the hotel restaurant the following morning at 8:00. Our first meeting was at the embassy at 9:00 with Marcus. I said good night to everyone, went to my room, and looked in the mirror. My face was flushed. I tried to make sense of what had happened, but I was on uncharted territory.

"I wonder if he's married? Somehow, I know he's not. A handsome, intelligent man in his thirties, who's still single. This may be another thing we have in common."

I smiled into the mirror and switched off the light.

* * *

The following morning, we discovered that the breakfast menu was more extensive than we had expected. There was bread, cheese, yogurt, butter, jam, eggs, and tea. To my delight, they had green tea, a drink I had gotten in the habit of drinking in Japan the previous year. We finished breakfast and went into the lobby. Marcus was waiting at the bar.

"I thought we were meeting at the embassy," I said, puzzled.

"I changed my mind," he explained. "We can meet quickly here and then go directly to the Foreign Affairs Ministry."

A few minutes later we were on our way to the Foreign Affairs Ministry. It was already hot and I removed my jacket. At the meeting, I continued to observe Marcus. His sporty, brown shoes with the thick rubber soles revealed a practical nature. He spoke excellent Russian. At the conclusion of the second meeting, as we were walking downstairs, Marcus asked, "How about lunch at the dachas? I'll show you where I live."

"I'd like that," Tim said, "but I have to go to the Embassy to catch up on some work."

"You do that Tim," I said. "I want to see the dachas."

The dachas were located in an orchard ten kilometers north of Tashkent. In addition to the dachas, the compound included an entertainment center and a swimming pool.

"This used to be a playground for senior Communist Party officials," Marcus

5

explained. "The Department leased the dachas as temporary housing for Embassy personnel."

We took two cars to get there. Sean, Marcus, Ivan, and I rode in one. Paul, Diane, and the interpreter rode in the other one. Marcus sat in the back seat between Sean and me. Ivan was in the front, next to the driver.

I wonder if he skis, I thought, looking at Marcus, who was engrossed in conversation with Sean.

"Is there skiing around here?" I asked.

Marcus turned and said, "My skis are coming."

I didn't ask whether his skis were downhill, or cross-country. In my mind, I got a picture of both.

At lunch, in the restaurant of the compound, I sat on Marcus's left. He ordered vegetarian soups for himself, Diane, and me.

"Janet speaks seven languages," Sean volunteered.

"Really," Marcus marveled. "That's quite unusual for an American."

"Well, I'm not the run of the mill gringo. I grew up in Greece, and did a stint in Italy," I said.

"By your looks and your accent, I wouldn't have guessed Greece," Diane remarked.

"Well, I'm German on my mother's side," I explained. "To make a long story short, I'm a living international affair."

Everyone laughed.

"I went to school in Italy," Marcus revealed.

"SAIS, Bologna Center?" I asked.

"Why, yes. How did you know?" Marcus looked at me, his blue eyes wide.

"I went to the same school. Soviet studies?"

"Yes. You too? That's amazing," Marcus said. "I was there in '79. When were you there?"

"'75. How did you like it?"

"I loved it," Marcus said. "It's incredible I haven't been back. What a coincidence to meet here someone who went to SAIS, Bologna."

"I didn't finish though," I went on. "I wanted something quantitative, so I dropped out the second year and enrolled in a Ph.D. program in Economics."

"Are you kidding? I was glad there were no numbers in that program. I'm definitely not a numbers man," Marcus commented.

"Well, you know what they say: 'Figures lie and liars figure,' but that's what I wanted to do at the time," I said.

Marcus and I spent the rest of lunch reminiscing about Italy and other countries we had visited. Everybody else had faded into the background.

After lunch, Marcus suggested we go for a ride around the compound and invited us to see his dacha. It was spacious, but far from luxurious. I imagined something cute, made out of wood, like Siberian houses I had seen pictures of. It was nothing like that. It was stucco with a flat roof. I guessed that wood was scarce in a country that was mostly desert.

"Photo op," I said, as we were leaving Marcus's dacha.

While taking a picture of the group, I noticed that Marcus seemed uncomfortable in front of the camera. He stood apart from the others, right hand in his pocket, a faraway look on his face. Odd. I gave the camera to Tatiana, the interpreter, and posed with the others.

We had another whirlwind of meetings after lunch. Marcus arranged to sit next to me in every meeting. As we were walking to the Finance Ministry from the Privatization Committee, he walked up to me and asked, "What did you say your name was?"

I looked at him astonished. I was the only woman on the delegation and we had been talking practically non-stop since last night. How was it possible that he did not remember my name?

"Bradley. Janet Bradley. It was in the country clearance cable you approved," I said.

By the last meeting, I was awfully tired, hot, and thirsty. We had to use interpreters, so the meetings were going very slowly. I really wanted some water. At that precise moment, Marcus reached for the pitcher of water to his left, filled a cup and gave it to me. I took it wide-eyed, whispering, "Thank you."

What's going on here? Was Marcus reading my mind? I blushed at my thoughts.

Mercifully, the meeting ended shortly thereafter. By then, it was after 6:00 and our next function, a dinner hosted by the Foreign Ministry, was at 7:00. There was no time to go to the hotel and change. I got into the car. Just what I needed, an official dinner without the benefit of a shower. Maybe I could sneak into the bathroom before dinner and wash up.

The Navrus restaurant was on a huge square downtown. A group of Uzbek officials waited for us and shook hands at the bottom of a staircase. We climbed a flight of stairs covered with the ever popular, politically correct, red carpet and found ourselves in a foyer with a coat check. I excused myself and found the bathroom. I washed up as best I could, then followed the noise to the private room reserved for the dinner. A large table, overflowing with food, was in the center of the room. No cheap cocktail party this.

I sat across from Marcus between two Foreign Ministry officials who kept filling my plate with the local delicacies. I recognized the vegetables, but had no clue as to what the other stuff was. For the good of my country, I was violating my dietary code. I noticed, however, that Marcus did not violate his vegetarian regime. Plate after plate of food appeared in front of us. Toast after toast was called. The heat, alcohol, and food took their toll on my mood, but I noticed that Sean seemed to thrive on playing the part of diplomat.

Mercifully, the dinner ended before I ran out of patience. Marcus ushered me into his car, then slipped into the back seat next to me. The car windows were open and a pleasant breeze played through my hair. I pushed flying strands of hair from my face and turned to Marcus.

"Have you seen the Aral Sea?" I asked. "I did a paper on it when I was an undergrad. I want to know how much it's shrunk."

"No, not yet," Marcus said, smiling. "Access is very tightly controlled."

"Well, then it must be in far worse shape than we think. Are you going to come to our meetings tomorrow?"

"No, I can't. I have to go to Termez for a ceremony in connection with Operation Provide Hope."

"Really? I thought that was over earlier this year," I said.

"This is Part Two. I have to get up at 4:30 to catch a 7:00 o' clock flight."

"Wow! You won't get much sleep then," I said. "Do you always work this hard?"

"I seem to," Marcus admitted.

Unfortunately, we soon arrived at the Hotel Uzbekistan. I was in a near panic. This is it. He's not going to be around tomorrow and we're leaving Thursday. I may never see him again.

To my surprise, Marcus followed us inside the hotel. We had a short meeting at the bar downstairs. Marcus wanted to know what kind of reporting we wanted and how we were going to clear the cables. It was agreed that he would send an OI (official informal) to Alma Ata and, after we looked it over, it would be sent out of Tashkent. All too soon, it was time to say good night. I shook Marcus's hand. "Thank you so much for all you've done for us," I said. "I'll be in touch about the projects. Do you have my card?"

"I think so," Marcus replied.

"Here's another one, just in case," I said, handing it to him. "Good luck tomorrow."

As I walked to my room, I realized that Marcus was Gerry's opposite. Getting along with Gerry was easy. He always deferred to me. But it had become awfully boring. I would never be bored with someone like Marcus. The risk there was getting burnt by the fireworks. It was a risk I was willing to take.

* * *

Early in the morning, I woke up with a stomach ache, cramps, nausea, and diarrhea. I was paying the price for being diplomatic the night before and not questioning what was being served. I took some Imodium A-D pills and prayed for relief before the day's round of meetings. I also swore off meat for good.

I dressed and went to breakfast with my travel companions and Paul Norris. I wanted some tea and plain rice liberally sprinkled with lemon. These were sure fire diarrhea stoppers. The pills seemed not to be working. Unfortunately, neither rice nor lemon could be had that morning and I had to settle for bread and tea. I told my colleagues that I would have to skip today's meetings and concentrate on getting better.

Ivan, always full of opinions, said, "You made a fatal error, boss. You didn't drink any vodka. It kills everything."

"That's just it, Ivan," I explained. "I wanted to spare my brain cells and liver and thought I'd let my immune system deal with the germs."

Back in my room, between trips to the bathroom, I mulled over the events of the last two days. I was going to postpone my marriage to Gerry in order to get to know Marcus better. That much was for sure. I would immediately start the process of trying to get an assignment in Tashkent, although this would be awfully hard to do because Uzbekistan was not a priority country.

Mercifully, the diarrhea subsided toward the afternoon and I was able to get some sleep. I woke up when I heard a knock on the door. It was Tim. I put on my bathrobe and opened the door.

"How are you feeling? I brought you a Pepsi. Are you coming to dinner?"

"I feel a little better," I said. "But I'd better skip dinner. I'm afraid of ingesting more germs. I'll stick to bread."

"We have to leave for the airport tomorrow at noon. Sean wants to go to the bazaar in the morning. Do you want to come along?"

"Sure, if I'm strong enough. If not, I'd like you to get me some lemons," I replied. "I'll see you at breakfast in any event."

I slept rather well that night, but was surprised to see how weak I felt when I got up in the morning. It was to be expected, of course. I had hardly eaten anything the previous day. Thankfully, the diarrhea and the cramps had stopped. Some tea with bread and jam would give me a bit of energy.

Alaiski bazaar was a bustling place. I was fascinated by it. Dozens of people were selling flowers, fruits and vegetables, nuts, spices, and bread in open stalls. Little stores on the edges of the bazaar had meat, groceries, clothing, and household items. Most of the people had Asian features. The men wore little square black hats and western clothing. Most of the women, however, wore long flowing skirts with bloomers underneath. My search for lemons proved fruitful, although the price was outrageous by local standards: two for a dollar.

Back at the hotel, we got ready for the Bishkek portion of the trip. The flight to Kyrgyzstan, another former Soviet Republic, was considered a domestic flight under the old regime, so it departed from the domestic terminal. This was actually more pleasant than the dingy international terminal. It reminded me of an airport I had been to in the Caribbean. The shuttle bus came to take us to the plane; we were the only ones aboard. When we got to the plane, however, a whole crowd was waiting to get on board. Then I got the message: there were separate lounges and buses for foreigners and locals. A remnant of the old regime, no doubt.

The little turbo prop did fine. We landed in Bishkek at 1:15 and went to the front of the plane to collect our luggage. As I was walking toward the terminal, a tall, blond, stout man approached me.

"Hi. I'm Allen Marenko from the Embassy," he said. "Are you Janet Bradley?"

"In person," I said. "This is the rest of the team: Sean Scaggville, Tim Bassett, and Ivan Bergman. Thanks for meeting us."

"We did the best we could with appointments," Allen explained. "But it's August and a lot of people are on vacation. You're only staying until Saturday, aren't you?"

"Yes. We're driving to Alma Ata on Saturday morning and flying back to Istanbul on Tuesday."

Allen told us that the Embassy had made reservations for us at the Hotel Issyk Kul. It was the former Communist Party hotel a few minutes outside of town and offered the best accommodations.

The hotel looked magnificent on the outside. It was an L-shaped high-rise behind an impressive iron fence and gate, and had a wonderful view of the Ala Tau mountains. We got very excited. This looked much better than we had expected. We went to the registration desk and said we were the people for whom the U.S. Embassy had made reservations. We checked in and got receipts with the price of the rooms on them. Mine said 330 rubles per day. It must be a mistake, I thought. At, say, 140 rubles to the dollar, this works out to slightly over $2.

I hurried over to where my colleagues were standing, chatting.

"It's no mistake," Ivan assured me. "I double checked. This must be the old commie price. Enjoy it while you can."

"Wow! I can't believe it," I marveled. "What a bargain! This place looks much better than that dingy Hotel Uzbekistan. Now I feel ripped off for paying $13 over there. And look at these beautiful, snow-capped mountains. I wish we could stay longer."

Our rooms were on the fourth floor and all of them had mountain views, some better than others. My room was next to Ivan's. Sean and Tim were on the other side of the hallway. We changed into business suits and grabbed something to eat at the top floor bar. Our first meeting at the Ministry of Economy and Finance was at 4:00 and was over at 6:00. I expected another formal dinner, but found out that the Embassy had made dinner reservations for us and that was it. I felt let down.

"They treated us much better in Tashkent," I said on the way to the restaurant. "Marcus was with us from morning to night."

"That's because Marcus is married to his work," Sean retorted. "Normal people have to go home to their families after work. You were taken with him, weren't you?"

"Well," I said, "I think he's a dedicated FSO with lots of energy."

We found the restaurant and were led to a private room. Even so, the noise from the live entertainment was deafening. Cautious because of my recent close encounter with Central Asian microbes, I picked food that was safe. After dinner, we went back to the hotel and the guys went to the bar. I went to my room and made plans to call Marcus the following day. Then, I fell asleep with great anticipation.

In the morning, I got up early and went jogging in the direction of the mountains. There were mountain streams flowing on either side of the road in front of the hotel. The air was fresh and crisp. I knew Marcus would love it here. I couldn't wait to call him later in the day.

We stopped at the Embassy after lunch. Tim headed for the room with the satellite phone and I for an empty office with a phone. Fortunately, Allen was out and I was told I could use his office. Sean followed me.

"I'm calling Tashkent," I said. "I'm going to ask if they got the documents we asked for. Do you need anything?"

"Are you calling him?" Sean asked. "I'd better go to the other room."

I ignored him and dialed the phone.

"American Embassy," Diane answered.

"This is Janet Bradley calling from Bishkek. May I please speak with Marcus?"

"Just a minute, Janet," Diane replied. "He's right here."

"Marcus!" I said. "I can't believe these phones. I almost broke my finger dialing."

He laughed. "How are you feeling?"

"Much better. I went jogging this morning. It's great over here. There are mountain streams in front of the hotel. The air is cool and crisp. And our rooms are $2.30 a day! Have you been to Bishkek?"

"Not recently. I was there in 1986."

"Did you by any chance get the documents we requested from the Privatization Committee?"

"No, not yet. We're still trying," Marcus explained.

"Well, that takes care of business," I said. " Now, about fun. We're driving to Alma Ata tomorrow through the mountains. I don't know what the flights are like, but would you like to meet us here and drive with us?"

"I'd love to," Marcus said. "But I can't leave the country. I'm Charge."

"Bummer," I said. "Some other time, perhaps."

I hung up the phone and went to the reception area where Sean was sitting.

"Well," he said. "Is he coming to meet you in Alma Ata?"

"Boy, you're nosy," I said. "If you must know, he would love to, but he can't leave the country because he's Charge."

"Well, don't worry," Sean remarked. "I'm sure you'll be seeing more of him, somehow or other."

After our meetings that day, we took a sightseeing tour of Bishkek. The town lay 2,400 feet above sea level at the foot of the Kyrgyz Ala-Tau ridge. The Russians had named the city Frunze, after a Russian general who had been born there. After the breakup of the USSR, the city had reverted to its original name. It was smaller than Tashkent and boring according to Allen. There was practically no social life.

"Ah, but look at those mountains," I had said. "You can go hiking every weekend and skiing in the winter. Then, there's lake Issyk Kul. I would like living here. I don't care if there's only a handful of embassies around. I would make friends with the locals."

We took pictures of the giant Lenin statue in front of the Agriculture Ministry. Lenin was pointing toward the East. The interpreter took a picture of us in front of the statue pointing West. He said the local joke was that Lenin was pointing toward the Agriculture Ministry saying, "Feed me."

After dinner that night, it was party time in Ivan's room. He wanted to cut and share the melon he had bought at a roadside stand earlier in the day. Sean contributed a bottle of local cognac. During the party, we made plans for the trip to Alma Ata. Tim decided to leave early, but agreed to meet us at the Hotel Kazakhstan.

The following morning, we had breakfast at the bar. The dining room had been taken over by an Italian movie company making a movie on Genghis Khan. Soon after, we started on our three-hour drive to Alma Ata. It was not what I expected. There were no mountain roads with hairpin bends. The terrain was pretty flat.

We stopped along the way and took pictures of the steppe with the Ala Tau mountains in the background. I imagined Genghis Khan and his troops galloping through those steppes a few hundred years ago. I had read that the Mongols would place a piece of meat under their saddle, ride on it for a few days, then eat it raw. Stories like these made me glad I was vegetarian.

As we approached Alma Ata, we noticed that it was a lot bigger than Bishkek. Kazakhstan is the second largest country in the area after the Russian Federation. Germany, France, Spain, Great Britain, Norway, and Sweden could fit within its territory. I gave our driver a baseball cap from the U.S., which would probably fetch a good price on the black market, then paid him $100 for the ride. It was not much by U.S. standards, but a very handsome sum for a Kyrgyz. I felt sorry for the driver, an earthquake engineer, and people like him. These highly educated people were forced to do menial jobs in order to survive the demise of the USSR. Economic restructuring was tough on human capital.

The rooms at the Hotel Kazakhstan were a lot more expensive than those at Bishkek's Hotel Issyk Kul. There were two sets of elevators. One stopped on even-numbered floors and the other on odd-numbered floors. Go figure. I liked the full-size refrigerator in my room, but a cursory test of the mattress revealed problems. The mattress actually consisted of three cushions set on springs, an orthopedic nightmare. It looked like I would have to sleep on the floor. The first order of business, however, was to throw my bags in the room, get my backpack, and rush to catch my ride to the party cruise organized by the Ministry of Energy. The cruise was at a lake about an hour away from the city. Ivan declined the invitation so he could meet some friends.

On board the Ministry's boat, I realized that I was the only woman there. In addition to Sean and Tim, there were eleven Kazakhs on board, most of them ethnic Russians. After a splendid meal served on deck, the Kazakhs got drunk on the countless toasts. The captain anchored the boat on a remote part of the lake and announced that it was swimming time.

"I didn't bring my suit," I said.

"We don't need suits," the captain said.

The Kazakhs and Tim stripped down to their underwear and jumped into the blue water.

"Come on Janet," Tim called out. "The water is great."

"Thanks, but no thanks. I don't want word to get around in Washington that I went swimming in my underwear with a bunch of drunken guys."

Given everybody's intoxication level, it was a miracle we made it safely back to the dock and to the hotel. A picnic in the mountains had been planned for the following day. It consisted of roasting a lamb, then eating it inside a yurt with gallons of vodka. I excused myself, saying I had to work. I caught up with Tim and Sean when they returned.

"How did the lamb roast go, guys? You're still standing, so it must have gone all right," I said.

Tim was beside himself with laughter. "You won't believe this, but it's customary to reserve the lamb's head, eyeballs and all, for the senior guest of honor. Guess who that was?"

"Sean?"

12

"Right. So after they roasted the lamb, they cut off the head and put it on a platter in front of Sean," Tim explained.

I burst out laughing.

"Well, Sean. Did you at least try it?" I asked.

"Are you kidding? No way," Sean said. "I can't eat something that's staring at me."

"Oh no," I said in mock horror. "You insulted the host country. They may never let us in again. How are we ever going to start projects here?"

"I'm not coming back here anyway," Sean said. "I want to work in Russia and Ukraine."

He handed me a draft cable, marked immediate. "Marcus sent this. Could you see if it needs any changes and call him up tomorrow with them?"

I rejoiced. Another chance to talk to Marcus. I looked at the date on the cable: August 5. He had drafted it the day before we left the country. He was not just dedicated, he was driven.

Monday's schedule was light because of Kazakh officials' vacations. In addition, there was no urgency to schedule as many meetings as possible, since we had a rep in town who could see Kazakh officials at his leisure.

At the office the following day, I found out that one of the FSNs was going to Tashkent on Tuesday and asked him to carry a letter for Marcus. That afternoon, I took a break from redrafting my cable on the Istanbul meetings to call him.

"Marcus Metamarro, U.S. Embassy."

"Hi Marcus. This is Janet Bradley. I'm calling with changes to your cable."

"Hi, Janet. How's the trip going?" He sounded thrilled to hear from me.

"Unbelievable. We went on this cruise where I was the only woman. Most everybody got drunk and some guys, Tim included, went swimming in their underwear. Yesterday, Sean was supposed to eat a lamb's head, but he demurred. I found an excuse not to go to that event," I said.

"Sounds like all you do is party. Do you ever do any work?" he teased.

"This was during the weekend, Your Excellency," I said. "In fact, I was working on a cable Sunday night. Now, about these changes to your cable. In paragraph one...."

After we agreed on the changes, I asked Marcus's opinion about an assignment for me in Tashkent. He thought it was a good idea. I decided to start the transfer process as soon as I got back to Washington. At the thought of Washington, I remembered Gerry. How could I go on with him as before? All I could think about was Marcus.

CHAPTER TWO
On The Silk Road Once Again

Time and distance did nothing to take my mind off Marcus. As soon as I arrived home, I put together a package for him, including a book called _Ecocide in the U.S.S.R,_ by Feshbach.

It seemed that everywhere I turned there were reminders of Marcus: the upcoming ski season, Sean and his request that I pick a region to work in, the pile of work waiting on my desk. The biggest reminder, however, was Gerry. The differences between the two men reinforced my feeling that Marcus was the man for me.

"You seem preoccupied. Something wrong?" Gerry asked. "You haven't been the same since you got back."

"There's been a lot of changes at work. I'm not sure I like my new boss."

"Are you sure you're not mad at me for some reason?" he asked.

"What makes you say that?"

"Because," he said, "I see less of you, and when I do you're not here - mentally or emotionally. It's like you're alone, even when we're together."

He was right. I was punishing him; punishing him for not being Marcus. Something had to give. I was ruining a long-term relationship for a man I might never see again. I could not help myself. Try as I might, Marcus was constantly hovering around my thoughts.

To make matters worse, communicating with him was difficult due to the obsolete, tapped phones. The one time I managed to reach him on the phone, we were cut off minutes into the call. My letters went unanswered and even the cable traffic after a while made no mention of Marcus. When I called to inquire about him, I was told that he was out of the country.

Just when I was ready to give up, a letter arrived in early November. I opened it eagerly. Marcus wrote of the beauty of the mountains and the wonderful skiing. He thanked me for the book I had sent, saying he had looked everywhere for a copy before he moved to Tashkent. But best of all, he was eager for me to get transferred there. I nearly danced for joy. He liked me! He couldn't wait to see me again! A knock on the door startled me out of my reveries. My secretary came in and handed me a priority cable from Tashkent. It was an urgent request for my presence. It meant I would have to organize the trip, hire a consultant, and get there and back before Christmas. As much as I wanted to see Marcus, the urgency puzzled me. It also seemed strange that the Embassy had requested my presence, when Sean was the Office Director. I took the cable to him.

"What do you make of this?" I asked.

"I think he's as anxious to see you as you are to see him," he said with a sly smile.

I blushed. "I asked for your professional opinion, not your personal opinion."

"Make your travel plans."

I dropped everything else and started putting the trip together. It was a miracle I found a consultant willing to travel between Thanksgiving and Christmas. The pressure, however, was getting to me. The letter from Marcus, the priority cable, the travel plans all made the distance between Gerry and me that much wider. Even spending one night a week with him became intolerable. I tossed and turned all night.

The weekend before Thanksgiving, Gerry and I were lying in bed watching TV. Gerry said that his family was already making plans for Christmas. If we bought a big house by then, the family could come to Washington for Christmas. I was taken by surprise. It was true that we had been looking for houses with the intent to fold our two houses into one, but we could never agree on what to buy. I had gotten increasingly skeptical about the house and Gerry, and now this.

"Gerry, we can't buy a house and move in by Christmas."

"Not this Christmas; the next one."

"What? Your family is already planning over a year in advance?"

"Why not?"

"You're asking me to make plans for Christmas '93!! My goal is to stay alive for this Christmas. I'm putting together this trip. Work is piling up. I'm a wreck. I have no clue as to how I'll do Christmas shopping or send cards this year. Next Christmas is nowhere near my radar screen. And as far as the house goes, I don't think so. We never once agreed on a house. How can we live together?"

Gerry turned from me, pain etched on his face.

"I'm sorry," I said, putting my arms around him. "I'm under tremendous pressure. We'll talk about it when I get back. OK?"

Thanksgiving Day provided a break from tension. We spent it with my adopted family on the Eastern Shore of Maryland. The tension resumed Friday in Washington when my car was broken into and my luggage was stolen. Saturday, I ran around trying to replace my stolen contact lenses, driver's license, and credit cards. Tuesday, another problem cropped up.

"Have you heard? The Uzbeks are requiring foreigners to provide certificates showing that they are HIV negative before they admit them into the country. Foreigners without certificates are tested at the airport," said a co-worker.

"You're kidding, right?"

"No, I'm serious," he said. "Check out the cable."

I went through my stack of cables and found the one mentioned. My face fell. It was true. I could not see how the consultant and I could get certificates by close of business Friday.

I checked with Diedre, the State Department's Uzbekistan desk officer. She said that diplomats would not be required to provide certificates, which took care of me, but still left Sandra, my consultant. I called her and asked her to check into getting tested. Sandra called back to say that even if she got tested that day, the results would not be ready until Monday, when we were scheduled to be in Frankfurt. I did not see how I could solve the HIV certificate problem in three days. Having Sandra tested at the Tashkent airport was out of the question. I decided to postpone the trip and called Marcus to tell him about it. The secretary said he was at a meeting. At my insistence, she called him to the phone. I explained my predicament and told him of my decision to postpone the trip.

"No, don't postpone," he said.

"What's the rush?" I asked. "I don't think three weeks would make any difference. It's not like the Uzbeks are on the cutting edge of reform."

"Don't postpone. The rule is not being enforced. We'll help you at the airport to insure there are no problems."

"OK, put it in a cable," I sighed. Why was he so insistent?

The cable was on my desk the following morning. I could go ahead and finish processing my travel orders. I warned Sean, however, "I'm at my SNAFU limit. If one more thing goes wrong, I'm dropping this crap and going skiing."

I took a cab to the airport. I could not bear to play the goodbye scene with Gerry.

My excitement climbed with the plane's ascent. I didn't mind the back-to-back overnight flights, the stringent security procedures in Istanbul's Ataturk airport, or the promise of another stay at the Hotel Uzbekistan. All I could think about was that with every mile flown, I was that much closer to Marcus.

By the time the plane arrived in Tashkent, I was a basket case. I was the first one out of the plane. Sandra had to struggle to keep up with me.

I tried to look over the heads of my fellow travelers for a familiar face from the U.S. Embassy. I did not see anybody I recognized. As we were waiting for our luggage, I spotted a woman standing by the exit holding two bouquets of red carnations. She called out my name.

"Welcome to Tashkent, Dr. Bradley. My name is Tanya Tepilova. I'm here to greet you and take you to the Embassy."

She gave me one of the two bouquets.

"Thank you," I said. "We're going to the hotel first. We took two overnight flights and we're really tired. We need to rest."

"Mr. Metamarro wants you to go to the Embassy right away," Tanya said.

"Straight from the airport? With our bags in tow? I even brought my skis." I was surprised at the urgency.

"You may check into the hotel, but then you have to go straight to the Embassy. These are my instructions," Tanya insisted.

I was irritated. Marcus was being unreasonable. Then, I looked at the carnations and smiled. Nice touch.

"OK," I said. "We'll do as Mr. Metamarro says. We don't want to get you into trouble."

At the hotel, Tanya helped us check in, while one of the drivers waited. I had dismissed the other one, saying we did not need two cars to drive to the Embassy. While we were waiting to register, I asked, "Are you sure we can't take a little nap? We're really tired."

"No," Tanya insisted. "Mr. Metamarro said you had to go to the Embassy right away."

"OK," I said. "I just don't see what all the rush is about."

My answer came when we arrived at the Embassy. Marcus had come to greet us in the reception room. Gone were his big smile, the sparks in his eyes, and the spring in his step. He wore a pained expression on his face and his shoulders were stooped, as if he carried the weight of the world on them. I tried to lift his spirits by being cheerful.

"Hello, Marcus. Nice to see you again. This is Dr. Walsh, the revenue forecaster you asked for. How can we help?"

Marcus shook hands with us, forcing a smile. Then he led me to his office.

"Janet, I'll be right back. Just bear with me a minute."

Marcus left the room. Exhausted from the long trip, I rested my head on his desk. I had to fight to keep my eyes open. I looked around for something to take my mind off sleep and noticed a passport on the desk. I reached over and flipped it open. A picture of Marcus stared back at me, his blue eyes huge and frightened. I looked at the birth date. He was almost six years younger than me. Rats!

I heard Marcus's steps, put the passport back, and resumed my sleepy posture.

"I'm sorry. I know you're tired. I just needed to go over your schedule before morning." Marcus sat at his desk and rummaged through a stack of papers.

"Do you think you can keep the weekends clear for me? I want to go skiing one weekend and to Samarkand the other."

Marcus pointed at the paper. Samarkand was already on the schedule. He had even hired a car and driver for the trip.

"How did you know I wanted to go to Samarkand?" I asked, flabbergasted.

"I don't know," he replied, avoiding my gaze.

"How did I know you were looking for the Ecocide book?" I went on, peering at his face.

"I don't know."

I let it go.

"At any rate, I want to go skiing this weekend and to Samarkand next weekend. You've scheduled Samarkand for this weekend."

"I may have to go to Paris this Friday," Marcus said. "Sylvana suggested I attend the CG for Uzbekistan. If I go, I'll be back next Saturday."

Sylvana Vargas was the World Bank's economist for Uzbekistan. She had no business selecting U.S. delegates to meetings sponsored by the International Financial Institutions, such as Consultative Groups (CGs). Marcus had asked for my presence in Tashkent ASAP. Now, he was planning to go to Paris at Vargas's suggestion. And the Ambassador was going along with this. This was highly irregular and I was more than a little incensed. I stood.

"I need to go to sleep, Marcus. I'll see you at the meetings tomorrow."

Marcus escorted Sandra and me to the parking lot. Our car had not arrived yet. While we waited for it, I noticed Marcus shivering in his summer suit. I offered him my trench coat to put over his back.

"I'm plenty warm in my jacket," I said. He declined.

"What's going on, Marcus?" I asked. "You gave me country clearance before I even asked for it. What's the rush?"

"I hate this place," he said. "I'm putting in sixteen-hour days and the Uzbeks are a pain in the ass. I've got to get out of here."

"Wait a minute. You applied for this job. You weren't drafted. You've barely been here four months, how will you get out? You can cut back on the long hours. At least, you can protect your weekends. I'm sure you'll feel better when we go skiing."

He wasn't making sense. He was obviously depressed and appeared to be on edge.

"My life is a Greek tragedy," he said. "I'm depressed, I can't sleep."

"I know a lot about Greek tragedies," I laughed. "I don't think your life qualifies. Why don't you join us for dinner at the Korean restaurant tonight? We can discuss the schedule some more." Over dinner, I tried to draw Marcus out. I was careful not to let Sandra know of my personal feelings toward him.

"I don't see how you could be burnt out so soon," I began. "You've only been on the job four months and you've already had a vacation."

"Ha! You mean in October?"

"Yeah, I tried calling you, but your secretary said you were out of the country."

"I was at my youngest brother's wedding. I'm one of seven kids; five boys and two girls. They're all married now. I guess that makes me the black sheep."

"What do you mean?" Sandra asked. "Just because you're not married?"

"I'm single too," I said. "It's better to be single than to have a lousy marriage. Once, I was engaged to a guy who turned out to be manic depressive. I thank my lucky stars I found out before we tied the knot. It cost me an arm and a leg to break it off. It would have cost me more, if we had gotten married."

"Oh, God. Really?" he asked.

"Yes, really," I laughed.

"I guess I'm just feeling sorry for myself. Being stuck here has me depressed. I'm an American and I want to live in America," he said. "I'm going to quit and live in California by the ocean or in the mountains. That's what David, my best friend, did."

"You're very good at what you do," I said. "Maybe quitting isn't the best decision."

"Last time I was in California, I joined a men's encounter group," Marcus said.

"Really?" Sandra asked. "What was that like?"

"Well, we sat in a circle and talked about things. We talked about women. I had to do something. My parents know. Oh, they know." Again, he wasn't making sense.

"Know what? What are you talking about?" I asked, puzzled.

"Never mind," Marcus said, knitting his brows. "How did we get into this conversation anyway?"

It was obvious that he had revealed something he had not intended. I looked at Sandra. She shrugged. I left dinner more confused than before. Marcus's whole mood had changed. He was obviously in distress and I suspected there was more to it than the long hours at work.

* * *

The next three days passed in a flash. We attended several meetings to collect

18

information on Uzbekistan's economy and on technical assistance provided by other donors. Marcus attended some of the meetings, but seemed distracted and on edge. He was kind enough, however, to invite us to a dinner in honor of a trade mission from the U.S. Department of Agriculture. Dinner turned out to be at the Tion, allegedly a mafia-owned restaurant. The dinner was in a private room and the food was plentiful and delicious.

Marcus, the workaholic, came late, but managed to sit next to me. He was flirting with me and oozing charm. There was no resemblance to the previous day's whiny brat. By virtue of our vegetarianism, Marcus and I became the center of attention.

"I love that cartoon you sent Marcus," Sonya, another Embassy officer said. "How did it go? 'Let me buy you a chicken leg, stranger?'"

I arched my eyebrows. In one of my letters to Marcus, I had included a Gary Larson cartoon picturing two cowboys in a bar in the Old West. "I don't think you heard me stranger," one was saying to the other. "I said I'm going to buy you a chicken leg." The caption underneath said: "They shot vegetarians in the Old West." Had he also shared with his colleagues the contents of my letter?

"That reminds me," Marcus said handing a postcard to Sonya. "Look what a friend sent me."

When I was handed the postcard, I saw the picture of a large, rare steak. The caption said: "Screw vegetarians. Let's eat meat." I turned the postcard over. It was addressed to a Lisa Bayer in Washington, D.C. Had Marcus become vegetarian because of her? Was she a girlfriend?

Marcus was blowing hot and cold and I had had enough of it. I waited until I could talk to him alone.

"Have you decided about skiing next weekend?" I asked.

"Not really. I'm still not sure what my plans are; I may be out of town."

"Look, it's fine with me if you don't want to go skiing. I can go both to Chimgan and Samarkand this weekend, switch my flight, and get out of here before you get back."

That got his attention.

"I'm sending you mixed signals, aren't I?" he asked.

"You certainly are."

"OK. OK. I'm pretty sure I have to go to Paris this weekend, so why don't you go ahead with the Samarkand trip....but don't switch flights! I promise we'll go skiing next weekend."

"All right; I'll stay. But, I'm going skiing next weekend, with or without you." Things were beginning to look up.

* * *

Saturday morning, promptly at 9:00, our escort met us in the lobby of Hotel Uzbekistan. He was a twenty-year old student named Ulugbek and, at six feet four inches, the biggest Uzbek I had ever seen. He led us to a black Volga that was waiting in the parking lot. We sat in the back of the car with our luggage. The trunk was full of supplies. Apparently, there was no road service in that part of the country. Even though the roads were in good condition, travelers had learned to

19

carry food, water, spare tires, and extra fuel. I felt like I was riding in a moving bomb.

There was a dusting of snow in the fields outside Tashkent; I imagined that the skiing would be good in Chimgan. Hopefully, the snow would stick around until the following weekend. We passed huge cotton fields. Ulugbek pointed out rows of mulberry trees on the edge of the fields. Their leaves are used to feed the silk worms that produced the other cloth Uzbekistan was famous for. I thought it bizarre that this arid country had been assigned by Stalin the job of producing cotton. Water was being diverted from the Amur Darya and Syr Darya rivers for irrigation. This, coupled with the inefficiency of central planning, was causing the Aral Sea to shrink to a small portion of its original size. Foreign donors were trying to address the issue, but a comprehensive solution would require the cooperation of all Central Asian countries siphoning off water from these two rivers. Such agreement was not forthcoming, so the Aral Sea kept shrinking. Redirecting Uzbekistan's economy away from cotton production would help, but this was a massive, long-term project.

We were reminded that the old regime had not completely disappeared upon arrival at the Hotel Samarkand. The woman at the reception desk told us we could not register because we did not have visas for Samarkand. I said I was there on a U.S. government mission. Nobody had told me another visa was needed for Samarkand. At any rate, we planned to leave the following day.

"Very well," the clerk said. "You may register, as long as you leave by noon tomorrow."

Kasim, the driver, and Ulugbek had to provide documents showing they were authorized to be there.

"They're with us," I intervened. "This should be proof enough."

As was true in Tashkent, foreigners were charged in foreign exchange a price that was several times higher than the price in local currency charged Uzbek citizens. Diplomats had a slightly preferential rate compared to tourists. Sandra and I exchanged glances. Up in the room, I let loose. "Can you believe these people? We're the cash cows and they're treating us like dirt. They could be making a mint out of the treasures they have around here and they're all hung up on visas."

"They have a lot to learn about incentives and how the free market works," Sandra remarked. "But let's forget about them. Let's go check out the sights."

The first stop was Gur Emir, a short walk from the Hotel Samarkand. It was a building with a magnificent fluted dome that contained the tombs of the Timurid kings, Sultan Mohammed, Ulugbek, and Tamerlane (Timur in Uzbek), the founder of the dynasty. Tamerlane's 500 year-old tombstone is made of rock jade, made to order by Ulugbek. The tomb had suffered rather badly from the ravages of time, but it had been painstakingly restored to its old splendor. We took some magnificent photographs of the splendid dome silhouetted against a clear, blue sky.

The second stop was Samarkand's most famous sight, Registan Square. Building of the Registan began in the 15th century and was completed more than two hundred years later. Ulugbek's madrasa (school for Muslim clerics) was completed in 1420. The Shir Dor madrasa, an imperfect copy of Ulugbek's madrasa, was erected between 1619 and 1636 on the sight of the covered bazaar of the hat makers. The third building on the square was perhaps the most famous of all, Tillia Kari. Yalangtus-Bij started building the gold-decorated edifice in 1646, but it wasn't completed until after his death. The building contained elaborate murals, but the famous colored tiles, damaged in an earthquake early in the 19th century, were never replaced.

Next, we stopped by the Bibi Khanoum mosque. It was the biggest mosque in Central Asia and one of the most beautiful monuments of the Muslim world. Now in ruins, the legend around it still captures the imagination. Bibi Khanoum was a beautiful Chinese girl; Tamerlane's favorite. In 1399-1401, when Tamerlane was away on campaign, she undertook to build a magnificent monument in his honor and hired a famous architect to do the job. The architect fell madly in love with the beautiful Bibi Khanoum and threatened to leave the work unfinished, unless she gave him a kiss. Bibi Khanoum gave in, but the guilty kiss left a mark on the architect and, upon his return, Tamerlane put him to death. He then ordered all the women in the kingdom to wear veils, so as not to arouse men's passion.

After Bibi Khanoum, we visited the nearby bazaar. It was picturesque, but not as large as the bazaars of Tashkent. I took the opportunity to buy some dried fruit, nuts, and bread. In that part of the world you had better fend for yourself, especially if you are a vegetarian. Restaurants are scarce and often closed for mysterious reasons. If they are open, they may have very limited menus. The most frequently available item is beef Stroganoff. Usually, that dish is made with luscious noodles mixed with pieces of beef in white sauce. The Uzbek version, however, consists of french fries and a hunk or two of tough, grisly meat. Whether the meat is beef, the cook only knows for sure. I survived on the famous plov, salads, and various soups.

The last stop for the day was Shahi Zinda, one of the most magnificent architectural structures of its time. It consists of a group of mosques and tombs built between the 13th and 15th centuries for the great men of that period; mostly army generals and court favorites of Tamerlane. It sits high on a hill on the outskirts of town. The sunset cast a mystical spell on the place as Sandra and I walked in the narrow passages and took pictures. Somehow, taking pictures seemed sacrilegious, but we wanted to capture the magic of the place. I stood transfixed watching the last rays of the sun touch the tombstones. I thought Shahi Zinda was a fitting resting place for Tamerlane's favorites. I also felt there was a romantic side to Tamerlane, the brutal conqueror.

With the major sights covered and the impending nightfall, our thoughts turned to nourishment. I had heard about a restaurant with a rather extensive menu and suggested we try it. Ulugbek, however, was adamantly opposed. He said the restaurant was owned by the mafia and that great harm would come to us if we frequented it. After protesting for a while, I gave in. We ended up eating a less than memorable meal at the hotel restaurant.

The following morning, after breakfast at the hotel, we drove to Ulugbek's observatory. It was an impressive monument to that great astronomer. After some picture taking, we visited the nearby gift shop. I bought a beautiful silk bed cover, called susane, for the equivalent of $15. I was quite pleased with the purchase. I expected such bargains to disappear, as Uzbek prices caught up with the rest of the world. The guys bought several loaves of bread saying that Samarkand bread was superior to that of Tashkent. Despite all the fun we had, we were somewhat anxious to return to Tashkent to prepare for another week of meetings.

* * *

The week flew by as we ran from meeting to meeting gathering information for the tax project. Tanya, our interpreter, was invaluable in confirming appointments and in providing moral support when appointments were canceled.

The day before Sandra left, she, Tanya, and I went to Tashkent's Old Bazaar, where we bought silk fabric and decorative Uzbek knives. The dusting of snow, rapidly turning gray, seemed out of place on the bazaar's large blue dome.

I waited anxiously for Marcus's return. I hired a car and driver and went to the airport to meet his flight. I tried to get into the international arrivals building, but a hefty Uzbek waved me away. I positioned myself outside the window so I could see the arriving passengers as they got off the shuttle bus.

Soon, a group of people entered the building and I looked for Marcus among them. I spotted him right away. He was wearing jeans and his blue ski jacket and carried his luggage carrier in his left hand. He was rushing to passport control and looked sad. I went back to the door. I pulled out my diplomatic passport and told the hefty Uzbek that I had to go inside to meet my friend from the U.S. Embassy. This time the Uzbek relented and let me in. The chauffeur from the Embassy had to wait outside. Marcus had cleared passport control and was waiting for his luggage. He seemed surprised to see me.

"Janet, what are you doing here?"

"I wanted to make sure you hadn't forgotten about the ski trip. Also, I thought you might be depressed about coming back, and wanted to cheer you up," I said.

"You're right. I'm depressed already. Paris was wonderful. I hated to leave. Where's the luggage? I don't have all day," he said impatiently.

"If you were traveling light, you would be out of here already," I commented.

The Charge from the French Embassy came over to chat. He had come to meet his wife and children who were coming for the holidays. Marcus introduced me.

"I made plans to go to the local lake," I told Marcus. "You're welcome to join me."

"Thanks, but I'll have to pass on that. I have to move today," Marcus explained. "I can meet you for dinner though. How about the Korean restaurant at seven?"

"Sounds good to me," I said.

The carousel started moving, signaling that the luggage was about to be deposited on it. Marcus's large, blue Samsonite suitcase soon appeared. He grabbed it and walked out the door, where the Embassy chauffeur was waiting. I waved goodbye and walked toward my car saying, "See you at seven."

It took about an hour to reach the lake. I was disappointed. The lake seemed to have shrunk. I suspected another siphoning off exercise. The driver claimed, however, that the lake's shrinking was a seasonal event. It was just after the cotton harvest and a lot of water had been used to irrigate the cotton. The lake would fill up again for the following growing season. I found it hard to believe that this was a recreation area for the city of Tashkent. The facilities were sparse and run down. A solitary restaurant was closed. It was a good thing I had brought my usual stash of dried fruit, nuts, and water. I looked sadly at the lake. I got the feeling that this lake too would go the way of the Aral Sea, unless the country diversified its economy away from cotton. Otherwise, the rapid population growth and the shortage of water would create serious problems in a few years. Seeing no opportunities for a nice hike, I asked the driver to return to Tashkent. This would give me a few hours to relax before meeting Marcus for dinner.

Back at the hotel, I took a shower and changed clothes. Since dinner with Marcus was not an official event, I put on my black wool slacks, cream blouse, and Indian vest. The blouse revealed a hint of cleavage. The broad, black belt with the big, gold buckle accentuated my tiny waist. A double strand of pearls and clip pearl earrings completed the outfit. I dabbed some Givenchy perfume on my wrists and behind my ears. I examined myself in the full-length mirror and smiled with satisfaction. I looked very alluring, to say the least. I was eager to see Marcus's reaction.

Five before seven, I took the elevator to the lobby. Marcus arrived promptly at seven. He was even more informal in a sweater and jeans. He did not comment on my appearance. He seemed anxious and distracted. I wondered if that man was capable of ever relaxing. We took the elevator to the top floor of the hotel and sat at a table by the window.

"Tashkent looks beautiful at night, doesn't it?" I said, looking at the city's lights.

"The filth doesn't show at night," Marcus countered.

We ordered what had become our usual: kapamaki, tempura udon, and two beers. Marcus started quizzing me about my meetings during the week.

"Remember our agreement," I said. "No business talk after six p.m. It's now past seven. This will have to wait until Monday. Let's talk about something else like why you're vegetarian."

"It's a healthy lifestyle." He shrugged. "That's why I like India. It's heaven for vegetarians. I went hiking there."

"And where did you acquire your taste for Asian food?"

"I spent time in Japan after college, teaching English. I had a Japanese girlfriend. It was wonderful." Marcus's expression brightened at the thought of Japan.

"I was in Tokyo last year," I said. "I was part of the U.S. delegation to the Asian Development Fund meetings. I loved the noodle shops and the efficiency of the Japanese. Belief systems in that part of the world are based on reincarnation. Do you believe in reincarnation?" I asked, looking closely at his face. I was thinking of the visions I had experienced when I first met Marcus. He gave me a blank stare.

"I haven't really thought about it. Do you?"

"I think it makes sense," I said. "Everything in nature comes in cycles. Linear

23

time is contrary to nature. One life, then heaven or hell, depending on how you've lived, strikes me as overly simplistic. Besides, I've had an experience that I can only explain in terms of reincarnation."

"Yeah? What?" Marcus leaned forward.

"When I first saw you, I had a very strong sense of deja vu," I said, carefully choosing my words. "I felt you were a kindred spirit and that I've known you for a very long time. Within seconds, two images flashed through my mind. They were like movies, really. In the first, two teenagers, a boy and a girl dressed in white togas, were galloping in a golden chariot with the wind on their faces. The chariot was drawn by a white horse. The sky was bright blue and the fields were covered with little white daisies with yellow centers. The boy was holding the reins and the girl stood behind him with her arms around his waist. They were laughing and the girl was asking the boy to go faster. The second image was of a young Asian couple inside a dark room with torches on the walls."

I left out the part about the couple kneeling naked on a mahogany bed and the man kissing the woman's neck. Marcus was staring at me incredulously.

"This was in a cave?" he asked.

"No, it wasn't a cave. It was a room with dark walls and oriental furniture. I felt we were those ancient people. The only way this could happen is if reincarnation is possible and we're soul mates."

Marcus looked at me somberly.

"Where did you learn about this stuff?"

"I've read oriental philosophy," I said. "According to this philosophy, there are soul mates, twin souls, and karmic connections. I feel we're soul mates. We were so happy then. Why aren't we happy now?"

Just then, Alain Bellon, the European Union's representative, approached our table and asked if he could join us.

"Sure. Pull up a chair," Marcus said. "I have to go soon, anyway. My car is waiting and I've promised Diane I'd give her a ride home."

I forced a smile, but cursed Bellon under my breath.

The conversation turned to more mundane subjects, like the performance of Uzbekistan's economy. In a few minutes, Marcus got up and threw his share of the tab on the table.

"Don't forget. Eight o'clock tomorrow," I said.

He nodded and swiftly walked out. I stayed long enough not to appear rude to Bellon, then went down to my room. Marcus's behavior puzzled me. Usually, men could not keep their eyes and hands off me. He was totally unmoved. And he was constantly on edge. Hypervigilant was a good word for it. I finally meet my soul mate and he turns out to be a cold fish. I promised myself that I would not allow any interruptions on our ski trip. With that comforting thought, I changed into my night shirt, slipped under the covers, and quickly fell asleep.

The following morning, I was in the lobby at the appointed hour, skis and backpack in tow. Marcus came in and helped me carry my stuff to the van in the parking lot. He wanted to have breakfast at the hotel, so I went along to keep him company. I watched Marcus, as I sipped my tea. He was not the picture of a man looking forward to an outing with an attractive blonde. He seemed to be sitting on pins and needles and his blue eyes darted nervously right and left.

"How did you sleep?" I asked. "Are you jet lagged?"

"I slept much better, thanks," he replied. "It's only four time zones between here and Paris, so the jet lag is not as bad as between here and the States. Shall we go? Chimgan is normally two hours away and we can't make record time in the van I've hired."

The van could seat ten, but we needed something long enough for the skis. The skis lay on the floor of the van and our bags in the back. I sat on a seat big enough for two, hoping Marcus would sit next to me. He opted for a single seat across the aisle from mine. He sat crossing his legs and placing his left hand in the strap on his right. His whole body was turned away from me.

"So, where do you hail from?" I asked, trying to get him to relax.

"Baltimore," he replied.

"Baltimore?" I burst out laughing.

"Yes," he said looking at me curiously. "What's so funny?"

"First of all, you keep talking about your family being in California," I replied. "Second, Baltimore is in my back yard. I live in Silver Spring."

"I grew up in Baltimore," Marcus said. "Then, when I started college, instead of going away, I sent my family away. They got fed up with Baltimore's crime. They love it in California."

"So you went to Hopkins for your B.A., too?" I asked.

"I was in an accelerated five-year program. At the end, I got a Master's in International Relations."

"Five years of International Relations! I couldn't stand more than one. I needed something more concrete," I said. "What kind of name is Metamarro? Italian?"

"Yes."

"What part of Italy did your ancestors come from?" I asked. I began to feel like an interrogator.

"Sicily. And yours?"

"On my father's side a place near Corinth, Greece. On my mother's side Munich, Germany," I replied.

Marcus seemed surprised. "And where did the name Bradley come from?"

"I made it up," I replied. "My father was always afraid that I would embarrass the family, so I changed my name."

I looked at the scenery outside. Not a speck of snow.

"There's not going to be any snow for skiing," Marcus said, verbalizing my thought.

"We're not there yet, Mr. Pessimist," I retorted. "Besides, if we can't go skiing, we can go hiking. I'm equipped."

I leaned forward to ask the driver how far Chimgan was from Tashkent. I also wanted Marcus to know that I could hold my own in Russian. I asked whether there was normally snow this time of year. The man replied that Chimgan was a hundred kilometers away from Tashkent and that normally chains were needed to get there in late December. This year was unusual. I sighed. I settled back in my seat and watched two men fishing in a nearby river. I couldn't understand them. As far as I was concerned, fishing was the most boring sport.

"Fishing has got to be the most boring sport," Marcus said.

I swung around astonished. "Do you always do this?"

"Do what?" he asked.

"Read people's thoughts," I said. "You did this twice already today. You also did it last time I was here. You're spooking me."

"It must be a coincidence," Marcus said and continued to stare outside. "Do you dive?" He changed the subject.

"Just snorkel," I replied. "I've always wanted to take the Y diving course, but it's ten weeks long and recently I haven't been in town ten weeks straight. How about you?"

"I went diving in the Red Sea when I was in Saudi," he explained.

"Wow! What was that like?" I knew that was one of the best diving spots in the world.

"Spectacular. It's a different world down there," Marcus said.

"One day I'm going to get my license," I said. "And I usually get what I want."

The old van was struggling up the mountain and still no snow in sight. I had to admit that Mr. Pessimist was right. As we approached the town, I also understood why Marcus had opted for a day trip. The place looked like a wreck. No fancy ski lodges anywhere. The driver parked the van near the ski lift, which wasn't running.

Marcus and I went looking for the lift operator. There was not enough snow for skiing, but at least we could ride the lift to the top to check out the view. The lift looked flimsy, but chances were we could survive the round trip. Marcus paid the operator the required fare, fifty rubles each. At current exchange rates, that worked out to thirty three cents. One could ski very cheaply in Uzbekistan if one were willing to risk one's life riding the dilapidated lift.

As we started up, Marcus started to grumble, "This place is so pathetic. I don't know why I came back."

"To please me perhaps?" I said, leaning against him.

There was not much room at the top to go hiking, but the view was spectacular. Mountain peaks were scattered all around, some of them snow capped. We walked around taking pictures of each other. We tried to include as many patches of snow as possible. I noticed rags tied to the fence like I had seen in Japan.

"These look like the rags I have seen near Buddhist temples in Japan," I said. "What do they mean around here?"

"I don't really know," Marcus confessed. "Maybe they're tokens of thanks for riding up the lift safely. Or, maybe people leave reminders that they've been here."

"What's that lake down there?" I asked, pointing to my right. "We could go hiking around there."

"That's lake Chervak."

He agreed to go hiking. We rode the lift down. Marcus offered to take my picture on a patch of snow with skis on. I asked whether I could use his skis. It was not worth taking my skis out of the bag.

As soon as I put Marcus's boots and skis on, I slipped on an ice patch and landed on my rear end. I quickly recovered and skied up and down the ice patch a few times, then took Marcus's skis off.

"Now I can say I've skied in Uzbekistan," I said laughing. "I just won't say how far."

We loaded the skis on the van, got in, and took off for lake Chervak.

We reached the lake, but did not stop, as I had expected. Instead, Marcus asked the driver to continue higher up the mountain. The van struggled up a narrow, dirt road.

"This road is very narrow," I said. "What if a truck comes from the opposite direction? How is this guy going to turn around, anyway?"

"Don't worry. Our Embassy drivers are very good. They can turn on a dime. We'll go just a little farther."

"You know best," I shrugged. "I'm new to these parts."

Finally, Marcus asked the driver to stop. He could not have picked a worse spot. The van was on a bend of the road and the wind so strong that the van shook. I took my backpack and stepped out of the van. Marcus gave some additional instructions to the driver and followed me.

We had gone only a short distance, when we spotted an army truck headed toward us. It seemed to come out of the mountain.

"I sure hope we're not on forbidden territory. I brought my diplomatic passport, just in case," I said.

"A lot of good that will do you, when the bullets start flying," Marcus said.

"In that case, I'll hide behind you, Your Excellency."

The truck passed without incident, but I thought of the van parked on the road a short distance away. Was there enough room for the truck to pass?

Marcus soon overtook me. He easily jumped over a ditch in the road. I did not want to look wimpy, but my legs were shorter than Marcus's. I needed help to jump.

"Hello. I need help back here," I shouted.

Marcus hurried back. He reached across the ditch and took my right hand, while averting his eyes. I was puzzled by his behavior. I had met many men from many cultures. Marcus's behavior did not fit any model I was familiar with. I wondered if he were gay. But then I knew gay men who were openly affectionate with women, in fact more so than straight men. Besides, he had mentioned a Japanese girlfriend. Something else was going on here and I was determined to find out what it was.

We continued walking up the mountain with Marcus charging ahead, oblivious to my presence. I was not oblivious to his, though. His long, slender, muscular legs and round buttocks were easily distinguishable through his tight jeans. The wind was blowing through his dark hair. I thought how boyish he looked. I found myself aroused by his fit, youthful body.

Although the gray mountains were bare other than a few evergreen bushes, there was a stark beauty about them. The snow on the top enhanced it. Down below, lake Chervak looked like a triangular emerald. We were protected from the wind as we climbed up the side of the mountain, but, at the top, the wind was gusting furiously. I sat down to reduce the wind's resistance.

"Good thing I wore my Gore-tex pants over my tights," I said. "The wind is strong enough to blow me away."

"Let me take a picture of you," Marcus volunteered.

I posed, then asked if he wanted to have his picture taken. He agreed. He stood crossing his arms, as if to hug himself, his left leg almost crossed in front of the right one. He did not smile.

"Why are you standing like this?"

"I'm cold," was his reply.

I took his picture wondering if he realized how defensive his body language was. The cold started to creep in. We were eager to get back to the warmth of the van, so we scampered down the mountain. We jumped in the van, drove to the edge of the lake, and parked. The driver was still shaking from his encounter with the truck. In an effort to let it pass, he had gotten off the road causing the right rear wheel to spin in the air. The soldiers had pushed the van back onto the road. He opened a big thermos and offered us some very welcome hot tea. While we were parked, Marcus sat next to me on the double seat. Once the van started moving, however, he moved again to the single seat. Soon after, he closed his eyes and napped. I watched him as he slept, or pretended to. I could not shake the feeling that I knew him quite well. When he opened his eyes, I said, "I can't get over the feeling that I know you. Remember what I told you happened when I first saw you?"

"I don't believe in that crap," Marcus replied.

"I'm not talking about beliefs, I'm talking about an experience. May I see your right hand?"

He extended it without a word. I noticed long life and head lines and a heart line similar to mine, long and shaped like a chain. The head and life lines intersected on the right side of the palm.

"You're shy."

"Yes, I am. How can you tell?"

"By the intersection of the head and life lines."

I showed my palm. The head and life lines did not intersect.

"See this?" I asked. "I'm not shy."

"I don't need to look at your palm to know that."

"But I needed to look at yours to tell," I commented. "You come across as a take-charge kind of guy, while you're actually shy. Your head and life lines are long, indicating long life and intellectual activity. Your heart line is a lot like mine; you're passionate, but still searching."

"Once, a gypsy read my palm," Marcus said. "Suddenly, she stopped talking."

"That's not a good sign."

"Do you really believe in that stuff?" He asked.

"Well," I replied, "I like to observe people and every hand is unique. For instance, a thumb that curves outward indicates an untrustworthy person. You have such a thumb."

I kept the rest of my observations to myself.

We were silent the rest of the way. Soon, we were at Marcus's temporary quarters. With the leaves gone from the trees, the dachas were clearly visible. They didn't look pretty. The place definitely looked more depressing than it did in August. I kept my thoughts to myself, but Marcus, as if on cue, verbalized them.

"I hate this place," he said. "It looks so depressing."

"In August I got the impression that you liked it. Why else would you drag my whole delegation here to show it off? It seems to me that your mood has changed, causing you to see the glass half empty instead of half full."

Marcus didn't respond. He was moving to more luxurious accommodations closer to town. Most things had been moved the previous day, but a few items still remained. We used every box and bag we could find to pack the remaining things, then resorted to carrying things loosely in our arms. It was quite a hike from the dacha to the edge of the property, where the van was parked. Between the hike in the mountains and the weight lifting of the move, I was building quite an appetite.

"I'm getting kind of hungry," I said. "Do you have anything to eat at your new place?"

"I have tons of pasta and tomato sauce," he replied. "No cheese, though."

"That's great," I said. "Carb loading is exactly what the doctor ordered after all this aerobic activity."

We finished loading the van, got in, and drove to Marcus's new house. It was dark by the time we got there. The driver helped us unload the boxes. Once, while I was handing Marcus a box, our faces came close and I thought of kissing him. The fear in his eyes made me pull away.

Marcus's house was a typical Uzbek house with a walled-in yard. One nice thing about it was a cellar, which he planned to use for his food stash and his sports equipment. Like most Uzbek houses, it had an inconvenient layout. One had to cross the dining room to get from the master bedroom to the bathroom. To get from the kitchen to the dining room, one had to cross the living room. I suspected that the placement of the bathroom next to the kitchen had to do with saving on pipes. The master bath had a dip pool for the sauna. It was definitely not designed for the handicapped; one had to go down a ladder to use the shower. Marcus showed me the master bedroom. I noticed that, like the dacha's bedrooms, it had twin beds instead of a double bed.

"What's with the twin beds in this country? Don't people cuddle around here?"

"I don't know," Marcus replied. "I'm expecting a friend for Christmas and I'll have to move one of these beds to the den. The bed there is too small for a big guy like him."

"I saw a double bed in the bazaar," I said. "You can put that in your bedroom and the twin beds in the guest room."

The house was well made, but grim. To be polite, I said, "It's very nice."

Except for the linoleum, the wall paper, and the gypsum stuff on the ceiling, I thought.

As if on cue, Marcus said, "Except for the linoleum, the wall paper, and the rococo crap on the ceiling. I hate wall paper. I like off-white walls."

"I was just thinking the same thing. Maybe the linoleum is a sign of prestige around here. I don't like wall paper, either. You would love my house. Off-white walls, no wall paper. You know it's amazing we have so many things in common. You even have the same pattern sheets I have."

"Yeh, amazing," Marcus said without much enthusiasm.

"So, where do you want to start?" I asked pointing at the stacks of moving boxes in the living room.

"How about the kitchen?" Marcus suggested. "We have to find something to eat later."

"Fine with me. Speaking of kitchen stuff, I brought you some herbal tea."

"Thanks," Marcus said. "I'm well supplied in that department." He pointed to a cardboard box full of herbal tea.

"I guess I've carried coals to Newcastle," I laughed. "The herbal tea is another one of those 'coincidences.'"

I started unpacking the boxes in the kitchen and got the strange feeling that I was unpacking my own kitchen. Marcus was a vegetarian, so he ate pretty much the way I did: rice, pasta, legumes. Soon, I had all kitchen items neatly in place. My stomach had been reminding me for a while that it was supper time.

"I'm done," I called out to Marcus "and I'm awfully hungry. What do you want to eat?"

Given the urgency with which our stomachs demanded to be filled, we decided on noodle soup. Marcus had bought some noodles at the local market and a big container of powdered vegetable broth in Paris. Soon we were sitting down to a supper of noodle soup and local flat bread. After dinner, Marcus cleared a chair and the sofa of items lying on them and motioned me to sit on the chair. He sat on the side of the sofa farthest away from the chair. If I did not have a healthy dose of self esteem, I would have felt like an untouchable. I thought of asking him if he would feel more comfortable with me sitting in the dining room. Marcus's aloofness, combined with the twin beds in the bedroom augured ill for a romantic night. Since he didn't drink, I was stumped for a way to loosen him up. His public face showed that he was attracted to me. His private face showed that he was afraid of me. What was he afraid of? I could only speculate. I did not know him well enough to ask. I started to feel uncomfortable myself.

"I brought you a Christmas present," I said. "Where do you want me to put it?"

"Thanks, but you shouldn't have," said Marcus. "Put it in the bookcase in the den."

I put my present on the empty shelf of the bookcase. I pulled out a book and said, "I noticed you have Peck's book. "Have you read it?"

"Oh yes!" Marcus said. "It's a great book. I go by what he says."

"Me too," I said. "I especially like his definition of love: 'Love is the will to extend one's self for the purpose of nurturing one's own or another's spiritual growth.'"

I thought it was encouraging that Marcus had read Dr. Peck's book, but I believed that actions spoke louder than words. Based on his performance to date,

Marcus did not show a will to extend himself. He reluctantly accepted gifts. He seemed to have built thick walls to insulate him from severe pain. I bet any money he had never been in love. With romance out of the question, and not feeling like unpacking more boxes, I was looking for a gracious way out. In perfect synch with me, Marcus said, "I don't feel like unpacking more boxes. I'd better call for a car to take you to your hotel."

"Good idea. Tomorrow is my last full day in the country and I have tons to do."

We waited for the car making small talk. I wondered how to say goodbye. A handshake seemed silly. A wave of the hand likewise. A hug seemed appropriate, but what if he went into panic mode? I would leave it up to him. Soon, we heard a car drive up and a brief honk.

"There's your car."

"It's goodbye then," I said, getting up. "I really enjoyed spending the day with you. Please remember to bring my skis to the embassy tomorrow."

Marcus approached me and put his arms around me.

"Good night, Janet. Thanks for all the help. See you tomorrow."

As I returned the hug, I noticed how tense Marcus's body was. It felt as if every cell in his body was screaming with fear. Hugging him felt like hugging a concrete post. I looked into his eyes and saw pain and fear. What horrible thing happened to make him like that?

I put on my jacket, picked up my bag, and walked out into the cold, starlit Tashkent night.

* * *

The following day, I stopped by the Embassy to pick up my skis and to give Marcus the $1,000 in cash I had promised him. Uzbekistan was a cash economy and Embassy officers gathered cash every which way they could. I was ready to give him the cash when he said he couldn't write me a check.

"I forgot my checkbook at home," he explained. "I'll go get it and be right back. Don't go anywhere. Do you have plans for lunch?"

"No, I don't," I said.

"Join me?"

"Fine by me."

He rushed out the door, while I waited on the first floor of the Embassy. I watched the staff trim the Christmas tree. It was rather skimpy and funny looking, but in a country that was mostly desert, it was amazing they had found a tree. Marcus was back in a flash and we went upstairs to his office. I counted out $1,000 in cash and he gave me a check from the State Department Credit Union. I took the check and smiled. On it, in huge orange letters was written 'MONEY.'

"Why are you smiling?"

"Your check," I explained. "It looks as if you're making fun of money."

"Oh, no," Marcus said. "I take money very seriously. I've saved quite a bit."

Sonya, the other embassy officer Marcus had invited to lunch, came in and asked when we were leaving.

"Right now!" Marcus said.

We walked the short distance to the restaurant. Marcus seemed much more animated in Sonya's presence. He was looking at me seductively, full of smiles.

It was an interesting transformation. Alone with me, he acted like a scared kitten, in a group, he became a ladies' man. Sonya discussed the embassy's preparations for Christmas.

"It sounds nice," Marcus said. Then, turning to me, "Would you like to spend Christmas in Tashkent?"

I was dumbfounded. He couldn't be serious. I decided to make a joke of his offer.

"If the plane doesn't fly, I'll stay," I said. "And you can bet your life that I will come straight to you. You're the one who has my money."

* * *

On my last day in Uzbekistan, I stopped by the Embassy for the final debrief and to say goodbye to the Ambassador.

"Do you want to know about another coincidence?" I asked Marcus.

He looked at me quizzically.

"Your phone extension is the same as my luggage combination. J is the tenth letter of the alphabet and B is the second."

"Now this is a crucial coincidence," Marcus laughed.

"Well, I've got to run," I said. "I have a plane to catch. See you next time."

I did not know when next time would be, but I knew there would be a next time. I walked into the hallway. Marcus caught up with me and gave me another one of his stiff hugs, while Diane watched.

I went downstairs and outside, where my car and driver were waiting to take me to the airport. Turkish Airways arrived and departed on time. I would spend Christmas in Greece, as planned, not in Tashkent with mysterious Marcus.

CHAPTER THREE
A Professional Opinion

I spent Christmas in Greece with my mother and brother. I slept quite a bit, recovering from my visit to Tashkent. I also wanted to avoid old family issues. The highlight of my stay was a hike on unseasonably snowy Mount Penteli. I thought how much Marcus would have loved being there.

I returned to Washington in time to celebrate New Year's Eve with Gerry. It felt good to be among friends and ringing in the New Year, but it took a lot of effort to put Marcus on the back of my mind and concentrate on Gerry. I planned to ask Ashley, my psychologist friend, for advice.

Back at the office on January 4, 1993, I felt I had been gone for a year, instead of a month. Things had piled up and I had brought more work from Tashkent. The number one item on my agenda was to bring Alisher, the bright deputy tax administrator, to the States for a study tour. Sean agreed and I started the process. I had mentioned my plan to Marcus before I left and was sure he would bug me about it. Two days later, Bob Griswold, a colleague from the Office of Humanitarian Assistance, dropped by my office and handed me an envelope. I noticed Marcus's handwriting on it.

"Did you spent the holidays in Tashkent?" I asked, surprised.

"Yep. I was on my way back from Tajikistan. Marcus Metamarro asked me to hand this to you. It must be very important," he said with a wink.

I tried to appear nonchalant.

"Oh, it must be about that official we're trying to bring to the States. Thanks for playing messenger."

I opened the envelope and saw a letter from Marcus and some official looking documents. I noticed the date on the letter and smiled: December 28, 1992. That was the day I had written him also. In the letter, he thanked me again for the Christmas gifts, wrote that he enjoyed my visit, and that he would read the book on reincarnation I had given him. Hearing from Marcus made my day. It gave me the impetus to speed up implementation of my projects, starting with Alisher's visit.

The plan was to bring Alisher to the States by the end of the month. I had only three weeks to pull this off. On January 8, I cabled Tashkent and the AID mission in Alma Ata the official invitation and information on fund sites. When I returned to my office from the cable room, I saw a cable from Tashkent inquiring what was being done to bring Alisher to the States. The date on the cable: January 8, 1993. Not only had Marcus's and my letters crossed, our cables had too. This was too much. I burst out laughing.

"Rita you have to hear this," I called out to my secretary. "I just sent a cable telling this guy in Tashkent about the plan to bring this tax official to the States. He sent me a cable on the same day asking me what the plan was. Am I in sync with this guy, or what?"

By the end of the month, the plans to bring Alisher to the States had been successfully completed. Naturally, several SNAFUs emerged, but were successfully overcome through Marcus's and my ingenuity and determination. Alisher was expected to arrive at Dulles airport on January 31. I would pick him up and deposit him at Guest Quarters near the State Department.

The day before Alisher's arrival, I received a card from Ashley. I opened the envelope filled with anxiety.

Regarding your question about the man who is so much like you, I consulted a psychic friend, a man of deep wisdom. After reading what you wrote me, he said that this man is your soul mate. He said that sometimes, we are lucky enough to find someone who is either just like us or our exact opposite. In either case, there is a powerful and enriching flowing of energy between the two. He encourages you to cultivate the relationship, which may or may not be compatible with your relationship with your significant other. One can have more than one major relationship at a time, though it is tricky. Life is not always simple! I guess my own addition to what he says is that unconditional love is never wrong. Giving and receiving love allows us to soften our armor and become more deeply who we are. Follow your heart. Love, Ashley.

I read Ashley's card several times to ensure I understood it perfectly. Ashley talked to psychics and confirmed my feeling. Marcus was my soul mate. My head was spinning. I sat on my bed trying to make sense of it all. What is the world coming to? You ask a shrink for advice and she tells you about soul mates and unconditional love. At least, she doesn't think I'm nuts. Maybe we're both nuts.

The following day, I drove my old station wagon to Dulles airport to pick up Alisher. He surprised me by speaking English as he entered the arrivals hall. He said he had been practicing by talking in front of the mirror. He had first started learning English by listening to Beatles songs. I smiled. Alisher was no ordinary Uzbek. I had read him right. If the U.S. Government could identify and support more progressive Uzbeks like him, the pace of reform in Uzbekistan would accelerate. I helped Alisher check into the Guest Quarters Hotel, then took him to Wallenski's for dinner. After I dropped him back at the hotel, I rushed home to call Marcus. I was glad I caught him. Sometimes he would leave for the office at 7:00 a.m.

"Alisher made it all in one piece," I reported. "I can't believe we pulled it off. Pat yourself on the back."

"Do you have his schedule all set?"

"For the most part, yes. I have only a couple of holes to fill," I said.

"He wants to go to California," Marcus said. "Can't you arrange it?"

"I would have to change the travel orders and add more money. Besides, I've already made arrangements for him to meet with tax officials in Harrisburg. Pennsylvania's economy resembles that of Uzbekistan and its tax system is simple; it's a good model for Uzbekistan. I'll drive Alisher there myself next Sunday. We'll stop at Gettysburg on the way up for a lesson in American history. It'll be much cheaper. The technical interpreter alone is costing us an arm and a leg."

The following two weeks I practically lived for Alisher. He had arrived with a big furry hat, but no wool sweater or gloves. I had to borrow some from my friend Warren. After his meetings were over, Alisher would call from his hotel and tell me he was lonely. I would spend some time with him after work, then would tell him that I had to go home to walk my dog. I wished Uzbekistan had an embassy in Washington, so Alisher would not be so alone. Alisher's trip to Pennsylvania provided me with a welcome two day break. I drove him and the interpreter to Harrisburg, then drove right back to Washington.

On Friday night, February 12, I called Marcus to tell him that the trip was a success and that Alisher was checking out of the hotel tomorrow.

"Your toffees are here," Marcus shouted, excited.

"Already?!!" I was shocked.

The pouch had gotten there fast for once. I had mailed him a box of chocolates and a card only ten days ago. It was a card I had picked up sometime ago not knowing to whom I could send it. On the cover, it had a hiker with a backpack standing on the Earth. The caption said, "I wandered all over the world....." On the third page, it said: ".....and finally found you. Finders Keepers."

Underneath, I had written, "A male version of myself: vegetarian, jock, and lousy drinker. And you're on the other side of the world. Boo Hoo."

The following day, things got a little messy with Alisher. I went to his hotel to help him check out and he surprised me with a bouquet of red carnations and a kiss on the lips.

"What was that for?" I asked.

"Valentine's Day," Alisher said. "Red carnations are my favorite."

"How did you know about Valentine's Day?"

"TV. You said I should watch to improve my English."

"Yes, of course. Thank you," I began to feel uneasy. "Are you ready for the Eastern Shore?" I was anxious to leave Alisher's hotel.

"I don't want to go to the Eastern Shore," Alisher said.

I started to get irritated, but I had to be polite.

"Alisher, you have to check out of the hotel today. My folks in Easton are expecting us."

"I don't want to go," Alisher insisted. "I want to go shopping."

"All day?" I was not enthused. I hated shopping. "And then? Where are you going to spend the night?"

"Your house? You said you would invite me."

I was not at all pleased at the turn of events. I could understand, however, why Alisher wanted to go shopping. There were no decent stores in Tashkent. The idea of him spending the night at my house made me very uncomfortable. But I had no doubt I could defend myself. Alisher was not much bigger than me. I agreed to both his requests, but felt on edge. I was pulling out of the parking lot after the last shopping stop when Alisher put his head on my shoulder and expressed a desire to snuggle. I set diplomacy aside and said firmly, "Alisher, if you don't cut this out, I will drop you off at the nearest motel. What you're doing is against government rules."

"Who would know?" Alisher asked.

"You and I would know," I said.

In the morning, Alisher apologized for making a pass at me.

35

"Are you Catholic?" he asked.

"No."

"Baptist?"

"No."

"Then why?" He looked puzzled.

"It has nothing to do with religion, Alisher. It's personal ethics."

The concept eluded him. I still felt uncomfortable. Fortunately, my Russian-speaking colleague, Helga, had agreed to join Alisher and me for brunch in Annapolis. After a quick peek at the Chesapeake Bay and some picture taking, I drove to Dulles airport. I had changed Alisher's travel orders to allow him to travel Business Class, so check-in was a breeze. Alisher went through security and blew kisses to Helga and me. I had mixed feelings about seeing him go. He was smart, but also very innocent. I had been tempted to take him up on his offer of a roll in the hay and teach him a few tricks. My conscience, however, forbade it. I had a reputation for integrity, which would be undermined if word got around that I had hopped in the sack with a foreign government official.

"Phew!" I said to Helga as we were walking to the car. "There goes a load off my back. Thanks for playing chaperon."

"You owe me," Helga said. "Big time."

"OK, OK. At least you didn't have to spend the night. It wouldn't have surprised me though if he had suggested a threesome. He's like a horse who has gotten out of the barn and wants to try this and that. Up to now, he's led a very sheltered life. I can't say I wasn't tempted myself, but I didn't want to lend credence to the blonde bimbo stereotype."

I started the car.

"So how come you're not with your toy boy, today?" I asked Helga.

"He's out of the country."

"Well, did he call, did he send flowers?"

"He's not the type," Helga said.

"I think this man of yours is all brains and no heart," I said. "This solves the running around problem, but augurs ill for passion. I want passion."

"What about your man?" Helga retorted. "Is he passionate?"

"Let's just say that he's technically correct. He's an engineer after all. But I can't seem to connect with him emotionally. It's the weirdest thing. I keep feeling that something is missing."

I dropped Helga off at her apartment, then drove to Gerry's house. He was already grumpy about being hungry. The dozen peach roses I gave him did little to improve his mood. Gerry was on a six hour cycle: breakfast at six a.m., lunch at noon, dinner at six p.m. Any deviations from his schedule upset his system. He gave me a box of my favorite candy and a raunchy card. That was another thing about Gerry: he was very earthy. Maybe it was because he had grown up on a farm watching the animals.

"I feel like Italian food," I said. "If you want to go to Sergio's, I'll have to change. If you want to go right away, we could go to Vicino's."

"I want to go right away. I'm hungry." Gerry sounded like a whiny three-year-old.

"Vicino's it is then."

As was to be expected, there was a rather long waiting line at Vicino's and more grumbling from Gerry.

Somehow, I don't envision a happy ending to this evening, I thought. Gerry's next comment confirmed my feeling.

"I used to enjoy counting the gray hair on the back of your head," he told me. "I don't see any now. Are you coloring your hair?"

"I am NOT," I replied. "Sometimes, gray hair is a sign of stress and nutritional deficiency. I must be doing something right if the gray is disappearing."

Finally, we were shown to a table. I ordered manicotti and a salad. Gerry opted for the lasagna. I wanted garlic bread too, but I abstained, knowing Gerry's views on garlic. I ate some plain bread until my salad arrived, then dived eagerly into it. Gerry made a face.

"Now what?" I asked.

"It's Valentine's Day and you're eating onions," he said disapprovingly.

"At least I am not eating garlic," I retorted. "You know I love them both. You should learn to like them too. They're great blood purifiers, among other things."

"You know they upset my stomach," Gerry said frowning even more.

I have a feeling that not only is the evening doomed, but this relationship as well, I thought, while continuing to eat my salad.

After dinner, we drove back to Gerry's house. I had left my car there.

"I have to go take care of Barney," I said. "Feel free to follow me, but I don't have the energy to come back. I've driven at least a hundred and fifty miles today. Besides, I have onion breath."

"That's all right," Gerry said. "I'll see you next weekend."

"We have to get a ski trip together," I said. "It's March in two weeks."

"Let's do that."

I drove home smiling. Barney comes in handy in more ways than one, I thought.

I looked at the time: 9:00 p.m. EST, 7:00 a.m. Tashkent time. I had time to try calling Marcus. By 9:30, I had finished walking Barney and was dialing Marcus's number.

"Hi, it's me," I said. "I'm happy to report that Alisher is on his way back. He's flying Business Class this time. There's a treat for you in his luggage."

Marcus wanted to know the latest on Alisher's visit.

"You can debrief him when he gets back," I said. "I have to get some shut eye. I'm bushed. By the way, did you polish off all the candy I sent you, or did you save some for yesterday?"

"I still have some," he replied. "It was very popular with my colleagues, I must say."

It was time for Marcus to leave for work, so we ended our conversation.

"Wow! What a Valentine's Day," I marveled. "Brunch with one guy, dinner with another, and the last talk of the day with yet another. Nobody can say my life is boring."

CHAPTER FOUR
Crises On Two Continents

I barely had time to catch my breath after Alisher left, when Marcus started pushing for a follow up on the tax project, as well as for an economic advisor for Uzbekistan's president. Almost every single day there was a cable from him addressed to me. If I had only one country to worry about, that would not have been so bad. But I was responsible for all economic projects in five countries and was putting together a financial sector project for twelve countries. I felt more and more frazzled. I had to get to the mountains for some R&R. I asked Gerry if he could make it the weekend of February 27. He agreed. So did Helga. I checked the ski conditions in New Germany State Park and reserved two rooms at the Casselman Inn in nearby Grantsville, MD.

Gerry and I left Saturday morning and picked up Helga at her apartment. We drove without incident to the State Park and put our skis on. I marched ahead, eager to immerse myself in the experience and leave all my worries behind. Gerry followed and Helga brought up the rear. Gerry would stop to wait for Helga and I would wait for both of them. Things were going fairly well until we started climbing.

"I can't do this," Helga said. "I've only skied on flat ground. How am I going to get back down?"

"You could take off your skis and walk," I suggested. I noticed Gerry wincing with pain. "Your hip?"

He nodded yes. His old football injury was acting up again.

"O.K.," I said. "It's getting close to lunch time. We can all ski back to the lodge, have lunch, and you guys can sit around while I go for another spin after lunch."

"It's not safe to ski alone," Gerry said.

"Who's alone?" I asked. "There are tons of people on the trails. I won't do blacks. Just greens and blues."

After a lunch of bagels, cheese, fruit, juice, and hot chocolate, the grumpy duo felt better. I left them chatting by the fireplace and went outside to put my skis on.

"And now for some serious skiing," I said, racing down the trail.

I wanted to race up and down that long hill a couple of times. There is nothing like cross country skiing to erase every bit of tension from one's being. It's not just that every muscle in the body is getting a workout; the beauty of the environment adds to the therapeutic effect. Ski conditions were perfect that day. Fresh snow, bright blue sky, hardly any wind, temperatures in the twenties. I saw a woman from my ski club and shouted a greeting.

The sun was low on the horizon when I skied back to the lodge. I chatted with Helga and Gerry for a while. Then, we all put our skis back on and skied to the car. The motel was about a half hour away. Helga and I checked in while Gerry waited in the car. After we unloaded the bags from the car, we agreed to meet in an hour and walk to the main house for dinner. At dinner, things started to unravel. Gerry started teasing me about my vegetarianism. I got back at him by saying he left too big a tip. I took a dollar off the table and handed it to him as we were walking out the door. He walked back to the table and redeposited the dollar bill on it. The tension was mounting and Helga was feeling uneasy. In the room, Gerry finally lost it. He shoved me and shouted, "You bitch! You always want to have your way."

"If you think I'm a bitch, why did you stick around for eight years?" I shouted back. "We do what I want because you can't make up your mind. I think we've tortured ourselves long enough. For Helga's sake, let's try to save the weekend. We can part company afterwards."

Fortunately, the room had two beds, so we each retired to our own. Shortly thereafter, I heard Gerry sob. I went to his bed and put my arm around him, as he lay on his side.

"This is not about the tip, is it?" I asked gently. "What's on your mind?"

"You're not the same," Gerry said. "You haven't been the same since last August. And you won't tell me what happened on that trip."

"You're right," I said. "I didn't tell you everything. I was afraid it would be too far out for you. It's too far out for me, but I'm trying to cope as best I can."

Gerry turned to lie on his back and was silent. I lay on my back next to him and began to speak.

"I told you I met a man in Tashkent. He works at our Embassy there. What I didn't tell you was that pictures from ancient times flashed through my mind, as soon as I saw him. One seemed to be a scene in ancient Greece. There was a young couple riding in a chariot in a field. The other one appeared to be in ancient China. There was a young couple in a room with brown walls lit by torches. I felt he and I were those couples. The only way I can explain it is through past life recall. We seem to read each other's minds. He fascinates me, but also scares me."

"Janet I love you and want to spend my life with you," Gerry said softly.

"Oh Gerry, now you tell me," I said. "All these years you were busy keeping me at arm's length. Remember how upset I was eight years ago when you engineered that assignment in Newport? When you got back, I asked you to move in with me and you refused. Two and a half years ago, after my broken leg healed, you didn't even try to keep me from moving out of your house. If we had gotten married, this would never have happened."

"It would have happened," Gerry shot back, "and we would have gotten divorced. I can't stand another divorce. The first one just about killed me. Now you have to hunt this down and find out what it's about."

"I'm not sure," I responded. "This guy is almost six years younger than me and appears to have serious health problems. But I need to find out what it all means. I have been reading about metaphysics to try to understand what's happening between him and me. Ashley says we're soul mates."

I lay a little longer next to Gerry, then went back to my bed. There was nothing else to say. I felt sorry for Gerry, but not too sorry. He got what he expected all along. I had known him only a couple of months, when he had told me, "I'm an S.O.B. and eventually you'll leave me like the others."

"That's a nice way of talking about yourself," I had joked.

That had been my introduction to Gerry's self-deprecation. I had been amused by it at first, but it began to irritate me more and more. Here was a handsome, intelligent, sensitive man, who thought he was no good. I had suggested we go to couples' counseling seven years ago, but Gerry had refused. He was the only one who could change his belief that he was no good. I had told him over and over that a person who can't love himself, can't love another. I sensed his confession of love at this time was a control tactic more than anything else.

* * *

The following morning, I asked Gerry whether his hip could tolerate more skiing. He said he could go for a couple of hours. We dressed for skiing and packed our bags. I called Helga when Gerry went to load the car. Helga came into the room.

"As you can see, both beds were slept in," I said.

"What happened?"

"In diplomatic jargon, we had a frank and open exchange of views. In layman's terms, we're through."

"Maybe it'll blow over," Helga said.

"I don't think so. We've been headed in this direction off and on for at least two years. We both knew it. The situation wasn't painful enough for me to take action. Gerry's not the type to make decisions."

After breakfast, we headed for the State Park. The weather continued to cooperate and I expected to get in a few good runs. Helga said she was awfully sore and didn't think she could go too far. In the end, I skied a little longer than the others, then met them at the lodge for rest and hot chocolate. We headed back to the Washington suburbs right after lunch.

The ride was pretty enjoyable while Helga was in the car. Things rapidly deteriorated after we dropped her off.

"The way things are between us," Gerry said, "I think we should call off the trip to Vermont."

We planned to go skiing in Vermont for a week in March. I had found a wonderful resort that served vegetarian meals and had hundreds of miles of trails. Reality was starting to hit. Gerry was getting out of the picture and things with Marcus were iffy, at best. Fortunately, I was busy enough at work to be without a boyfriend for a while. I would miss Gerry, though. He had been good to Barney and me.

Gerry dropped me off at my house and hugged me goodbye. As soon as I closed the door, I dissolved into tears. I had lost my best friend. I sat on the floor hugging Barney until the tears stopped flowing. Then, I got up, went to the bathroom, and washed my face. On the positive side, with Gerry out of the picture, I could have my hair cut really short.

* * *

Marcus was becoming bothersome about following up on the Uzbeks' request for an economic advisor. I tried to comply, but the guy Sean had suggested did not meet with the Uzbeks' approval. I had come up with another candidate, then heard

Marcus was sick. I waited until April 1 to call him.

"Guess, what?" I asked.

"What?" Marcus said.

"I won $20 million in the lottery. I'm quitting the government, buying a farm in Vermont, and adopting six children."

He laughed faintly.

"What's the matter with you?" I asked. "You sound awful. I thought you had gotten used to those Uzbek bugs by now."

"I don't know," he said. "I've never felt this bad before. I have a splitting headache, my joints ache, I'm nauseated and too tired to move. I'm not going to work today."

Marcus not going to work? I was alarmed. Something must be seriously wrong with him. "Take it easy for now," I said. "You have to be up and about by Tuesday. The new man is coming."

"I'll try," said Marcus weakly. "Thanks for calling, Janet."

I hung up the phone with a knot in my stomach. I stood up and felt nauseated. I thought about the letter I had included in the consultant's briefing package. In it, I had asked Marcus to quit sending so many cables and asked when he was going on vacation. Now, I felt guilty about what I had written.

On April 5, the day before the candidate was due to arrive in Tashkent, I was telling Rob Howard, the head of the Central Asia division, that the consultant was on his way and that Marcus should be happy.

"Marcus is getting medevaced," Rob said.

"What?" I exclaimed, my knees buckling. I sat down, trying to stop my head from spinning. "When?"

"Tonight our time. He's taking the same plane out that's bringing your guy in. Do you know Marcus?" he asked, sensing my anxiety.

"Yes, I do," I whispered. "I knew he was sick, but I didn't know it was that bad. Do you know what hospital he's going to?"

"A hospital in Frankfurt, I assume. I don't know which one."

"Thanks a lot for telling me, Rob. I don't know what's going to happen to my projects with Marcus out of the picture. His health comes first, of course."

I was frantic after I hung up the phone. After I calmed down somewhat, I called up the Uzbekistan desk officer to find out what she knew.

"Hi, Diedre. It's Janet. What do you hear about Marcus?"

"I don't know for sure, but it might be hepatitis," Diedre replied.

"What type? A or B?"

"It might be A," Diedre said. "I think it's something he ate at a reception."

"Do you know which hospital he's going to be admitted to?"

"The 96th military hospital in Frankfurt, I think," Diedre said.

"How do you like that?" I said. "Of all the people assigned to that post, it's Mr. Health and Fitness who gets medevaced."

"Ironic, isn't it?" said Diedre. "Look, I've got to run. If I hear anything more, I'll let you know."

After more calls and more referrals, I finally got the numbers I needed. I waited

41

until 5:00 a.m. the next day to call the medevac coordinator in Frankfurt.

"My name is Janet Bradley and I'm calling from Washington to confirm that Marcus Metamarro is being medevaced."

"Washington? You're up early," the woman on the other end of the line said. "What is your relationship to the patient?"

"Friend."

"Yes, he's expected on Lufthansa flight 3321, which is scheduled to land in 20 minutes," the woman said.

"Can you tell me, if arrangements have been made for him to be admitted to the hospital?"

"I can't tell you that," the coordinator replied. "He has to be evaluated first. He may be able to stay at some apartments we have here."

"So how do I find out, if he was admitted or not?"

"You can call me later today."

"I certainly will. Thanks very much for your help," I said, hanging up.

I sighed with relief. At least, there was some doubt about whether Marcus was sick enough to require hospitalization. I tried to get some more sleep before I got up to get ready for work.

I called the medevac coordinator again as soon as I got to my office. By then, it was afternoon in Germany. What I heard filled me again with anxiety. Marcus had indeed been admitted to the hospital. The next step was to call the hospital and try to locate Marcus.

I tried to concentrate on my work, but the picture in my mind was of Marcus alone, lying in a hospital bed in Frankfurt. Finally, 1:00 p.m. rolled around and I, heart pounding, dialed the number of the hospital. I mentioned Marcus's name and they transferred me. It was ringing!

"Hello?" Marcus answered.

"Marcus! It's Janet. I know you wanted to get out of Tashkent, but don't you think getting medevaced is a bit extreme?"

He laughed. "They just served me dinner. Grilled cheese sandwich. That's the best they can do for a vegetarian."

"How are you feeling? What's the diagnosis? What's the prognosis?"

"Well, it was funny," he giggled. "When I walked out of the plane, they chased me with an ambulance."

"You could actually walk?"

"Sure, but they have a law here that if you have hepatitis you must be in isolation. It's contagious, you know."

I imagined Marcus being chased on the tarmac by an ambulance, lights flashing and siren blaring, and chuckled.

"Now what?" I asked.

"Well, they'll run some tests. Then, they'll tell me what to do. I sure hope they won't ship me back next week," he said.

"You sound much better than you did last Thursday," I remarked. "Take care. I'll call you later for an update. Bye for now."

"Bye Janet. Thanks for calling."

After I hung up, I remembered that Easter was coming up. I could juggle a few things and fly to Frankfurt to spend Easter with Marcus. I could be there Friday and come back Tuesday. I called up United Airlines and made a reservation. Then, I called Marcus to tell him I would be in Frankfurt Friday morning and to ask directions to the hospital.

"Hello?" Marcus sounded annoyed.

"Hi. It's Janet again."

"Janet, don't call me so often, OK.? You woke me up."

"I'm sorry. It didn't occur to me that you would be asleep at 7:30 p.m. It won't happen again," I said.

I hung up fuming. I was willing to spend megabucks to visit this guy in the hospital and he was chiding me for waking him up. Forget that idea! I called up United and canceled my reservation.

By the following day, my anger had evaporated. I got Marcus a get well card and a Gary Larson book and sent them to the hospital by DHL. Three days later, I called the hospital again. I was told that Mr. Metamarro was no longer a patient there. When I got to work, I checked with Diedre.

"Yes, he's out of the hospital. He flew to California," she replied.

"I'm glad," I said. "He should be with his family at a time like this."

True to my word, I didn't call Marcus again. I found out how he was through Diedre. I was puzzled when Diedre said that Marcus had not gone to his parents or any of his six siblings. He had checked into a series of hotels.

Oh well, cherchez la femme, I thought. He must be shacking up with somebody.

I had just hung up from calling Diedre two weeks after the medevac, when my phone rang.

"This is Medical Services," a female voice said. "I have a Mr. Metamarro on the line who wants to get transferred to your office. For some reason, the call won't transfer. Would you mind calling him back?"

"No, not at all," I said. "What's the number?"

I was given a number in San Francisco. I dialed it.

"Hello?"

"It's Janet, returning your call. You won't believe this, but I was asking Diedre about you a couple of minutes ago."

"Those coincidences keep piling up, don't they? I have a great view here, but the beds are lousy," he said.

"Where are you?"

"San Francisco Marriott, on Market Street. I'm on the thirty first floor. Great view of the Bay."

"I'm jealous," I said. "I'm stuck here in D.C. taking care of business, while Sean is globe-trotting. What are you doing at a hotel? Are you shacking up with somebody?"

"No such luck. I'm doing Performance Appraisals. How did it go with the consultant?"

"You're working?" I raised my eyebrows. "That's not what medevacs are

43

for."

"I don't feel sick all the time," he explained. "This disease is strange. Usually, I feel pretty good in the morning, but by evening I feel so tired, I can barely move."

"Well," I said, "maybe you feel lousy in the evening because you overextend yourself the rest of the day. You have to pace yourself. The consultant bombed, by the way. We're back to square one. I wish I could come visit, but I'm stuck here until Sean gets back. But I'll be in Tashkent for the Consultative Group next month. You and I are part of the U.S. delegation. So, you'd better be fit as a fiddle by then."

Sunday, April 25, 1993, was Gay Pride Day. Thousands of gays and lesbians were in Washington, D.C. for the festivities.

"Is anybody left in San Francisco?" I joked when Marcus answered the phone.

"Yes, there are people here."

"How are you feeling today?"

"Not so well, actually. I think I overdid it yesterday. I had brunch with my brothers and sisters," Marcus said.

"Did you eat or drink anything you shouldn't have?" I asked.

"I don't think so."

"Marcus, why don't you go to your parents? A hotel is no place to recover. You can't control your diet that well there."

"I don't want my mother hovering over me," he replied.

"Did you get the fax I sent you with information on liver function?"

"I got it, thanks."

"You know," I went on, "this illness is giving you the opportunity to sit still and turn inward. You normally lead such a hectic life, you have no time for introspection. Remember what Socrates said 'Know thyself.' Here's your chance to get started."

"It's not in my nature to lie still. My mind races."

"Well, maybe this is a warning that you have to modify your nature. I don't want to get preachy. I'll let you rest," I said.

I hung up feeling that something was seriously wrong between Marcus and his mother. His comment, combined with his behavior toward me and the absence of long-term relationships with women pointed to a mother problem. His recovery from the hepatitis was priority. The mother problem would have to wait.

* * *

The following Wednesday, I called up Marcus's hotel and was told that he had checked out. "Did he leave a forwarding number?" I asked the switchboard operator.

"No, he did not," the woman replied.

I felt a knot in my stomach. Marcus had felt worse on Sunday. Did this mean that he was back in the hospital? I called Medical Services.

"I know you can't give me an employee's number. But can you tell me if the number I have is the same as the number you have?"

The woman on the other end agreed. I gave her the number of the Marriott.

"We have the same number," the woman said.

"Well, this number is no longer any good," I said. "Mr. Metamarro has checked out of that hotel."

Now I had an excuse to call Marcus's mother, but did not know exactly where in the Bay Area his parents lived. I didn't want to ask Diedre, either. I decided to check the phone books in San Francisco and Oakland. The State Department library had copies of out of state phone books. There were Metamarros in both San Franscisco and Oakland. I xeroxed the relevant pages. Which number should I call first? I chose a listing in Oakland that included the same middle initial as Marcus's. A woman answered.

"Are you related to Marcus Metamarro who works for the State Department?"

"I'm his mother," the woman said.

Bingo! I explained who I was and why I was calling.

"He should have left a number," Marcus's mother said.

I got Mrs. Metamarro's version of how Marcus was, then said, "You know it's critical to his recovery that he get enough rest. This running around from one hotel to the next doesn't do him any good. He may sustain permanent liver damage. Can't you do something to help him keep still for a while?"

"You talk to him," was the answer. "Parents lose influence after age twenty." I was irked.

"We're expecting Marcus here this afternoon," Mrs. Metamarro continued. "You can call him then. We'll try to get him to stay."

"Please do," I said. "I'd like to send him something. Where can I send it?"

"You can send it here care of my husband," Mrs. Metamarro said and gave me the address. I called back at 3:30 PDT and a man answered. I identified myself and asked for Marcus.

"I'll see if he's available," the man said.

Marcus came to the phone. His tone was flat.

"I was worried about you," I said. "I thought you were back in the hospital."

"No, I just go in for tests every week," he said. "I show steady improvement."

"I'm glad to hear it. I had a talk with your mother. She wants me to talk to you about getting enough rest."

"What?" Marcus said.

"Forget it. Are you going to stop by Washington on your way back?"

"I could," Marcus said, "but the Ambassador would not like it."

"OK, then. I'll see you in Tashkent," I said.

* * *

I had a lot of things to do before my departure date of May 15. Sean had agreed to let me attend the Consultative Group meetings in Central Asia. I would be gone for three weeks. Fortunately, I could leave Barney with Gerry. My breakup with him had lasted only three weeks. He called up saying he missed his "little Janet," and we had reconciled, for now. But I was still determined to unravel the Marcus mystery. I would take full advantage of my three weeks in Central Asia to proceed with my research.

On the day of my departure, I dropped off Barney at Gerry's, went back home and finished packing. Gerry had insisted on driving me to Dulles airport. He was picking me up at 3:00. He fussed when I was not ready to walk out of the door at the appointed hour and was furious when I asked him to stop at a drugstore for travel shampoo.

I tried to control myself. I knew he was upset that I would be away for three weeks. We drove to the airport practically in silence. Gerry dropped me off at the curb, gave me a hug, and took off.

Once again, I was flying to Tashkent via Frankfurt. Now, however, I did not have to fly to Istanbul too. Lufthansa had started service to Tashkent and Alma Ata from Frankfurt the previous month.

When the plane landed in Frankfurt, I checked my suitcase at the luggage check and approached an attendant at the Lufthansa counter.

"I would like to confirm two reservations on flight 3320 to Tashkent."

"Names?" The attendant asked.

"Bradley and Metamarro."

"Yes, you're on the manifest."

"Mr. Metamarro is ill. Could you please assign him a comfortable seat and put me next to him?"

"He has a window seat."

"Could you make this an aisle?"

"As you wish."

The next day, I was back at the airport after a refreshing night in Wiesbaden. I had collected my suitcase from the luggage check and had checked it on the flight to Tashkent. I took a seat near the Lufthansa counter and watched the people going by, hoping to see Marcus. In a little while, I saw Barbara, the executive officer at the U.S. embassy in Tashkent, take a seat in the vicinity. Before long, I saw Marcus walk up to Barbara. My heart skipped a beat. I waited to see how long it would take him to spot me.

Suddenly, he focused on me. His eyes bulged out of their sockets.

"Janet! You pop up at the oddest places," he said.

He sat next to me.

"What's odd about this?" I asked. "This is the fastest way to Tashkent."

"You're going to Tashkent, too?" Marcus was surprised.

"Of course, I am. Don't you remember? I told you when you were in San Francisco that you and I are on the Consultative Group delegation."

"I was mentally impaired then," Marcus said. "But I do remember getting your get well card and the Larson book. That was great, thanks."

"I hear you were in Prague," I said. "When did you get back?"

"This morning. It was great. I hadn't been there in twenty years."

"Twenty years! You must have been a mere child the last time you were there," I remarked. "I was fifteen," Marcus said. "I flew with my brothers to Paris, but I left them there and toured Eastern Europe on my own."

"You did? And what did your parents have to say about that?"

"They said, 'We got the postcard you sent.'"

"That's it?" I asked. "My father would have skinned me alive."

In a few minutes, Marcus excused himself to make a phone call and I took the opportunity to do the same. I had to make sure that the two consultants I had hired were arriving in Tashkent the following week. With the phone calls out of the way, Marcus, Barbara, and I started walking toward the gate.

"What's your seat number?" I asked Marcus as we were waiting to board the plane.

"28A. And yours?"

"32A," I responded, miffed.

Marcus had changed his seat assignment. I had goofed. I should have left his original selection alone and asked for the aisle seat next to him.

"Let's try to sit together after we board the plane," Marcus suggested.

Marcus asked his seat mate to move, but he refused. My seat mate did the same. Undaunted, I approached Barbara's seat mate. The woman agreed to switch seats. Now I was sitting next to Barbara. Marcus asked Barbara to move after the meal service.

"Under one condition," she said. "That you two don't talk business."

"You have my word on it," I said.

We both got settled into our new seats.

"What was it like growing up in a family with seven children?" I asked.

"Awful," said Marcus, smiling.

I noted the mismatch of the verbal and body language. "Why?"

"You compete for attention. I'm screwed up. Thirty five years old, never been married."

"What about me? I've never been married, either."

We watched the movie, then talked some more. We had just closed our eyes for a bit of sleep, when the chief attendant announced that breakfast was being served. After a stop in Alma Ata, the plane took off for Tashkent.

Soon, we were on the ground. We rode the familiar bus past the unfinished building to the dark corridor that led to passport control. Then, there was waiting and praying that our luggage would show up. I had a rather fancy suitcase now and I was somewhat worried. Diane, from the Embassy, had come to greet us. She gave us each a hug.

"I bet you're thrilled to see Marcus," I said. "Your work load will be lighter."

"Ain't that the truth," laughed Diane.

"Fortunately, the big meeting is tomorrow," said Marcus. "We have this afternoon to prepare. But first, I have to stop by my new house."

The Department had moved Marcus to yet another house. He hoped this was the last time he had to move until his tour ended next August. After the luggage arrived, Marcus and I got into two different cars. I headed for my hotel, he for his house. We agreed to meet at the Embassy in the afternoon to prepare for the next day's meeting.

* * *

The following morning, I wore my navy suit, white blouse, and blue pumps, and put my briefing materials in my blue briefcase. I had to look the part of the U.S. delegate. As the only woman, I stood out. After breakfast downstairs, I went to the lobby to meet Marcus. He was wearing the blue plaid suit I liked.

"I dreamed you were standing on the edge of a cliff and you shouted at me,

'Watch me Janet. I'm going to jump.' I screamed, 'Noooooo,' but you jumped, anyway," I said as we walked to the car.

"Maybe that's what you wanted me to do," Marcus observed.

"Then why did I scream 'no?'"

We went into the parking lot, where the Embassy car was waiting.

"You brought the Toyota?" I asked, looking at the four wheel drive incredulously. "And how do you suppose I'm going to climb up in this tight skirt?"

I tried this and that way, but the car was too high. Neither Marcus nor the driver gave me a hand. In desperation, I hiked up my skirt to mid-thigh and climbed in the back seat next to Marcus.

"The guys in the parking lot enjoyed the show," Marcus said, laughing.

"And how about you? Is this why you didn't help me? You wanted me to hike up my skirt?"

Marcus turned his head away and stared outside.

"How do you like my hair?" I asked.

He turned around and looked at it.

"It's short."

"Yes, and?" I insisted.

"It's OK," he said.

"A friend of mine told me to stay away from priests," I said.

"Why?"

"He said I looked like an altar boy," I said, smiling.

Marcus was silent.

"On the other end," I continued, "I expect you to lift me up and deposit me on the ground, so that I won't have to hike up my skirt again."

My request fell on deaf ears. Once we arrived at the conference, Marcus jumped out and charged ahead leaving me to fend for myself.

A Consultative Group is what is known in government jargon as a pass-the-hat exercise. A developing country presents a reform plan and tries to raise funds from the international community to implement it. Ambassador Curtis and the aid mission director sat at the table and behind them sat Marcus and I, and Ned Bennett from the regional aid mission in Kazakhstan.

"So what do we do?" Marcus asked. "Just sit and look pretty?"

"I will sit pretty," I said. "You have to take notes because you will write the cable."

One delegate after another spoke. My eyes were glazing over. The only bright spot was when Alisher spoke. I leaned over to Marcus and whispered in his ear, "If you were me, which one of the men in this room would you choose?"

He made a face. "I'll leave that for you to decide," he said.

"First off, you have no sense of humor," I said. "Second, you must be devoid of a male ego."

He looked at me puzzled.

"At least you should have voted for yourself," I whispered.

Marcus lowered his head and continued taking notes.

Mercifully, the meeting was over at 5:00 p.m. The delegates had two hours to get to the outskirts of Tashkent for the reception Uzbekistan's government was hosting for them. I had enough time to stop by my hotel, drop off my briefcase, and change clothes.

"Are you coming to dinner?" I asked Marcus.

"Yeah, sure," he replied.

"You'd better not stay long," I said. "Remember, you're supposed to be resting."

This was not a cheap little reception. It was a sit-down dinner with live entertainment. Very loud live entertainment. I kept my fingers in my ears as much as I could.

"How undiplomatic of you," Marcus said. "The only way to avoid the noise is to leave the room."

"I care more about my ear drums than about diplomacy. Let them take a hint and lower the volume," I said.

Soon, the singers were replaced by a belly dancer. Unfortunately, the music that accompanied her was as loud as before. At least the woman's gyrations were more entertaining than the unintelligible songs. The delegates were paying close attention. Except for Marcus that is. The deafening music notwithstanding, he was trying to talk to the man across the table from him. The dancer approached Marcus and put her long, transparent veil around his neck. Marcus kept on talking. She then started gyrating in front of his face. No reaction. I nudged him with my elbow. "Look," I whispered.

Marcus looked up for a second, then continued his conversation.

The dancer was motioning to the delegates to join her on the dance floor. A Polish woman got up first. She did an excellent job of imitating the dancer.

"Let's dance," I whispered.

"I'm sick," Marcus replied.

I got up and danced with the ILO guy. It was very funny watching a bespectacled, overweight guy in a suit trying to belly dance, but I gave him credit for trying. Marcus watched us, smiling.

"I had forgotten my blouse was a bit see through," I told Marcus after I sat down.

"That was nothing," he assured me. "You should have seen Penny's blouse. It was disgusting."

"Disgusting, eh?" I remarked. "Another man would have found it sexy."

I looked at my watch and stuck my wrist under his nose.

"Time to go home," I said.

He nodded. Within a few minutes, he was gone.

I stayed until the music stopped. Afterwards, I caught a ride to my hotel with another delegate. On the way, I thought about Marcus. Obviously, his problems went way beyond the hepatitis. He wouldn't dance and thought sexy blouses were disgusting. He worked compulsively, although this endangered his health. He pretended to be a playboy, while he was terrified of being close to women. Serious behavior modification was definitely in order. And only he could bring it about. Nobody else could do his work for him. I was determined to learn more about Marcus when I returned from Alma Ata and Bishkek; the next stops on my itinerary.

Despite the demanding schedule, I managed to go shopping in Bishkek. I decided on an ornate wooden tray for Marcus and a chess set with local figures for myself.

Ned and I left Bishkek for Alma Ata Friday morning. I had to go to the regional office to tie up some loose ends before I left for Tashkent. My ticket to Tashkent was waiting for me at the travel office Friday afternoon. I had survived two intra Central Asian flights so far; I could survive another. I called Marcus.

"Are you getting enough rest, or are you back to your sixteen hour days?" I asked.

"I'm trying to take it easy, but you know how things are around here," he said.

"You're in clover in Tashkent," I said. "Bishkek was freezing cold, there was no hot water, and I went hungry."

"Really?"

"Really. I'm coming back tomorrow to enforce rest and relaxation," I said. "Now, listen. Our Ambassador to Tajikistan wants me to extend my stay in the region by a few days. I need an extension on my Uzbek visa. May I give you my passport data over the phone?"

"No, you have to send a cable."

"Darn it Marc, I don't know if I can get a cable out today."

"Well, then it'll have to wait until you get here."

"Thanks a lot," I said, sarcastically. "I look forward to seeing you tomorrow."

I returned to my hotel early enough for a sauna and bath at Arasan, the public bath house around the corner from the Hotel Otrar. This was a huge place where customers had a choice of Russian, Finnish, or Turkish baths. Men were separated from women, but private baths were available for couples with proof of marriage and small, segregated groups of men and women. At the entrance, vendors sold bunches of branches, usually birch, with which some of the customers beat themselves to promote lymph and blood circulation. I preferred the Finnish bath. First, I got a bath sheet from the locker room lady, undressed, wrapped myself in the sheet, and put my clothes in a locker. The attendant locked it and I went into the sauna. It was huge. At least a dozen adults would fit comfortably there. After sitting in the sauna as long as I could stand it, I cooled off by doing a few laps in the dip pool. It was large and round and located in a round room with a domed roof. The room had benches all around where naked women sat or lay down. I was the only western woman there, so I drew quite a few stares. I tried to be discreet as I examined the local female anatomy. Resting on my bath sheet on the bench, I smiled. I felt as if I were in a harem.

After a few rounds of the sauna and dip pool, I felt completely clean and relaxed.

"Why can't we have something like this in the States?" I wondered. "Maybe, it goes counter to our Puritan hypocritic tradition."

It was getting close to 6:00 p.m. I had to get to the locker room before the locker room lady left. I dressed and briefly dried my hair. I walked out of the bath house toward my hotel. I still had to pack and have dinner. Tomorrow, I would be having dinner with Marcus.

Saturday morning, I went jogging through Park Pamfilova and along Gogol Street toward Tsentralnyi Park. On the way back, I stopped at the market to look for bananas. Marcus was crazy about bananas and oranges and they were not always available in Tashkent. To my delight, I found bananas. I was ready for my next meeting with Marcus.

CHAPTER FIVE
Commuting to Tashkent

I was looking forward to spending some quiet time with Marcus. I had so much to tell him. I was hoping he would be more relaxed for a change. I was about to hitch a ride to Hotel Uzbekistan on a bus full of French tourists, when Azim showed up at the airport. He had dialed arrival information and was told my flight had been delayed by half an hour. He apologized profusely and wheeled my luggage to an old Volga, telling the driver to head for the hotel. Azim helped me check in and rolled my suitcase to the room. He insisted on giving me his home number, just in case. I thanked him and ushered him to the door. I could not wait to call Marcus.

"Hi. It's Janet. I've just arrived. What are you doing?"

"I'm riding my Lifecycle. On the top level, yet," he bragged.

"Are you? I thought vigorous exercise was out in your delicate condition. You might have a relapse. Are you hungry yet? Now that the meetings are over, I'm dying for onions and garlic. I could stop by the bazaar and pick up some."

"I have tons," Marcus said. "Just come on over."

"How do I get there?"

"The Embassy driver knows where I live. Just tell him you're coming here."

"I've dismissed the driver. I don't want the Embassy types to know where I'm going and what I'm doing," I replied. "I'll take a cab."

Marcus gave me directions. I opened my suitcase to get his housewarming present, the ornate tray I had bought in Bishkek. At the last minute, I decided to give him the chess set instead.

Marcus's new house was to the north of the city, about five miles from the hotel. The cab driver found it without any problem. I rang the bell. A few seconds later, Marcus opened the gate. He was wearing jeans and a blue, button down shirt. His dark hair was slightly wet and he smelled like soap. Apparently, he had just showered. He looked delectable.

"Hi," I said, smiling. "Nice place."

I could see a court yard with grass and roses in the center. A dog house stood in the car port close to the gate.

"Come on in, I'll give you a house tour."

"Look what I got," I said, reaching into my backpack and pulling out a bunch of bananas.

"Bananas!" Marcus exclaimed. "Where did you find them?

"At the market in Alma Ata. From Ecuador yet!"

The house was luxurious by any standards. It had a large living room with parquet floor, a good size dining room, three bedrooms, large kitchen, study with an indoor fountain, two bathrooms, a sauna big enough for six, and an indoor marble swimming pool. A circular staircase led to a loft. The house was furnished in Queen Anne style, courtesy of the U.S. government. Marcus had put his Lifecycle in the study.

"Wow!" I remarked. "When you go back home, you'll feel like a pauper."

We went to the kitchen. Since we were both hungry, we opted for pasta. Salads were a risky proposition in Tashkent, so we steamed a cauliflower. I sauteed a bunch of onions and fresh garlic and added them to the tomato sauce. I made garlic bread using fresh garlic, olive oil, and the Uzbek flat bread. No leisurely meal this. We both gulped everything down in a few minutes. For dessert, I had raspberries and Marcus a banana, which he ate with a fork and knife.

"Mmmmm. The perfect fruit," he said as he polished off the last piece.

"You're like a monkey with those bananas," I laughed.

"Now, how about some..." Marcus began.

"...peppermint tea," I interrupted.

"That's what I was about to say," said Marcus.

"Isn't it amazing how we like so many of the same things?" I said. "You don't know how wonderful it is for me to be able to eat onion and garlic without worrying about smelly breath. Gerry can't stand the stuff and he's constantly on my case for eating it."

Marcus put two tea bags into a white ceramic tea pot. I noticed that the handle of the tea pot was cracked.

"This tea pot looks like it's had it," I said. "I'm afraid it'll fall onto the floor and crash into a hundred pieces, if you hold it by the handle. Why don't you throw it out?"

"It belonged to an old flame," Marcus said. "I lived with her ten years ago."

"How long did you live with her?"

"One year."

"I guess that's long enough to get to know someone."

"Yes. Sex was great," said Marcus. He reached into a cupboard and brought out two teacups. "I'm sorry about you and Gerry. I guess it wasn't meant to be. I don't feel responsible, though."

"And you shouldn't. It was my decision," I said.

"Have you been in touch with him?"

"Sure, we're neighbors, but I could never connect with him. Not the way I connected with you. I'm still overwhelmed by what happened when I first saw you. The more I get to know you, the more the 'coincidences' multiply. The synchronicity between us is amazing. I've had instances of ESP with others, but never to this extent, and never with Gerry. He and I are like this." I placed my right palm six inches above the left.

"Who's higher?" Marcus asked.

"I'm higher," I said. "You can also think of it in terms of frequency. If I'm at 20 cycles per second, Gerry is at 10. You and I must be at the same frequency. This would explain why we're in such incredible synch. I can feel the changes in your energy field. This is how I know what's happening with you."

"Is my energy field disturbed?" Marcus asked.

"Sometimes," I lied slightly. In fact, since I had met him last August, I had never felt him to be at peace.

"I thought about it some more," said Marcus. "I don't believe in reincarnation."

"I'm not talking about a belief. Belief is of the mind. I'm talking about what I experienced. This experience doesn't fit into the one-life-followed-by-heaven-or-hell belief system. I'm studying metaphysics to try to make sense of it. By the way, why are you so attached to your body?"

"What do you mean?" Marcus asked.

"Well, you're a fanatic about diet and exercise. You even exercise when you're not supposed to. You act as if your body is the most important part of your being. Wouldn't it be nice to go in and out of your body at will? No bags, no passports, no visas. And you could be anywhere instantly. Avatars can do that, you know. I wish I could," I said.

"You certainly have a different way of looking at things," Marcus said. "Nobody talks to me the way you do."

I was hoping Marcus would invite me to use the sauna, but he made no such attempt. I tried to estimate his degree of shyness.

"Do you know that public bath in Alma Ata?" I asked.

"Yes, what about it?" Marcus said.

"Well, our Embassy people don't use it. They're too prudish to appear nude in public. Would that bother you?" I asked, observing his body language.

"No problem," he replied, smiling.

He's bluffing, I thought. I changed the subject.

"Monday is Memorial Day," I said. "Do you have any plans?"

"I'll go to the Embassy and read cables," Marcus said.

"You'll work on a holiday? Come on, let's do something fun. What fun thing would you like to do?"

"I don't know," Marcus shrugged. "I'll ask Diane to suggest something."

I was miffed that he needed a subordinate to tell him what to do on his day off.

"Let's sit in the living room," Marcus suggested. "I'm tired of sitting on this bench."

"Go ahead," I said. "I'll join you after I do the dishes."

There were two couches in the living room arranged in an L-shape. Marcus lay down on one. I finished the dishes and walked into the living room.

"I brought you something," I said. I took the bag I had left by the door and gave it to Marcus. "House warming present."

Marcus took the wooden box out of the bag and opened it slowly.

"It's beautiful," he said, examining the Kyrgyz chess set. "But you shouldn't have."

"I thought chess would be one game you could play in your weakened state. Do you want to play?" I asked.

"I haven't played in so long," Marcus said. "No, I don't think so."

He took five pieces from the chess set and placed them on the coffee table, next to the wall. OK, I thought. Sex and board games are out. Maybe he'll talk.

"What's your birth order?" I asked.

"Number two," Marcus replied.

"Two?!" I was surprised. "In a crowd you act like number one."

"My mother put me in my father's place," Marcus responded turning his face away from me.

Not too far, I hope, I thought with a shudder.

"Is number one a girl?" I persisted.

"No, a boy."

"So why did she put you in your father's place?"

"I was bigger and smarter," Marcus explained.

"And what was number one doing, while you were helping mother?"

"He was out doing what normal kids do, playing ball and such," Marcus said.

"And where was father?"

"He was working long hours to support a wife and seven kids. They decided to have seven kids," Marcus said. "That's too many. You can't give a child enough love and attention if you have seven of them. I'll do a better job with my kids."

"I agree," I said. "Two are enough. The planet is beginning to feel the strain of overpopulation."

"Yes," Marcus agreed. "Two are enough and you have to know what you're doing."

"Funny you mentioned your mother putting you in your father's place," I said. "My father put me in my mother's place. He said he was the captain of our family ship and I was first mate because mother was frequently ill. He was very strict. He beat my brother and me to a pulp. But mostly me, because I defied him. Did you rebel against your mother?"

"No," answered Marcus.

"Why not?"

"I knew what I had to do to get love and attention."

"Love," I remarked. "That was irrelevant in my family. The operative words were duty, honor, and hard work. You know, what you got was approval. Conditional love, at best. True love is unconditional. You're loved for being, not doing. Did your parents beat you?"

"No," Marcus replied, turning his head away.

I looked at Marcus lying on the couch with a sad expression on his face. I was moved with compassion. He had been hurt growing up the way I had. It seemed his wounds were deeper than mine, though. He was constantly on the defensive, as if expecting to be attacked. He had been enmeshed with his mother the way I had been enmeshed with my father. No wonder we were both still single. We were afraid a spouse would control us the way our parents had. I felt like holding Marcus and telling him that we were smart and could overcome our childhood trauma. We could help each other change. I was not sure, though, how to deal with him. His survival tactic had been to erect thick walls around him. If I tried to tear them down in my usual bull-in-the-china-shop way, he would get even more defensive. I would have to be gentle and patient, qualities that did not come easily to a former tomboy. After all, that's what soul mates are for: to challenge and help us grow.

"You know," I said, "when your parents put you in a spousal role, you can't see them as parents again."

"No, you can't," Marcus agreed.

Suddenly, for the first time in my adult life, I looked at an attractive man and saw much more than a sex object. I saw myself. I had thought of seducing him in August, but there was no time. In December, I had come prepared with sexy lingerie and condoms. But every time I went near him, I saw fear and pain in his eyes. I became more interested in knowing and comforting him than adding a handsome diplomat to my collection of lovers. Marcus touched me on so many levels, I could not see him as a mere sex object. Suddenly, the thought of sleeping with him frightened me. He had touched my heart and soul. If he touched my body too, there would be nothing left that was mine alone. I was afraid I would lose myself in him. I felt the urge to run to the door and out of the house.

"It's getting kind of late," I said. "I'd better go and let you rest."

"OK," Marcus agreed. "I'll call for a car. It should be here in a half hour."

We waited for the car listening to Marcus's favorite medley, a tape he had made himself. There was not one song on that tape I did not like. We heard the car pull up and give a slight honk. I got up and picked up my backpack. Marcus gave me a hug.

"Goodnight. Thanks for the presents and the company," he said.

"Goodnight. Sleep tight. Don't let the bed bugs bite. Do you want me to tuck you in before I go?" I teased.

"No," he laughed. "I can manage."

He escorted me to the gate. As I was walking to the waiting car, I heard the gate clang shut. Marcus had disappeared inside.

* * *

The following morning, I called Marcus from my hotel.

"It's a nice day," I said. "Do you want to go jogging?"

"I could barely get out of bed this morning," he said. "I feel awful."

"Do you think you might have overdone it with the Lifecycle, yesterday?" I asked.

"I might have, but I promise you I won't do that today. I'll just stay in bed."

"Do you promise, or should I come over and tie you to your bed?"

"I promise, I promise," he assured me.

"Can I get you anything?"

"No, I'm fine," he said.

"OK then," I said. "Rest up so we can do our fun thing tomorrow. Let me know what the plan is."

"I will," Marcus said, "as soon as I talk to Diane."

I hung up the phone, worried. I had the day to myself. What should I do? Try to find the consultants who had arrived a few days ago, or call Alisher? I rejected both ideas. If I contacted these guys today, I might not be able to shake them off by tomorrow in time to link up with Marcus. I had better lie low. I could combine jogging with a trip to the bazaar for my fruits and vegetables. In the afternoon, I could go to the opera. It sounded like a plan. I jogged along Lunacharsky Boulevard and toyed with the idea of dropping in on Marcus. I quickly dismissed it. He would probably feel smothered and I would feel resentful about his being laid up.

Marcus called that afternoon.

"I'm feeling better," he announced. "I went for a walk earlier today. I talked to Diane. She suggested we go to a place called Parkent, about an hour outside of town. She wants to come along and bring a British journalist."

"Fine by me," I said. "What time do we leave?"

"I'll come pick you up at 9:00, then we'll go by Diane's and pick up her and John."

"OK. See you tomorrow. Go to bed early, so you can get plenty of rest," I advised.

"Yeah, yeah," Marcus said.

The following morning, he pulled up into the hotel parking lot in his blue Audi.

"What no driver?" I asked, surprised.

"No, I'll drive."

"Are you sure you're up to it?"

"Yes, I feel fine," he said.

I slipped into the passenger seat next to him.

"So what do you know about the place we're going to?" I asked.

"Nothing much. It's a picturesque little town in the foothills of the mountains."

"That's good enough for me," I said. "It'll be good for you to breathe some fresh mountain air."

Soon, we were at Diane's. She and John were waiting and without much ado jumped into the back seat.

"Which way?" asked Marcus.

Diane looked at her map and told Marcus which way to go. We followed the road to Samarkand, before turning left toward the mountains.

"Say Diane, how are you going to go hiking in the mountains in a long skirt and flip flops?" I asked.

"I'm wearing the long skirt in order not to offend the natives," Diane explained. "I didn't think we'd do serious hiking."

"You think they'll get offended by my wearing slacks?" I asked.

"Well, at least you're not wearing shorts," Diane replied.

"I know better than to wear shorts in a Muslim country," I said.

By hook and by crook, Marcus found the road to Parkent. On the outskirts of Tashkent, we saw a bazaar. I asked Marcus to stop so I could check the prices and the goods selection. The bazaar looked almost bare compared to Tashkent's centrally located bazaars. Some dried fruits and nuts were available though. I bought some peanuts in the shell. We got back into the car.

"John, are you just passing through or do you live here?" I asked.

"I'm covering Central Asia from Tashkent," he replied.

"Interesting," I observed. "Are the Uzbeks censoring you?"

"Not directly. But I have to watch it. One unflattering story about Uzbekistan and I'm history."

"We're trying to introduce the authorities to the concepts of a free press and independent judiciary," I explained. "But it's slow going."

Marcus was trying to shell peanuts and drive a stick shift at the same time.

"Could you please concentrate on driving?" I said. "I'll shell the peanuts for you."

I shelled some peanuts and held out a handful. Marcus ate from my hand.

"I love having you eat out of my hand," I teased. "By the way, why do you like mountains?"

"When I was twelve years old, we went to Colorado," Marcus explained. "I was awed by those mountains."

"We had a summer place at the foot of a mountain," I said. "The house was at 3,000 feet and the peak almost 9,000 feet. I loved climbing that mountain. When I was at the top, I felt I was at the top of the world."

I looked toward the back. John and Diane were carrying on their own conversation. Marcus slowed down. The road patrol was signaling us to stop.

"Now what?" he frowned.

He stopped the car on the side of the road and the Uzbek official came to the driver's side. He peered inside the car. Marcus handed him his documents.

"*Voi passol*? Are you an ambassador?" the man asked.

"*Nyet, ftaroi.* No, number two," responded Marcus with a dazzling smile.

The man nodded and waved us through.

"What was that about?" I asked. "Did he think you had stolen the car?"

"Who knows?" Marcus replied. "Maybe this was the first time he saw a car with diplomatic plates."

We started climbing the foothills of the Tien Shan mountains. Green rolling hills extended as far as the eye could see. Ours was the only car on the road.

"Great place for biking," I said. "You should have brought a road bike. That way you could explore the country. With the Lifecycle all you do is spin your wheels. Have you tried roller blading?"

He shook his head.

"It's my favorite sport after cross-country skiing," I explained. "It's much easier on the joints than jogging."

A few minutes later, we were in Parkent. The main street was lined with trees and a variety of shops. Men in their typical little square hats were sitting cross legged on the porch of a tea shop, sipping tea.

"How quaint," I said, excited. "Let's go there later, shall we? Now, how about some lunch? I'm buying."

Everyone agreed it was a good idea to get a bite to eat before going farther. We went to the local state restaurant. If the menu had anything suitable for vegetarians, we would eat there. There was noodle soup, plov, and shashlik. Lunch for four came to $2.

After lunch, we crossed the busy street and went inside the tea shop. Instead of tables and chairs, there were platforms with floor mats arranged in squares. People sat on the mats and put the teapot in the middle of the platform. Marcus bought a pot of green tea and brought it out on the porch with four cups. He sat cross legged between Diane and me and demonstrated the proper way of holding the cup. John took a picture of the three of us, using my camera.

After tea Uzbek style, we stopped at the bookstore next door. The prices were ludicrous; books could be had for a penny. I bought a book about Samarkand, a Russian/Uzbek phrase book, and a Russian grammar book. It did not escape me that Marcus bought a poetry book.

"Where to now?" asked Marcus.

"We could drive a little farther and see what we can find," offered Diane.

"Yes, let's do that," I seconded.

It looked like Marcus was going whichever way the wind was blowing. A little farther up the mountain we came to a picturesque village called Soukok. Houses with mud walls and thatched roofs perched on green hills.

"Wouldn't it be nice if we could find a place we could come to on weekends?" asked Diane wistfully.

As luck would have it, there was a camp for factory workers nearby. It included a large building with a restaurant, game rooms, and several dorms. A man introduced himself as Suhrat and offered to show us around. He asked whether we were married.

"No," Marcus replied. "We're all single."

Suhrat walked us to the dorms. I was walking in front of him, when I felt him grab my right buttock. I gave him a dirty look and caught up with Marcus.

"Marc, Suhrat just grabbed my ass," I said. "I would slap him if you weren't here."

"OK, from now on everyone's married," Marcus said.

"You already told him we were single," I protested. "The issue here is sexual harassment, not marital status. Some protector you are."

Marcus was avoiding a confrontation. I would have to fend for myself if Suhrat misbehaved again. The dorms were on the top of the hill and had a beautiful view. They were not as run down as the ones in Kyrgyzstan, but unlikely to appeal to a Westerner. We thanked Suhrat for the tour and got back into the car to explore more of Soukok.

"Do you think you could handle a little hike Marc?" I asked. "We could take that trail up there."

I pointed to the hill across the creek.

"I could go for a little while," Marcus said.

We had gotten off the paved road. Marcus parked the car. We walked to the top of the hill. People came out to stare at us. I took pictures of the houses and the people, mostly women holding babies and young girls trailing behind them. Marcus spoke to them in Russian, but they did not understand. Diane tried out her Uzbek on them. An older woman responded and invited us into her house. I was surprised that a few miles outside the capital people did not speak Russian. Apparently, they didn't have to.

At the top of the hill, there was a beautiful view of the surrounding mountains. Unlike in December, they were green and lush.

"Wow! Look at that," said Marcus. "We'd better start back, though. I'm getting a little tired. Also, I'm worried about my car."

We took the dirt road back to the car.

"I prefer the smell of manure to the smell of exhaust fumes," I said. "At least it's natural. I'd rather be here than in Paris."

"Not me," said Marcus.

"Marcus Metamarro, you're full of contradictions," I said. "You were just wowing over the mountains and in the next breath you say you'd rather be in Paris. I'll figure you out yet."

Marcus need not have worried about his car. It was where he had left it and no parts were missing. The villagers waved at us as we drove off. We waved back.

"The Russians have been around here for more than a century and they haven't touched these people," I marveled. "They go on doing what they've done for thousands of years; live off the land."

As we were nearing town, John asked to be dropped off at the intersection of two major roads. He had to meet some friends at 6:00 p.m.

"You can't join us for dinner?" Marcus asked. "I thought we could fix something to eat at my place."

"Sorry, I can't," said John.

As we neared the intersection, I said, "I've been here before."

"In a past life?" teased Marcus.

"No, silly. Last December when I was driving to the lake."

After dropping John off, Marcus drove to his house.

"What have you got to eat?" I asked. "I'm starving."

"Look in the fridge and the cupboards," said Marcus. "I'm sure you'll come up with something. Diane and I have to go to the Ambassador's house for a few minutes."

"OK, I'll see you when you get back," I said.

In addition to the usual garlic and onions, I found cabbage and carrots in the fridge. There was some barley in the cupboard, as well as some of that French powdered broth. I decided to make barley and vegetable stew. The stew's aroma greeted Diane and Marcus as soon as they walked in the door.

"What are you making?" asked Marcus. "It smells great."

"I guess you can call it barley and vegetable stew," I said.

"It sounds delicious," said Marcus. "You can come visit any time."

Soon the stew was ready. I filled three bowls and set them on the kitchen table. Marcus brought out some seaweed he had bought in California to sprinkle on top.

"Yuck," said Diane.

"Yum," I said. "I love sea weed."

Marcus put some music on and started to reminisce about Prague. He thought Prague was fantastic and encouraged us to visit it.

"We listened to this music in Prague. It was wonderful," he said. "So, I bought the tape."

I made a mental note to find out what he meant by "we." We ate the stew with Uzbek bread and cheese. I was going to miss this bread in the States. They made it fresh every day and it had no preservatives. We all had seconds of the stew.

"I don't mean to eat and run," Diane said, "but I live at least forty five minutes from here and we have to stop by the Embassy first."

Marcus was working on Diane's performance appraisal. She was eager for him to finish it and put it in tomorrow's pouch to Washington.

"I can't believe you guys are going to the office at 9:00 p.m. on a holiday," I said. "This place is crazy."

In a few minutes, we all got into Marcus's car and drove off.

"I'll drop you off at your hotel first, OK?" Marcus told me. "No sense in dragging you to the office with us."

"Whatever's easiest," I said.

Marcus drove into the hotel parking lot and waited with the engine running and his hands on the wheel.

I picked up my backpack from the back seat. Diane helped me open the trunk and retrieve the books I had bought in Parkent. I walked to the door by the driver's side. The window was open. I kissed my index finger and touched Marcus's left cheek.

"Thank you for a lovely time," I said. "Goodnight."

"Goodnight," said Marcus, his knuckles white against the wheel.

I walked into the hotel lobby and took the elevator to the ninth floor. Going back to my dingy, little hotel room after leaving Marcus's luxurious home was always depressing.

* * *

The rest of the week went by in a flash. The consultants and Alisher had been looking for me all weekend. Alisher was especially curious.

"Where were you?" he asked. "I called you a hundred times."

"I didn't get any messages. You must have called the wrong room," I said. "I was out sightseeing."

"With whom?" Alisher demanded.

"A friend," I replied, amused at his apparent jealousy.

"Who is he? I will invite him to a duel," he said making a motion of throwing down the gauntlet.

"I wouldn't do that if I were you," I said laughing. "It would cause a diplomatic incident."

"I know who it is," Alisher said quickly.

"Good for you. Now keep your mouth shut," I advised.

I took the consultants to the Embassy to meet Marcus and explained the nature of the project they were working on. Marcus regretted not being able to join us for lunch. He had brought his lunch. I noticed he was holding a bowl of the stew I had made the previous day.

"A friend made this for me," he said smiling at me.

The following day, June 2, the consultants and I left early in the morning for Bukhara. After a meeting and dinner with the local tax officials, we spent the night at the home of a local official. This solved the visa problem. I had my own room; the consultants and the interpreter shared one. We all slept on the floor, on roll out mats.

First thing the following morning, our hosts took us to a wedding plov. This is an all male event hosted by the bride's father. I was allowed to go, due to my foreign status. Perhaps also because I wore slacks. The event consisted of eating as much plov as one could stand and making numerous toasts to the bride and groom. It was a remarkable event, considering it started at 7:00 a.m. After the plov, there was a meeting at the local tax office, followed by a tour of the old town.

"What's that tower for?" I asked.

"It is said," the tour guide explained, "that unfaithful wives were thrown from that tower."

"And were did they throw the unfaithful husbands from?"

Everyone laughed. Bukhara's old buildings were supposedly superior to those of Samarkand. Somehow, I preferred the latter. Maybe that tower had turned me off to the whole city. I had the chance to see Samarkand's Registan Square once more. Peter, one of the consultants, insisted we return to Tashkent via Samarkand. He had never been there before. That done, we headed back to Tashkent.

I called Marcus the following morning.

"Hi, I'm back. I want to come over to your house tomorrow to cook," I said.

"What are you going to cook?" he asked.

"I'll start with breakfast."

My plan included cooking a couple of pots of legumes and freezing them for Marcus to eat later.

"Fine with me," he said. "What time are you coming?"

"How about 9:00? I want to stop by the bazaar first."

"Nine is good," Marcus replied. "Oh, before I forget, I have a house warming brunch on Sunday. I want you to come and bring the consultants. Monday, I'm having a dinner for a bunch of Uzbek tax officials. You and the consultants must come."

"Marcus, you're overdoing it again," I observed. "Remember, you're not out of the woods yet."

"There's no other time," he insisted. "I have a reception to go to on Tuesday and you're leaving Wednesday for Bishkek."

"Yes, but I'll be back Saturday," I reminded him.

"Better do it sooner, rather than later," he said.

I smiled. He was as pigheaded as I was, perhaps more so. No doubt about it. We were soul mates.

Saturday morning, I left my hotel room at 7:00 a.m. I was at the bazaar at 7:15 and had first pick of the produce. Some vendors had not yet arrived and some were just unloading. I bought beans, lentils, garbanzos, carrots, onions, and garlic. At the grocery store, I bought cheese and noodles. I wanted to buy more stuff, but I was constrained by the size of my backpack. I left the bazaar and walked north toward Marcus's house.

As I approached the gate, I noticed a car with diplomatic plates pulling away. That was strange. I rang the bell.

"What was that car doing here?" I asked.

"They came to give me a ride to the office," said Marcus. "I told them I wasn't going this early."

"You were planning to go to the office today?"

"I have to go in for a couple of hours," he said. "By the way, your face is very red."

"It should be. I've just walked six miles with a twenty pound pack."

"You walked all the way from the hotel?" marveled Marcus. "I thought I was the only one who took long walks."

"Think again," I said. "I'm a cross-country skier. I have to train year-round."

"So what are you going to cook? An omelet?"

"I don't eat a lot of eggs," I said. "Ideally, I would like to cook waffles, but I don't suppose you have a waffle iron."

Marcus shook his head.

"In that case, I'll cook pancakes with whatever fruit you happen to have around."

Marcus took a box of pancake mix out of the cupboard. It was part of his recent purchases in Frankfurt. I mixed the batter and put some raspberries in it. Pancakes were just the ticket after my long hike.

"Mmmm. Good," Marcus said. As he ate, he looked out the window. He finished his breakfast and stood up. "I'm going to mow the grass. I like yard work."

While Marcus was mowing the grass, I boiled some water and poured it over the lentils and beans to speed up the cooking process. I paused to look out the window. I felt I had been forever married to Marcus. He came in shortly.

"I have to go to the office now," he said. "I should be back by 1:30. I'll call if I'm late. What are you going to do?"

"Well, I have to wait for the beans and lentils to cook," I said. "It'll take at least as long."

"Enjoy the house then," said Marcus. "I put out a towel. You may want to take a shower. Here's my bible, in case you want to read. I'll see you later."

I examined the 'bible' he had given me. The title was _Fit for Life_ by Harvey and Marilyn Diamond. I heard the door slam and the car start. Marcus was gone.

I was very tempted to snoop around, but restrained myself. Too bad the pool was empty. I could have gone skinny dipping. I settled for a nice long bubble bath. I noticed a long red hair, as I was wiping the tub before I filled it. I remembered one of the maids had long red hair. I finished my bath and put on the clean T shirt I had brought. I checked the beans and the lentils. Not ready yet. I went to the living room and picked up the book Marcus had left for me. Now I understood where the idea of eating fruit for breakfast had come from.

I looked at the time: 1:30. Marcus wasn't back. He hadn't called either. I thought of calling his office, but didn't want to sound like a nagging wife. I saw a set of tapes near his stereo entitled Creating Love by John Bradshaw. I played them while lying on the sofa. Once in a while, I would get up to check the beans and lentils.

I had almost played the entire set of tapes, when I heard a car pull into the car port. I closed my eyes and pretended to sleep. Marcus came in mumbling, "It's hot in here."

He turned on the air conditioner and went into the kitchen.

I opened my eyes, having given up on Marcus coming near me. "What time is it?" I asked.

"4:30," he replied. "I couldn't leave earlier. Our Ambassador in Kazakhstan was there with his wife. I had to spend some time with them. What did you cook?"

"Lentil soup with rice and beans with pasta," I replied. "I wanted to make humus with the garbanzos, but those things are still hard as rocks."

"I love humus," Marcus said.

"I thought you might," I said. "You love everything else I do. I listened to the Love tapes, by the way."

"The whole thing?"

"Well, I had time on my hands. Have you listened to them?"

"Not all of them," said Marcus.

"Who gave them to you?" I asked.

"My brother," said Marcus.

"Bradshaw made a lot of good points," I continued, summarizing key points of the tapes. "I particularly liked the exercises about healing the inner child. Speaking of love, if you had to choose between loving and being loved, which would you choose?"

"Loving, I think," said Marcus. "But it's not sustainable."

"I would choose loving too," I said. "Loving is active, while being loved is passive. I disagree that it's not sustainable. Love is its own reward. Gerry says he'll wait for me for twenty years, but it's been eight and things haven't clicked."

"He loves you and you don't?"

"I love him, but things are just not working. I don't know how to explain it," I said. "It's just that when I think of marrying him, I get this knot in my stomach."

"Things clicked between Hilda and me right away."

"So, why aren't you with her, then?"

"I run away from intimacy," Marcus said. "I'm sure it has to do with my parents. I feel nothing for them."

"You're blocking it," I said. "That's no good."

"I saw Hilda last summer," continued Marcus. "We talked and talked. We're still in love. I wrote her a long letter. She may come in August. We'll see. Then, there's the Czech woman. I met her at Stanford. She was a Fulbright professor. She pushed and pushed. She loves me desperately, she thinks I'm the one. I'm trying to decide. I got lonely, wrote her, and visited her in Prague."

"Fooling around with profs, are you?" I teased. "I did too. But not from the economics department. I didn't want people to say I got my As through couch diplomacy."

"Couch diplomacy," Marcus repeated, laughing.

"Do you have a picture of Hilda?" I asked.

I was trying to find out what Marcus's type was. He brought out a photo album with several pictures of Hilda.

"This is Hilda ten years ago," he explained.

I expected the stereotypical Swede with long, blond hair and big blue eyes.

Hilda was nothing like that. She had chin length brown hair and looked grim. She did have long, slim legs, though.

"Hilda has been doing yoga for twenty years," Marcus said.

"I'm impressed," I said. "I have been physically active all my life, but I just started yoga this year. I had to find a way of relaxing that didn't involve chemicals."

In my mind, I summarized what I knew about Marcus. He was smart, driven, and pursued by many women. I didn't think he loved any of them. He had shut down his feelings and had become a performer. He correctly pointed to his parents as the root of his, as yet unresolved, problem. There was little he could do about it here. But he could do something about it when he got back to the States.

A fixer upper, I thought. Do I walk, or jump into the fray? I love a challenge.

"Is dinner ready?" Marcus asked. "I'm hungry."

"Beans with pasta or lentils with rice?" I asked.

Marcus chose lentils. We went into the kitchen and I filled two soup bowls with lentils. After dinner, Marcus suggested we sit outside and take our chances with the mosquitoes. I agreed. We each picked a book and sat in the yard reading. We read until it got dark; then went back inside. Marcus called for a car.

"See you tomorrow at 11:00," he reminded me, as I was walking out the door. "Don't forget."

"Sure thing," I said. "Thanks for the hospitality."

I did some yoga in my room and took a shower. An odd feeling came over me. I felt there was something wrong with Barney. I tried to dismiss the feeling. What could be wrong? Gerry took excellent care of him. The feeling would not go away and I had learned to trust my intuition. I went to the lobby to use the satellite phone. It was early afternoon in the States. Gerry was probably lying around watching movies.

"Hello?"

"Hi, it's Janet. I'm in Tashkent. How are you guys doing?"

"OK, for the most part," Gerry answered carefully.

"What do you mean 'for the most part'?"

"Well," Gerry said slowly. "You know that cyst Barney has in his shoulder from the time that Great Dane bit him?"

"Yeah, yeah."

"It's oozing gunk and blood," he replied.

"Did you take him to the vet?"

"Yes. He says it needs to be drained, but I didn't want to do it with you away. Barney would need anesthesia and stitches," Gerry explained.

"Can it wait until I get back? I'm far from done here. In fact, they want to extend my trip another nine days. That would put me back on the 19th."

"I don't know what to tell you. It's up to you."

"Listen," I said. "I think we should leave it alone for now. Maybe it'll drain on its own and surgery won't be necessary. Just keep it clean. Call me if anything changes. I'll be here until the 9th. Then I'm going to Bishkek."

I usually saw the glass half full, but I was worried about Barney. Was I doing the right thing? The following morning, I asked Marcus for advice.

"What do you think I should do?"

"How should I know?" said Marcus. "You know what you came here to accomplish. It's up to you."

"Thanks, a lot," I said. "You're being very helpful." I thought for a moment. I had a responsibility and would stick to it. "I'll stay and pray. See you at 11:00, with the consultants."

I called the consultants, Peter and Allen. They'd better not have a big breakfast. There would be plenty to eat at Marcus's house. Although we took a walk around the neighborhood, we were still the first ones to arrive. Marcus opened the gate.

"We tried not to be the first ones here," I said, "but we got tired of looking at the sheep."

Marcus looked at me puzzled.

"We took a walk around your neighborhood," I said. "It looks positively bucolic."

We sat outside. Through the open door, I could see Marcus's cook and her redhead assistant walking back and forth from the kitchen to the dining room.

More guests came. Marcus gave everybody a house tour. The guests oohed and aahed at Marcus's decadent quarters. The tax consultants and I were the only outsiders. Everybody else was stationed in the country, either with the Embassy or the Peace Corps. It was the type of event at which Marcus excelled. He circulated in the room, making pleasant conversation and smiling a lot. Everybody appeared to be enjoying themselves. Before long, however, they ran out of small talk and started heading toward the door. Peter and Allen caught a ride back to the hotel with an Embassy official. Diane and I were the last ones to leave. She was scrounging around for leftovers. She had her own party later that day. Marcus declined to go; he wanted to rest. I accepted the invitation. We bid Marcus farewell and headed toward Diane's house.

Most of Diane's guests were not government officials. They were either journalists or academics doing research in Central Asia. I enjoyed their company and their relative freedom of expression. I was sorry when the party had to end.

* * *

June 7, was a busy day. The consultants and I met with the head of tax administration and various other tax officials. At dinner that evening, Marcus was as relaxed as I had ever seen him. At the dinner table, I took my favorite picture of him. He announced to everybody that this was the first official function in his new house. He offered a toast to U.S.-Uzbek friendship and to all the participants. Marcus did pomp well.

The party broke up at 11:00. At the door, Alisher took Marcus and me aside. He wanted to invite us, the Ambassador, and the two consultants to dinner at his house the next day. He told Marcus where to meet him. It was a good thing we all met Alisher and followed him home; we would never have found the apartment house on our own.

As was Uzbek custom, the table was overflowing with fruits, nuts, and various appetizers. It was impolite for guests to be greeted with an empty table. Alisher directed me to sit between him and the Ambassador. Marcus and the two consultants sat on the other side of the table.

"Why isn't your wife eating with us?" I asked.

"She's shy," answered Alisher.

"Please ask her to join us," I said. "It's not fair for her to do all the preparations and not to participate in the meal."

Nodira joined us for a while, but soon escaped to the safety of her kitchen.

It was a pleasant, relaxed evening for a change. We even watched a Russian TV game show. Soon, the Ambassador signaled that it was time to go. Next day was a work day. I had to repack my bags and drive to Bishkek.

A dark green Volga was waiting for me at the hotel parking lot the next morning. I rolled my luggage toward the trunk. One of the two drivers waived no. He opened the trunk. It was full of cans of gasoline and spare tires. I kept forgetting about the lack of services on the road. Once more, I would have to ride in the back seat with my luggage. It was pretty hot outside and I wondered what the temperature inside the trunk was. I told the driver I was worried about the cans of gasoline exploding.

" *Nyet, nyet,*" he assured me. "*Eta harasho zakrita*. It's closed well."

The fastest way of driving from Tashkent to Bishkek was through a town in Kazakhstan called Chimkent. The road was pretty flat for the most part and in very good shape, but it was still a ten hour drive.

Penny, the health officer from the aid regional mission in Alma Ata saw me at the hotel.

"We heard you were coming," she said. "Did you have a good trip?"

"Just two flat tires," I said. "Otherwise, I would've been here earlier. Can you believe my drivers turned around and are driving back as we speak? It'll take them all night."

"You're too late for dinner," said Penny. "The restaurant is closed."

"I'm fine," I said. "I had food with me. All I need now is a hot bath and a bed. Is there hot water?"

"Yes," Penny replied. "Evidently, they finished cleaning the pipes."

"I guess tomorrow we're driving back to Alma Ata together," I said. "Any idea what time we're leaving?"

"Around four, I think," said Penny. "It depends when Carl wants to go. Since you'll be going to meetings with him, you won't be left behind."

I did not look forward to spending the day with Carl Butcher, the regional mission director. I found him very cold and distant. He had no life outside work and was the consummate bureaucrat. Extremely turf conscious, arrogant, and insensitive to his subordinates, he was a world class bootlicker when it came to his superiors. He had risen very quickly to a rank close to Ambassador and had gotten bunches of awards for his hard work and dedication. I said goodnight to Penny and retired to my room.

The pace did not slow after the Bishkek meetings. I had to accompany Victor Escobar, the U.S. Ambassador to Tajikistan, to a tax conference in Khojent the following Monday. I was beginning to feel like a Gypsy. The good news was that the way to Khojent was through Tashkent. I took the same flight from Alma Ata I had taken two weeks ago. After arriving at the hotel Uzbekistan, I dismissed the driver and took a cab to Marcus's house.

"Meals on wheels," I said when he opened the gate. "How are you doing, sickie?"

"Not too well, I'm afraid." He followed me into the kitchen.

"What do you want to eat?" I asked. "The beans and lentils I made last weekend are still there. I see you have lots of veggies. I could throw some of these together with garlic and onion. Garlic is the greatest anti-viral agent, you know."

"Beans, I guess," Marcus said.

I took a bowl of beans and pasta from the freezer and microwaved it. I made toasted garlic bread with the local flat bread. Dinner was ready in a few minutes. I could tell Marcus was in bad shape by the slow speed he ate.

"Would you like some peppermint tea?" I asked. "It's good for digestion."

He nodded.

"Some fruit?"

"There are some cherries in the fridge," he said weakly. "I'm sorry. I can't sit anymore. I have to lie down."

"Go ahead, I'll bring the tea when it's ready."

Marcus went to the living room and lay down on his favorite sofa. I placed a pot of tea and two mugs on the coffee table. I filled one mug for Marcus and one for myself.

"I wish there was something I could do," I said.

"You can't do anything."

"Does anything hurt?"

"My head," he replied. "I have a splitting headache."

"There are acupressure points for headaches," I said, "but I don't know where they are."

Marcus didn't answer; he had fallen asleep. I lay down on the other sofa and closed my eyes. I dozed off too. As if in a dream, I heard Marcus's voice.

"Gosh, Janet. What time is it?"

I opened my eyes and looked at my watch. "Ten fifteen," I said.

"Darn, I have to call a car for you."

He got up and went to the kitchen to use the phone. He sat at the kitchen table and dialed the Embassy switchboard.

"There's no answer. I can't believe it. Answer damn it. They're supposed to answer twenty four hours a day."

I stood behind him.

"Does your head still hurt?" I asked.

"Yes."

I reached over and started massaging his forehead and temples.

I knew Marcus had a guest room and wondered if he would offer to have me spend the night. He was silent for a while, then said, "You could walk to Lunacharsky and get a cab."

"I see," I said.

I walked to the foyer and picked up my backpack. Marcus stood by the spiral staircase.

"I would walk with you," he said, "but I can't."

I gave him a hug. He did not respond. His body felt like a concrete post.

"I hate to see you like this," I said. "I hope you feel better tomorrow. I'll call you before I leave. Goodnight. Sleep tight. Don't let the bed bugs bite."

I shut the door and the gate behind me.

* * *

The next four days were taken up with the trip to Khojent. I had little time to think about anything other than the meetings I had to attend. I arrived back in Tashkent at 5:00 a.m. It was already light, since there was no daylight savings time in Uzbekistan. It was hard to sleep with the sun streaming through the window; the threadbare drapes did not provide much protection. I gave up at 7:30 and called Marcus.

"Hi. I'm back. How are you feeling?"

"Much better than I did over the weekend. Are you coming by the Embassy? I want you to look at something."

He sounded happy to hear from me.

"Of course, I'm coming. First, I want to make sure you didn't butcher the report I sent you from Alma Ata. Then, I have to do my Tajikistan report and cable it to Ambassador Escobar. He's really something, by the way. Not your regulation government issue."

"Before I forget," Marcus said. "I have a party Friday after work. Nothing fancy. Just beer and snacks."

"So thoughtful of you to have a send-off for me," I teased. "I'll buy stuff to make pizzas. I thought of a way to make them with Uzbek bread."

My last two days in Tashkent, Marcus was as I remembered him the first time I saw him, almost a year ago. Full of energy and smiles, especially in public. Thursday, I finished my Tajikistan report and gave it to Marcus to cable to Dushanbe.

Friday, I waited for Marcus to finish work. He had to pick up some beer before he got home. He and I donned our backpacks and walked downstairs and out the door.

"It's nice having you around," Marcus said, turning away from me.

"Nice of you to say so," I replied.

We got into the back seat of the Ambassador's car. Marcus was Charge again and could use the boss's car.

"Alisher wants to invite you to a duel," I teased.

"What?"

"He was looking for me when you and I were cruising in Parkent and Soukok. I told him I was with a friend. He said he knew who it was and wanted to invite him to a duel. I told him he'd better not. It would cause a diplomatic incident."

"He's married!!" Marcus exclaimed.

"He's a Muslim," I said. "He can have four wives. I, of course, would settle for nothing less than wife number one. Nodira can handle the household and Alisher and I will work together to reform Uzbekistan's economy. I kind of like the idea."

"You ARE crazy," Marcus said, laughing.

"I'd rather be crazy than boring."

Marcus dismissed the driver near a metro stop. He said he would drive the car the rest of the way and back to the embassy the following day. As soon as we got to the house, I got busy making my pizzas. One of the privatization advisors came to the kitchen to chat with me. Marcus came in and interrupted us.

"Enough pizzas," he admonished me. "Come sit outside."

"OK, just two more," I assured him. "I want to use up the ingredients."

Marcus's two cooks had prepared some additional dishes. There was more than enough food for the eight people present. After dinner, everyone retired to Marcus's fountain room to watch a movie.

At 11:00, I got up and walked across the room toward Marcus.

"I have to go," I said. "I have a plane to catch. It's been great spending time with you. Stay healthy and don't work too hard."

Everyone else stood, as well.

"You don't have to go," Marcus protested. "It's still early."

"Please don't take your cue from me," I said. "I have a plane to catch."

Unfortunately, the party was over. Marcus stood outside the front door saying goodnight to his guests. Smiling, he hugged me goodbye.

"Have a good trip, Janet. See you next time," he said.

"Next time may be in a few hours," I said. "Remember, I never got my visa extension. I may not make it through passport control."

One of the privatization advisors dropped me off at my hotel. I went up to my room, picked up my luggage and went to check out. The driver met me in the lobby a little after midnight.

So far, so good, I thought. If I make it through passport control, I'll be home free.

I carried with me the letter from the U.S. Embassy to the Ministry of Foreign Affairs, asking for the visa extension. Maybe that would help. I looked at the sleeping city and felt sad about leaving. Tashkent felt almost like home now. I wanted to explore Uzbekistan a little more. I felt drawn to this exotic country and not just because Marcus lived here. Somehow, it felt very familiar to me.

As I feared, I didn't make it through passport control on the first try, despite the letter. After a fruitless effort to find the chief passport officer, I bullied my way through passport control with the help of a Lufthansa flight attendant. The little blond Russian official took my passport and changed the expiration date on my visa from June 14 to June 19, mumbling all the while:

"*Ou menya boudyet problem, ou menya boudyet problem.* I'll have a problem." Then he stamped it.

"*Otchin, otchin balshaya spassiba.* Thank you very, very much," I said. "*Problem ne boudyet.* There will be no problem."

I grabbed my passport and ran to board the plane. After this trip, Foggy Bottom would be positively boring.

CHAPTER SIX
Failed Escape

There is nothing like a long overseas trip to make you appreciate your home turf. The passport woman at Dulles airport stamped my passport and said, "Welcome home."

"Thank you," I said, smiling. "It's great to be back."

After I collected my suitcase, I got a cab and gave the driver Gerry's address. I wanted to see Barney as soon as possible. I was so glad to be back, I found everything beautiful, even the Beltway, which I normally detested. Once at Gerry's, I paid the driver, left my luggage on the lawn and ran toward Barney's house. He was already outside, wagging his tail. "How's old Barney doing?" I asked, kneeling down to hug him. "Does your booboo hurt?"

I examined his cyst. It was no bigger than before. It just looked kind of ugly. Putting a bandage on it was pointless. He would bite it off within minutes.

"We'll go for a walk later, O.K.?"

I collected my luggage from the lawn and rang the bell. Gerry did his usual number of "Go away. We don't want any," but eventually opened the door. He did not seem thrilled to see me.

"What's the matter?" I asked. "Aren't you glad to see me?"

"You went to Barney first."

"Well, yes," I replied. "I wanted to check his cyst. Don't tell me you're jealous of a dog. Besides, if you knew I was here, why didn't you come out?"

Imagine if we had gotten married and had children, I thought with a shudder. He would be constantly competing for attention. It would have been awful.

"I brought you something," I said, changing the subject. "There isn't a heck of a lot to buy there, especially since this is my third trip."

I took out of my carry on souvenirs from Kyrgyzstan, Uzbekistan, and Germany. Gerry thanked me and said, "Let's go eat. I'm hungry."

I looked at my watch. Of course, it was 6:30. Gerry's dinner time was at 6:00.

"My treat," I said. "Where do you want to go?"

"You decide," said Gerry. "You're the one who has been out of the country for five weeks."

"What I would like more than anything else, is a good salad," I said. "Who has a good salad bar?"

"Big Boy?" Gerry suggested.

"Big Boy it is."

Over dinner, I gave Gerry a sanitized version of my trip, leaving out the Tajiks with the Uzis and the tete-a-tetes with Marcus. Gerry had not forgotten, however.

"What about that man from the Embassy? Was he there?"

"Yes, he was," I admitted. "He was just coming back from his medevac. He was sick a lot. He still hasn't recovered from the hepatitis he caught almost three months ago."

I bit my tongue as soon as I said hepatitis. That would get Gerry going. Sure enough, it did.

"Hepatitis? See what you can catch in these hellholes you're going to? Nothing is safe there. You can't eat, you can't drink, you can't breathe."

"Relax, Gerry. I didn't catch anything. I took shots before I left and I was careful. I always drank carbonated bottled water. I even brushed my teeth with it. I ate fruits that grew on trees because they're less likely to be contaminated."

I also ate tomatoes, cucumbers, beans, and carrots, but decided it might not be a good idea to reveal that. I reached over and touched Gerry's hand.

"Come on. You haven't seen me in five weeks. Why start picking fights about me seeing the dog first, and about diseases I didn't catch?"

I knew, however, that these arguments were partly due to Marcus-induced anxiety. Gerry and I were secure enough with each other to reveal lustful thoughts about members of the opposite sex. What upset Gerry was that my attraction to Marcus was not primarily lust. He could handle lust. An emotional bond was far more threatening. Suddenly, I understood the difference between lust and love that had perplexed me for years. I realized that I loved Marcus, and that the lust I had felt for Gerry was waning. Lust had kept us going all those years. Now, it was not working any longer. I was feeling things I had never felt before. Just thinking about Marcus made me feel I was flying. A look from him sent an electric current through my body. There had never been anything like that with Gerry, or anybody else for that matter. And now things were getting worse. In order to be able to sleep with Gerry at all, I had to close my eyes and imagine he was Marcus. I knew that this was only a short-term solution.

After dinner, we went back to Gerry's and walked Barney. It was almost like old times. Barney smoothed the tension enough for us to make love when we got back.

God forgive me, I thought afterwards. I'm only human and Marcus is far away and sick.

The following morning after breakfast, Gerry drove me home. I would come for Barney later. I had bills to pay and tons of mail to sort through. Gerry had mowed the grass, but weeds were growing in abundance in the flower beds. At noon, I called Marcus. It was 9:00 p.m. in Tashkent.

"Hello," Marcus answered.

"It's Janet. I thought you might want to know that I made it back safe and sound. It was touch and go at the Tashkent airport, though. I almost missed the flight."

"I'm glad you made it," said Marcus, his tone belying his statement.

"What's the matter? Aren't you feeling well?"

"I feel pretty good, except I'm a little down, I guess," he replied.

"Marcus," I changed the subject, not wishing to dwell on his down mood. "Do you know what day is today?"

"What?"

"It's Father's Day," I said. "Have you called your father?"

"No," Marcus answered.

"Did you send a card?"

"No."

"You can still call. It's morning in California."

"Yeah, yeah," he replied without enthusiasm.

"Your choice," I said. "I've found I always regret things I haven't done; never the things I've done. My greatest regret is that I didn't reconcile with my father before he died. Your dad isn't going to be around for ever. Besides, nothing gets your mind off your troubles like focusing on other people."

I hung up thinking that Marcus was a long-term, labor intensive project. He was behaving like a needy child, not a caring adult. He had a lot of developmental tasks to accomplish. Was I up to the challenge?

* * *

Taking the metro to the office Monday felt very strange. It was clean and comfortable and working perfectly. I looked at the expressionless faces of my fellow passengers. They followed their daily routine of going to work, collecting a pay check, raising kids. Did they have any idea why they were doing any of these things? Did they have any idea who they were? These people seemed to be missing something. Something crucial: Passion. Central Asian faces flashed through my mind. The Tajik with the Uzi who had laughed a gold toothed laugh at my diplomatic passport. He had passion. The guy who wanted a better prosthesis, so he could dance. He had passion. Alisher had passion. So did Ambassador Escobar. Marcus had passion, but only when he was angry. Gerry had no passion. His phobias had wiped it out.

The thought of my office at the State Department made me shudder. What made it bearable were the photographs of Central Asia I had made into posters: Marcus and the driver in front of lake Chervak, I on a mountain top in Chimgan, Samarkand's Registan Square, a creek in Bishkek, and the mountains near Alma Ata.

My colleagues were glad I was back. Their workload would decrease and they could travel. I looked at my in-box. It was overflowing with paper. Rita came in with a bulging folder. It held what would no longer fit in my in-box. I dove right in.

The week went by in a flash. My number one priority was the technical review of the bids on the financial sector contract. Then, I had to find two resident advisors for the Kyrgyz and one for the Uzbeks. Marcus would be bugging me about the latter, no question about it.

Among other things, I had to get a present for Gerry's nephew who was getting married in less than a week. I recalled the day last August when I picked June 27 to marry Gerry and how I put everything on hold a few hours later when I met Marcus. It turned out that I had to be at someone else's wedding that weekend.

I wanted to call Marcus to wish him a happy birthday, which posed a problem, since I would be sharing a room with Gerry. I would figure something out, though. The wedding was in Upstate New York, so Gerry and I drove up Friday evening and had dinner with the groom's parents. The wedding went off without a hitch except for the inevitable questions about when Gerry and I were going to get married.

I smiled and changed the subject. Back at the hotel, I located the pay phone nearest our room. I sneaked out at midnight to call Marcus. Fortunately, Gerry was sound asleep, so he didn't hear me leave. I dialed Marcus's number, but there was no answer.

Darn it, I thought. Where is he at 9:00 a.m. on a Sunday morning? At least he must feel OK, otherwise he would not be out.

I would have to try later. The following morning, when Gerry was in the shower, I tried again. Still no answer. Darn and double darn. If I did not find him by noon, I would have to call that evening, which would be too late. After breakfast, Gerry and I took a walk by the river. Then, I said I wanted to go for a swim before we checked out. On my way to the pool, I tried calling Marcus from the pay phone. This time he answered.

"Hi. It's Janet. What are you doing?"

"I'm riding my Lifecycle."

"You must be feeling fine then," I said. "You were out early this morning. I called you at 9:00 and there was no answer."

"I went for a hike with some guys from the Embassy," Marcus said.

"That was a nice birthday activity. Today is your birthday, isn't it?" I asked.

"Yes, it is."

"Well, happy birthday. Did anybody give you a party?"

"No," he said.

Darn that Barbara, I thought. She dropped the ball, although I circled the date on her calendar.

"Where are you?"

"I'm at a wedding near Albany," I explained. "You know what's funny? Almost a year ago, I picked June 27 for my wedding day. It's my virtual parents' anniversary. I thought it would be fun to have the same anniversary."

"I know, I know," Marcus laughed. "Another coincidence."

"I've got to go," I said. "I have to be out of this place by noon. Take care."

"Bye Janet. Thanks for calling," Marcus said, sounding pleased.

Gerry was going to spend some time in New York with his parents, so he drove me to the Albany airport for the flight back to Washington.

* * *

July passed very quickly with me busy putting together and chairing a technical review committee. In addition, I was trying to convince a professor Ambassador Curtis and Marcus liked to go to Uzbekistan as an economic advisor. I was constantly after the professor, even while he was on vacation. To make my case even stronger, I asked the Ambassador to give the professor a call. Evidently, that did the trick. The professor was duly impressed and agreed to go to Tashkent to meet the President. A trip was scheduled for August. I was in frequent contact with Marcus to schedule the visit. He was back to normal, as evidenced by his temper tantrums. Once, though, it was I who lost it.

"How are the birds?" I asked during a telephone conversation.

"They're dead," he replied.

"You're kidding, right?".

"No, I'm not," he insisted. "I left them out in the yard and the neighbor's cat ate them."

"For crying out loud," I shouted. "You're talking about becoming a parent and you can't take care of two little birds?"

I hung up in a huff. I was upset not only about the horrible death of the two canaries, but also because Marcus was alone again. His house was very well appointed, but lacked warmth. The two birds lent it some. Later, I regretted yelling at him, but it was too late to call back and apologize. I called from home that night.

"I'm sorry about yesterday's insensitive remark, but I was upset about the birds."

"You're calling me at 7:30 in the morning to talk about birds?" Marcus laughed.

"Well, it's 10:30 p.m. here and I can't go to sleep with this on my conscience," I explained.

"Which insensitive remark?"

"Which remark. You sound as if I made a bunch of them. The one about you being unfit to be a parent. You forgive me?

"Oh, that one. Yeah, I forgive you," Marcus chuckled.

"The poor little birds," I went on. "What are you going to do?"

"I got over it," said Marcus.

"So, you're not going to replace them?"

"No, I don't think so."

"Too bad. Well, I'd better let you get back to sleep."

"I'm going to get up. Somebody revised my plan to sleep late."

"Sorry, I didn't know you had such a plan. Have a good day."

The following day, a Saturday, I went to Hechinger's and picked up eight citronella candles in buckets, long matches, and pot holders. I planned to put them in the pouch for Marcus. The long matches were needed to light the gas oven. Regular matches were too short to do the job through the hole at the bottom. The cook lit the oven by lifting the panel at the bottom and igniting the gas with a rolled up newspaper she had lit with a match. I was appalled and had told Marcus this was a fire hazard.

In the meantime, Marcus was planning to fly to Pakistan, then take a bus to Western China.

"Pakistan in July?" I asked, surprised. "Don't they have monsoons or something?"

Marcus sounded like a broken record, "I've got to get to China, I've got to get to China."

He sent me a fax July 9, saying he was leaving the following day for Islamabad. "It will be an interesting, but difficult trip," he wrote.

I called him on July 18. "How was China?" I asked.

"I didn't make it. The monsoons had washed out the roads and I couldn't get there. I hung around Pakistan. Thanks for the videos, by the way. I ran into Todd Edwards on the flight from Islamabad to Tashkent and he gave them to me."

"He wanted to know whether they were XXX," I explained. "I said I would never corrupt an innocent youth like you. I didn't tell him you had actually asked me to put XXX videos in the pouch."

Marcus received my care package at the end of July. I was relieved. The pouch was notoriously unreliable. Once, it took four months for my thank you letters to Uzbek ministers to get from Washington to Tashkent. I was afraid the citronella candles would get there way past mosquito season.

"Oh, Janet," said Marcus. "You make me feel guilty."

"Guilty?" I was puzzled, although by now I should have been used to Marcus's unorthodox reactions. "Of receiving gifts? Why? You don't think you deserve them?"

"I do, I do," he said chuckling.

"Then what's the problem?"

"You give too much," he said.

"I'm a giving kind of person," I said. "Instead of feeling guilty of receiving, why don't you give something too?"

No question about it. Marcus needed reprogramming. He responded to kindness in a perverse way.

"So, how did it go with Ray?" I asked, changing the subject.

Ray was a colleague of mine, who had recently met Marcus in Tashkent. I had gotten Ray's version of how things had gone, "That Metamarro is full of shit."

Now I wanted Marcus's version.

"What a blowhard!" he exclaimed, then cautioned me, "Don't quote me on that."

"I won't, but I can tell you that he didn't like you either," I revealed.

"Yeah? What did he say about me?"

"I can't tell you over the phone. Maybe when I get there. What's it worth to you?"

"I will NOT be blackmailed," Marcus shouted.

"For crying out loud," I protested. "Where's your sense of humor? You act as if you're constantly under attack or as if attack were imminent."

* * *

August's main event was professor Conrad's interview with Uzbekistan's President and the latter's agreement to use him as an advisor. It was literally an earth shaking event. An earthquake hit Tashkent the very moment the president was saying, "OK, you may be my advisor."

I was overjoyed. This was one less thing I had to worry about. August was shaping up to be very busy for both Marcus and me. The latter was Charge d' Affaires because the Ambassador was out of the country. In that capacity, he bugged me even more over insignificant things. On August 24, I woke up from a dream that he was calling. I noted the time: 4:49 a.m. I called his office number.

"I just woke up from a dream that you were calling," I said. "What do you want?"

"It's in the cable I sent you," Marcus responded.

When I went to my office that morning, I found a cable from Marcus sitting on my desk. I checked the time: 9:49 a.m. Greenwich. It was the exact time I had waken up from my dream!

"The two of us would make a good experiment in parapsychology," I mused.

Three days later, there was another cable asking me to call Alisher in Paris. I started praying for Ambassador Curtis's early return. Obviously, Marcus loved to see his name at the end of the cables. He wanted to send as many as he could, while he was in charge.

Saturday morning, August 28, I woke up anxious from a strange dream.

I was putting shoes on a little girl. After I was done, I went by the bedroom and saw Marcus and Hilda, his old Swedish girlfriend. They were making love in an acrobatic kama sutra pose. They seemed to be in pain. Marcus's expression was a mixture of hatred and pain. Hilda was stone faced, apparently concentrating on the pose.

I awoke knowing Hilda was going to visit Marcus. I decided to check the accuracy of my intuition. I called Marcus at home. No answer. I called his office.

"American Embassy, Marcus Metamarro," he answered.

"Bradley residence, Janet Bradley," I mocked him.

"You're up early on a Saturday," he said.

"Yeah, well I had a weird dream. And what are you doing at the office on a Saturday afternoon?"

"I'm sitting here bidding on jobs for my new assignment and I have a splitting headache," he said, sounding anxious.

"Really? What are you bidding on?"

"Paris, Rome, and Ottawa. I want some place civilized," said Marcus. "If they send me to Ouagadougou, I'll quit."

"When exactly are you coming to Washington?" I asked, changing the subject. "I'd like to get some of your friends together."

"You don't know them," said Marcus abruptly. "Besides, I don't know exactly. I have to be in California for Dave's wedding on October 2nd and I'll be running out of leave by Columbus Day."

"Anything else new and interesting?" I didn't want to reveal my dream, unless absolutely necessary.

"Hilda is coming Monday. That's important, I guess. We're going to Thailand Labor Day weekend."

"You guess? You're not sure?" I asked. Might as well forget him, I thought. He's hopelessly screwed up. "Well, it's been nice chatting with you. Good luck with the job search," I said, hanging up.

I decided to get Marcus out of my life. I would plan to be out of town when he got to Washington. He even admitted to being screwed up. I had no obligation to help him. I was not a social welfare agency. All I needed to do was decide where, exactly, I would go.

Although I did not care for Greece as a whole, I felt drawn to Crete, especially the eastern part of the island. I had been there twice and not once to Rhodes and Corfu, two other famous Greek islands. Later that day, I called up United Airlines and made a reservation to Athens for October 1, returning October 17. Gerry wanted to go on vacation in September, but I could not make it. He, on the other hand, could not make it in October. Gerry had planned a bicycle trip to England the first two weeks in September.

By early September, my biggest worry was that Marcus would catch a tropical illness in Thailand. I called up the Department's Health Unit and asked what vaccinations were necessary for Thailand. Then, I faxed the information to Marcus.

Am I nuts, or what? This guy told me he's going to some exotic place with a leggy Swede and I'm worried about his getting sick during the trip. I'm not doing too well washing him out of my hair, I thought while sending the fax.

I didn't really believe Marcus would get these shots before he went. It just made me feel better that I had sent the information.

On September 4, I put Barney and a change of clothes in the car and drove to REI. I was going to pick up a sea kayak I had rented and head to Maryland's Eastern Shore for Labor Day weekend. None of the other kids were at the folks, so it would be quiet. Barney loved it there. He practically spent the whole day in the water. Once in a while, he would come toward the house to make sure everything was all right, then he would run into the water again. I was relieved Gerry was doing his thing in England. With Marcus on my mind, I could not focus on Gerry. He sensed that and felt hurt.

While kayaking on the Miles River, I thought about Marcus and Hilda in exotic Thailand. Why was I so upset about Hilda being with him? In my gut, I knew Marcus was not having wild sex with her. I imagined he was incapable of it. Anybody who was as tense as he was, could not maintain eye contact, and who could barely tolerate touching and being touched, could not possibly enjoy inserting any part of his anatomy into another being's anatomy. Hilda was an old, trusted friend. I shuddered at the thought of Marcus using her to his own selfish ends, including to promote his playboy image. Marcus wanted to appear sexually active, while being terrified of letting anyone get close to him. He had enticed Hilda to Tashkent and had asked the Ambassador for leave to go to Thailand with "his Swedish girlfriend." Diedre had told me about the Official Informal. Marcus had said about a colleague of mine, who he felt had crossed him, "I want to pull out every hair in her body." A misogynist would make such a comment, not a man who loved women. I suspected that Marcus's hidden resentment toward his exploitative mother had poisoned his relationship with the entire female gender.

I could relate to that. My violent relationship with my father and the unwanted attention of several men had poisoned my relationship with the male gender. To get back at men, I had toyed with them the way Marcus was toying with women. That's what hurt so much; getting a dose of my own medicine. Suddenly, I found myself hoping that Marcus would decide to settle down with Hilda. From what he had said, she seemed like a nice, caring person. Besides, she had legs that wouldn't quit. And he had known her for a long time. It would be easier for him to overcome his sexual hangups with Hilda as a partner. I felt I had made the right decision to get out of the picture.

Gerry came back from England on September 12, having enjoyed his bike trip.

"Would you be up to doing that bike tour around Deep Creek Lake on the 25th and the 26th?" I asked. "I've signed up both of us."

"I'll have to see how I feel by then," Gerry responded.

In the end, he did do the tour, but it was less than an enjoyable time for both of us. After Saturday's ride, there was dinner and dancing. Gerry said he didn't want to dance, so he went to the room. I found another cyclist who liked dancing and danced until the music stopped. Thank God, Gerry and I were sharing a suite with another couple. He gave me the silent treatment, instead of haranguing me about how selfish I was. I did not see how my abstaining from dancing would ease the pain in his hip. If I sat in the room with him, there would be two miserable people instead of one. I had asked him if he wanted to go for a swim before dinner and he had refused. When Gerry was in a down mood, the world's biggest forklift could not lift it. I was looking forward to my trip to Greece the following weekend and was quite perky as a result. Maybe my trip was another reason Gerry was down.

I got to Athens on October 2. After a couple of days visiting friends and a few days at my beach house, my mother and I took the ferry to Crete on October 10. I was quite calm and happy by then. I had finished the job of awarding the big financial sector contract, and I had gotten used to the idea of Marcus settling down with Hilda. Things were still hanging with Gerry, but I was certain we would part as friends at some point.

The boat docked at Heraklion early in the morning of October 11. My mother and I had breakfast at the restaurant on the dock and waited for the shops to open. I wanted to rent a car and drive to the eastern side of the island. For some reason, I had no interest in the western part. The eastern part drew me like a magnet. I did not know exactly where we were going to stay. We were going to play it by ear. That was one of the beauties of traveling in the off season. I wanted to visit Aghios Nikolaos. A friend had suggested that we also stop by a little town in the vicinity called Elounda. Evidently, it was the Greek Prime Minister's favorite.

My mother and I walked to the car rental place and rented a little Suzuki. Then, I drove in the direction of Aghios Nikolaos. It was already getting hot.

"Can you imagine how hot this place must be in August?" I asked Mom. "I don't know how these Scandinavians can stand it."

Crete was a popular destination for many Scandinavians. Charter flights made getting there easy. I was not very interested in the large town of Aghios Nikolaos. I drove around a few minutes and decided to head straight for Makris Yalos, a town on the south shore an English friend had suggested. I had just left Aghios Nikolaos when I saw a road sign with Elounda's name.

"What the heck," I said. "Let's swing by there to see what all the fuss is about."

Driving along the sea, I noticed plenty of rocks indicating good snorkeling. My interest piqued, I drove to a hotel on the beach on the outskirts of town.

"How would you like spending the night here, Mom?" I asked. "It seems like a nice place and it looks like the snorkeling will be great."

"I don't know," Mom said. "You decide."

Having lived with a controlling mother and husband for decades, my mother could not make decisions. This made traveling with Mom easy, but sometimes frustrating.

"Let's see if they have any rooms," I said.

Mom sat on a bench under a tree, while I went to the reception desk to ask about a room.

"We have one room left," the clerk said. "Mountain, not ocean view."

"That's fine," I said. "We're only staying one night."

Room key in hand, I went back to the car to collect the luggage and to the bench to collect my mother. The room was fairly pleasant, having been decorated in island style with stucco walls and native fabrics. There was no television.

We had lunch at the restaurant by the pool, then Mom went to the room for a siesta. I put my snorkeling gear on and dived into the blue Mediterranean. The water was refreshing this time of year and just right for me. I liked snorkeling in tropical waters because of the beauty of the reefs, but found the water too warm. This was just right.

The sun had already set when Mom and I walked to town for dinner. We had walked no more than half a mile when I saw the sign: Fast Food MAM. I was stunned. I had gone half way around the world to avoid Marcus. I was in a town I had not planned to be in and here were Marcus's initials! Talk about a sign. And this time I had not asked for it. What was this all about? Marcus must be leaving Washington now, wondering why I wasn't there. I had to do a meditation to try to figure this out. It seemed everywhere I went, something reminded me of Marcus.

"After dinner I would like to buy some souvenirs," I heard Mom say.

"What? Yes, sure. The shops must stay open late around here," I commented.

We had dinner at a restaurant by the sea. I had a lot of vegetarian entrees to choose from. Being a vegetarian was a snap in Greece. We visited a few souvenir shops after dinner. I had to get something for Gerry. Not only was he taking care of Barney, his birthday was in three days. I started looking at T shirts. A nice ceramic plate might be better for Gerry. As I was going through the T shirts, I noticed a peach one that seemed to be custom made for my peach shorts. I pulled it out and looked at the design on the front. My heart started to pound. The design was the same as on the tile Marcus kept in his bathroom: four dolphins in a circle.

"Have you been carrying this tile around the world with you?" I had asked him.

"Yes, I have. I like it."

"I like it too," I had said. "I've seen this design in Crete."

We both liked Crete. This was another 'coincidence' between us. Marcus had brought Hilda here ten years ago and I had brought Hugo. We had a series of awful fights and I had returned to Athens, leaving Hugo alone in Crete.

I bought the peach T shirt. There was no escaping Marcus. I might as well go with the flow. In a daze, I walked back to the hotel.

"I'm going to bed early, Mom," I said. "I want to have a good rest before I start driving around tomorrow. The way people drive around here, I have to be wide awake."

Mom had the same idea, so we both were in bed with the lights out by 10:30 p.m. Eyes closed, I appealed to my Higher Self for guidance. Our chat went like this:

J: "HS, why do all these weird things happen to me? I want to live a normal, peaceful life."

HS: "Ha! That's why at the age of eight you decided to go to America (Philadelphia of all places), become a U.S. citizen, and get a doctorate. Your mother used to say, 'Why couldn't you fall in love with a man like normal girls? You had to fall in love with a country.' Things do not just happen, you choose for them to happen; you chose to be born, you chose when and where, and you chose your parents."

J: "What are you driving at? That I chose to meet that heap of trouble who turned my life upside down and started driving me crazy as soon as I laid eyes on him?"

HS: "So, whose idea was it to go to Central Asia in late July last year? Not May or June, or even early July, but late July."

J: "Mine. It was perfectly logical: In May and June I was busy negotiating an Inter-Agency Agreement, and by the time I got Ivan on board it was July. I picked Central Asia because it was the poorest part of the NIS. After the initial trip, I was planning to quit the government, Gerry and I would fold our two houses into one and we would get married on June 27, 1993. That was my plan."

HS: "And how did you feel about marrying Gerry?"

J: "Well, I've always felt there was something missing. Somehow, we couldn't connect mentally, but I felt it was my duty to marry him after all these years. Everybody expected me to. Wait a minute. What are you implying? I subconsciously wished for someone like Marcus to appear? He's Italian, brunette, Catholic, from a large family, workaholic, reckless, impatient, full of contradictions, goes a mile a minute, inhales his food (and you know what that implies about lovemaking), and has an army of women chasing him. For all I know, even Harvey is after him. Whoever heard of a guy remembering another guy's birthday, let alone sending him a card? I have been avoiding his type like the plague."

HS: "And what are you?"

J: "I am NOT Italian, or Catholic, or come from a large family, or reckless; I take calculated risks. The rest I guess is the same. Wait. I guess Greek is pretty close to Italian, (but my German blood stabilizes my Greek blood), and I did go to Catholic church, and in my American family I am one of seven kids. All right, we're practically carbon copies. But this is just the point. I'm revved up as it is, and he revs me up even more. And when he's depressed or sick, he drains my energy and I feel like a discharged battery. Either way, I need him like a hole in the head."

HS: "Did you ever think that you need him to work out your karma?"

J: "Well, actually no. You suppose we left something unfinished in a past life and he followed me in this one to finish the job? It's possible, I guess. Or is he supposed to be my punishment for all the men I've hurt in this life? Oh boy! I sure hope it's not the latter, because the rest of this life is not enough to erase that karma, unless we both live to be 200."

HS: "How many men have you hurt?"

J: "Let's see. Wannabe husbands, six: two Greeks, one Dane, three Americans.

81

Miscellaneous lovers: out of a universe of seven or eight just Hugo. I cheated on him once, but I felt awful and never did it again. Wannabe lovers and assorted others: I can't even begin to count them."

HS: "And when did you start hurting men?"

J: "Since I was fourteen. That's when I got boobs and men started bugging me. No, it was earlier. When I was twelve, I punched Niko in the eye, but he was pestering my little brother. And in third grade, I beat up Yanni because he said in class that girls were weak. He was lucky the teachers lifted me off of him, or I would have smashed his face. Well, I had to prove to him that he was wrong. Oh, I forgot Tassos in second grade. He had those rosy, chubby cheeks that I liked to pinch or kiss, depending on my mood. OK, that was unjustified. Oops! I forgot my little brother. I started beating him up ever since he was born and I was twenty one months old then. And what about my father! I fought with him like cats and dogs until he died. Wait. There's one more. I didn't like getting baptized so I started pulling the priest's beard until it almost came off. (He thought I was a baby devil.) I was ten months old then. In short, I've been hurting men pretty much all my life."

HS: "You know how karma works."

J: "Yes. If I do something wrong and don't make up for it in one life, I reincarnate until I do. And if I go on doing bad things, I accumulate more bad karma and so on. OK, so maybe Marcus appeared to help me work off my bad karma. I've always been nice to him, although he has been driving me crazy and giving me nightmares, headaches, and insomnia."

HS: "Think again. When you got intrigued by the similarities between you and him, wasn't your plan to analyze him, label him, classify him, and then go off to marry Gerry? Did you ask his permission to use him as a guinea pig?"

J: "That was not my original plan. My original plan was to avoid him. When I saw on our schedule on that first trip to Tashkent 'Dinner with Charge and Embassy Officials,' I tried to get out of it. And I never finished analyzing him because he was so far away, and running around, or depressed, or sick. Then, I felt guilty and started giving him presents. Then, he started feeling guilty because of that. So it seems that we're accumulating bad karma when we're around each other. If this keeps up, we'll be chasing each other through many lifetimes just to work things out. How do I put a stop to this vicious cycle? I thought leaving him alone would do the trick, but again I find things that remind me of him."

HS: "This is because you're not finished with him, yet."

J: "Thank you very much. I could have told you that. I thought two weeks in December would be enough to get finished with him (ha! ha!) and here it is almost a year later and there is no end in sight. How do I get finished with him?"

HS: "Be patient, you'll know. This is also part of your karma. You have to learn to be patient."

J: "OK, I get it. I have to stick around, always be nice to him, and sometime, somehow, the situation will be resolved. If I'm not nice, more bad karma and so forth. This sounds like the taming of the shrew via karma. Thank you very much. Janet out."

I drifted off to sleep feeling I had barely scratched the surface of the deep connection I felt to Marcus Metamarro. I was certain beyond the shadow of a doubt that I had met Marcus for a reason. I was not quite sure what that reason was, but I was going to find out if it killed me. I knew I would see him again. I had to find out as much about him as I could.

The rest of my time on the island was spent swimming, snorkeling, and walking on the beach. I realized one my life's ambitions by visiting Vai, Crete's famous palm beach. The popularity of the place was proven by the packed parking lot. The beach was just as I had seen it on postcards. White sand, blue water, and lots of palm trees. What was not on the postcards, were the topless women. Entrance to the beach was free, but one had to pay a dollar to rent a chair. Mom and I settled on two recliners under the palm trees and I started to observe the people around me. All were foreigners. Most were Nordics, but I heard Italian and Spanish once in a while. I was trying to figure out a way to take pictures of the topless women to send to Marcus and Gerry. There was a heavy set German woman with melon-size breasts. Gerry, the boob man, would appreciate a picture of her. The problem was this woman never looked away. I had to settle for a picture of a well-proportioned, but less well endowed woman.

Seeing the sign with Marcus's initials was not the only event that shook me up in Crete. On our last day there, I decided to drive to the port of Heraklion via a different route. It entailed going up a winding mountain road and then down again on the north side of the island. It was on that road that I saw my life flash before my eyes. As I was rounding a bend, I almost had a head on collision with a huge truck that was taking up practically the entire width of the road. I threw the car into some bushes on the right side of the road. The trucker sped by without even slowing down.

"Are you all right, Mom?" I asked.

"What happened?"

"I had to throw the car into the bushes to avoid that truck," I explained. "I'll try to back out." Backing out of the bushes did not work. The wheels on the passenger's side were spinning in the dirt. What I needed was someone with a chain to pull the car out. As if by magic, a pickup truck stopped soon thereafter. The driver hooked a chain to the back of the rental car and pulled it out of the bushes. I thanked the man profusely. He would not accept any money. The car had a few little scratches, but otherwise it was in great shape. We had been extremely lucky. A near escape, on Gerry's birthday yet.

"God was watching over us," Mom commented.

The rest of the day, was uneventful. We stopped at Knossos for a look at the ruins. One of the reasons I liked the Minoan civilization was that women had equal rights with men. Girls wrestled with bulls alongside boys. Minoan women were the first civilized women to wear topless dresses. The palace at Knossos was an architectural and engineering masterpiece. In my opinion, the Minoan civilization was more advanced than that of Classical Greece.

After a late lunch on the roof of a restaurant near the ruins, I drove the few miles to Heraklion. I stopped on the way to wash the car a bit. The scratches from the bushes did not show on a clean car. I need not have bothered. The guy at the car rental did not even inspect the car.

On the ferry to Pireaus, I thought about my near miss with the truck. This was the second near miss in the last six weeks. At the end of August, I almost drowned when my whitewater kayak had overturned. Was there a message from above in these near misses? Was some behavior modification in order? I was not happy about the dual thing I was doing with Gerry and Marcus, but I was at a loss about how to resolve it. I had ended it with Gerry in February and then it started up again. In August, I resolved to get out of Marcus's life, even left town to avoid him. Then, I found all these reminders of him in Crete. At least, I had avoided Marcus this time. I would have been too rattled to see him now.

I arrived home the following day. My friend Kitty had insisted on picking me up at the airport. Kitty's daughter, Allison, wanted to see Barney, so I asked Kitty to drive to Gerry's house. Remembering his adverse reaction last June, I made a point of ringing the bell first, instead of rushing around back and greeting Barney.

With the pleasantries out of the way, we moved into the house, after I confined Barney to the back yard.

"Happy birthday, Gerry!" I fished into my bag and pulled out the presents I had brought for him, then gave Allison and Kitty their presents.

Gerry opened the box of chocolates I had bought at the Frankfurt airport, and the plate I had purchased in Crete. His fingers traced the octopus painted on the plate. "It's beautiful, Janet. Thank you."

I was relieved. It was so hard buying for Gerry; I was never sure how my gifts would be received. Allison and Kitty liked the jewelry with the Macedonian star, as well. They left for their dinner engagement shortly thereafter.

"Where are you taking me for dinner?" Gerry asked.

I laughed. "Some place close, quick, and easy."

The laugh died in my throat. By the look on Gerry's face, it was obvious he was looking forward to a cozy dinner for two, with dessert atop the bed sheets.

"Gerry, I hope you don't mind, but I'm beat. I've been up since 4:00 AM Athens time, and between the flight and the jet lag, all I want to do is get some sleep. Besides, tomorrow is a work day."

It was true; I was tired. But that was not the whole truth. I was anxious to get home and check my messages. I had to know if Marcus had called. Gerry accepted my decision without argument. There were no messages from Marcus at home.

At my office the following morning, the first thing I did was to check my voice mail. No messages from Marcus. I sat down and sighed in relief. At that moment, Rita walked in and handed me a yellow piece of paper.

"I didn't know you were back," she explained. "Here's a message for you."

I looked at it and got butterflies in my stomach.

"You were called by Marcus Metamarro. Please call."

The date was October 18 and the number was Diedre's number. He was still in Washington! How? Why? He was supposed to run out of leave a week ago. This was too much! No matter what I did, I could not avoid him. I took a few deep breaths, then dialed the number. Diedre answered.

"I'm returning the call of that vagabond diplomat," I joked. "Why is he still here?"

"He got promoted," Diedre replied. "He got a week's extension for consultations, in other words, he's looking for a job. Let me get him for you."

"When are you going to do a lick of work?" I teased Marcus. "You got medevaced for six weeks, then you took off a week in July and one in September and now you're taking off most of October!"

"I've done more work for this Department than anyone I know," Marcus said. "Are you free for lunch?"

"I guess so. I just got back. I haven't had time to plan a lunch date."

"Do you want to go across the street? I hate the cafeteria," Marcus suggested.

"My feelings exactly. Meet you at 12:45 at the Dip entrance?"

"OK."

I sat at my desk and considered my options. I could stand him up. I could call and cancel. I could show up and keep it light. I opted for the last option. Running away earlier this month had not solved a thing. I might as well face the music. I showed up at the Dip entrance at the appointed hour. Marcus came running from the opposite side. He was wearing a white shirt, striped tie, and light blue pants. He had his hair cut very short. He greeted me with a hug.

"What's this?" I teased, pointing at his hair. "The military look?"

"What about you?" he retorted, laughing. "Pretty short hair for a girl, I'd say."

"I may look like a girl," I said, "but I'm 50% male."

"I forgot. There's a man hiding in there somewhere," said Marcus, laughing.

"Of course, there is," I said. "And there's a woman hiding somewhere inside you. You just have to look inside to find her. Half of our chromosomes come from a male and half from a female. Don't you know anything?"

The cafeteria at the National Academy of Sciences was closed for a special function.

"Where should we go, then?" asked Marcus. "Our wonderful cafeteria?"

"Let's go to the Watergate," I suggested. "It's a nice day. We can buy something and eat it outside. I know a spot with river view."

"O.K., but I have to be back by 2:00," said Marcus. "I have a meeting."

"The way we eat? No problem."

We started walking north on 23rd street.

"So how's your liver these days?" I asked.

"It's working pretty well," Marcus replied. "But still not 100%."

"You know," I said with a serious expression. "The liver normally regenerates completely in six months. There must be some negative thoughts in your head that prevent healing."

"There must be."

"Well, get rid of them."

At the Watergate complex, we opted for the salad bar at the Safeway. I wondered if Marcus would buy me lunch, considering I had sent him a bunch of care packages and various gifts. I got ahead of him at the check out line. Marcus didn't make an effort to pay. I led Marcus to the upstairs court yard. Most people sat downstairs, so that part of the complex was relatively uncrowded.

"The only problem with this location is jets flying overhead," I said. "I can't believe people are paying megabucks for apartments on the flight path to National Airport."

"Well, it's a convenient location," Marcus commented. "I hate commuting."

"It depends on how you commute," I said. "I rather enjoy riding the metro. I usually find a seat and read, write checks or letters. I could never drive. The stress takes years off your life. Congratulations on your promotion, by the way. I didn't tell anybody you were thinking of quitting a few months ago."

"Thanks. Now I have to find a job for next year," Marcus observed.

"I think you should get something that would facilitate your eventual transition out of the Foreign Service," I said. "How about monetary affairs?"

"I'm checking into that and trade," Marcus revealed.

"I don't know about trade. I've done that and it's boring," I said. "You get involved in trade disputes. To change the subject. Did you hear about Diedre and Chad?"

"Yes. She told me. She must like younger men. She's out of my league," Marcus commented.

"Historical age is the least important," I said. "As a health freak, you should know that. Although younger in years, Chad may be psychologically older than Diedre. He's no wimp, that's for sure. If he were, he wouldn't have gotten mixed up with her."

In accordance with my plan, I did not bring up the Cretan coincidences. As we were walking back to the Department, I suggested we get Marcus's friend, Harvey, and my colleague, Helga, together.

"I saw him at the wedding. He only dates Jewish women," said Marcus. "Dave did too."

"I think that's narrow-minded on their part, but Helga qualifies. Will you set it up?"

"I'll mention it to him, and will let you know," Marcus promised.

"By the way," I said. "I've been reading some stuff on the mind/body connection."

"Chopra," said Marcus.

I shuddered. He was reading my mind again.

"Yes," I said. "Ageless Body, Timeless Mind."

"I bought the book when I was in California," Marcus revealed. "I'm reading it now."

When I had recommended the book to Gerry he had blown up at me, saying it was a bunch of crap and that I should not waste my money buying some quack's book. And here was Marcus reading the same book. Suddenly, Marcus stopped walking and faced me.

"Why did you go to Greece?"

"I wanted to visit my mother. I also wanted to get out of here. I went to Crete. That place soothes me."

"Oh, Crete. I've been there. I love it," Marcus said wistfully. "There's so

86

much history on that island."

"I dislike the rest of Greece, but I like Crete," I commented. "The Minoan civilization was more advanced than the Classical Greek one. Women were not second class citizens."

We entered the State Department building.

"I've got to run to my meeting," Marcus said. "You'll be around the rest of the week, won't you?"

"Yes, I will," I assured him.

"I'll see you later, then," said Marcus.

I went back to my office and thought about inviting Marcus to dinner at my house. I wanted him to meet Barney before he left on Saturday. I didn't have time to pull together a party and the thought of being alone with Marcus when he was not ill made me very nervous. I was afraid of doing something I would regret. Marcus and I were an all or nothing proposition. Either complete and unconditional surrender or arm's length. I was not ready for the former, so the latter would have to do. I could still go out with Marcus, Harvey, and Helga. That would be on neutral ground and on a superficial level. I could handle that.

I saw Marcus once more that week. He came to my office to return some of the videotapes I had lent him. He became serious when he saw the pictures on my walls: the one he had taken of me on the mountaintop and the one I had taken of him and the driver.

"I love that picture," I explained, pointing to the one Marcus had taken of me. "I enlarged the one of the lake because the colors were so amazing. Unfortunately, the enlargement does not do them justice." I decided it was safer to change the subject. "Just a minute. I want you to meet Helga."

I went to Helga's office next door and asked her to come meet Marcus. We chatted for a few minutes.

"What do you think?" I asked Marcus after Helga left. "Is she a good match for Harvey?"

"I told Harvey what you want to do," Marcus said. "He rolled his eyes."

"That was not what I asked you to do," I said, irritated. "I asked you to invite Harvey somewhere and then Helga and I would show up."

It was obvious Marcus was not interested in playing Cupid and Harvey was not keen on getting matched.

"The heck with it," I said. Why should I bother? For all I knew, Harvey was gay. I sought neutral ground. "Do you want to say hi to Sean?" I asked.

"No, he refused to see me," said Marcus.

"He did?!!"

"Yes. Diedre tried to set up an appointment for me and he said I should wait until you got back," said Marcus, getting up. "I'd better get going. I have tons to do before I leave. I guess I'll see you in Tashkent."

"Only if wild horses drag me there," I joked, getting up as well.

"Wild horses," Marcus laughed.

He gave me a hug and ran out the door. I watched him leave, wondering how I had ended up in such an odd relationship, if one could call it that. I vowed to level with him.

I wrote Marcus a five page letter telling him about thoughts and feelings I had not revealed before. After I put the letter in the pouch, it occurred to me that I had left out the punch line. I wrote another letter and mailed it later. I enclosed a tape on intimacy from Chopra's Higher Self set. In that letter, I wrote:

"...from information you have given me and by the way you act when we are alone, I got the impression that this nonstop movement and happy-go-lucky attitude is your way of covering up some pain you have been carrying around for a long time.....once you leave the Tashkent craziness behind, you should try to work it out and leave it behind, as well. I am willing to listen, if you are willing to talk. Do not fear that I will reject you. I promise I won't. In fact, I can't. You are so much like me that by rejecting you I would be rejecting myself. There is no chance of that."

The following week, I called up Marcus and told him that the letters and the tape were coming.

"I wanted to ask you about Chopra," I said. "When did you discover him?"

"A few years ago. I read his book *Perfect Health*," Marcus said.

"I read *Quantum Healing*," I explained. "It appealed to me a lot. Especially the part about Western medicine using a Newtonian model for the human body and ignoring its energy aspects. I have a physicist friend who cannot imagine the human body in terms of atomic and subatomic particles, although he has no problem with neutrinos in inanimate objects. As far as I'm concerned, $E=mc^2$ says it all. If you solve that equation for m, what you get is that mass equals energy. Mass is simply energy in a lower vibration. Just like water turning to ice when it freezes. The electrons are just moving more slowly. Once you accept the concept of an energy body, you have no problem accepting the immortality of the soul. The soul is energy and energy cannot be destroyed. Western medicine desperately clings to the Newtonian model because it can be observed. But to say that there's nothing more to a human being than what the eye can see is as silly as saying there are no infrared or UV rays. Besides, there are people who can see and sense the human aura."

"I got interested in Chopra because of the health aspects of his writings," Marcus observed. "You're going way beyond that. You're talking metaphysics."

"I certainly am," I said. "At some point, you have to get into metaphysics to understand physics. Do you accept that emotions influence body function?"

"I do," Marcus said. "It has been proven."

"Fine. Thoughts and emotions are energy, something metaphysical," I continued. "So you have something metaphysical affecting something physical. Now change the words. Use soul for metaphysical and body for physical. You have the soul influencing the body and vice versa. If memories are stored in the soul and the soul is energy that cannot be destroyed, you can see how it's possible to have past life recall. Are you still stuck in your one life belief?"

"I am. Reincarnation hasn't been proven."

"Marcus, have you listened to anything I've told you in the past ten months? I got flashbacks from past lives when I met you. All I have to do now is find a way of remembering more. I know I will remember when I can handle it. Past life memories are just like current life memories. They pop up when you're ready to handle them. Even two years ago I would not have been able to handle this. It just about wiped me out this time. I feel tormented, as if I'm repressing something that's struggling to come out."

"Well, we're not going to settle this issue today," Marcus said. "I have to get out of bed and do some chores."

"Isn't that funny?" I remarked. "We're both in bed, but you're getting ready to get up and I'm getting ready to go to sleep. Do you think the Uzbeks are enjoying our conversations? Maybe they'll learn something useful. Can you imagine the faces of the KGB types when they get a transcript of this conversation?"

In mid-November, I found out that Diedre was going to Tashkent for Thanksgiving. I called her up.

"Diedre, I have some things for Marcus that I can't put in the pouch. Can you do me a tremendous favor and take them with you?"

"What things?" Diedre asked.

"My special spicy cranberry relish and homemade pesto. I assume you're taking bananas and oranges. He's crazy about them."

"Sure, I can do it," Diedre said. "As long as they're not the Price Club size."

"No, no. You know I'm a reasonable person," I assured her.

Marcus had to spend another holiday away from home. At least, he would have something to remind him of home. The day before Diedre's departure, I took the cranberry sauce and pesto to her office.

"I've used plastic jars, but you'd better put these in your carry on, just to be on the safe side," I cautioned. "Thanks an awful lot for doing this."

"You know what I think?" Diedre said. "I think you're spoiling that man rotten."

"Impossible," I explained. "He's his own worst enemy. I'm sure he'll find a way to torture himself."

Thanksgiving was on the Eastern Shore again. This time, the crowd was smaller, so Gerry and I did not have to stay in a hotel. Maybe the excitement of the folks moving there was starting to wear off. I took Friday off and did the traditional thing. I went shopping with my virtual mother and sisters. Back in Washington, I put together a Christmas package for Marcus: some candles and decorations he could use, if he had a party. I was certain he would. Giving parties was part of his job description. It also helped him avoid the work he needed to do, like looking inside himself and getting in touch with his feelings.

I called Marcus before Christmas to wish him Happy Holidays.

"I got the two letters you wrote in October," he said. "They were two months in transit. Fascinating. I got the second letter first, so I didn't know what to expect. I watched Switch, the movie you sent. I thought it was weird. Is there a message I should be getting?"

"If you're not getting it, you're not ready for the message," I said. "All in good time. I expect a suitable response to my thought-provoking letter. Not some pap about the weather, OK? I'm going away for Christmas and New Year's to find some snow. Also, I'll be coming your way next month. You'll get a cable, as soon as I firm up the travel plans and the composition of the team."

I made a quick run to the Eastern Shore to drop off my Christmas presents, then headed to New York with Gerry and Barney. Barney loved it there. He had a girlfriend and could run around without a leash. There was not that much snow in Upstate New York that Christmas, but there was a lot of wind. Strong winds straight from the North Pole created wind chills of -50 Fahrenheit. Yet, Gerry and I went cross country skiing.

For me it was a test of how much cold I could endure. The wind was a bother, but if you could ski in such a way as not to head into it, it was not so bad. Skiing near trees helped. The wide open spaces were the worst. There, the human body was the only wind breaker, and not a very good one at that.

Back in Washington on January 2nd, I called Marcus to wish him a Happy New Year.

"Is there any relish and pesto left?" I asked.

"Are you kidding?" he responded. "I took half of the relish to Sonya's for Thanksgiving and then polished off the rest. The pesto was used up today. I had twenty five people to dinner tonight. They loved it."

"I'm not going to keep you long. I just wanted to know what I could bring when I get there. Tashkent will be my third stop, so fresh bananas are out. Maybe dry ones."

"Never mind," Marcus said. "You don't have to bring anything. How was skiing?"

"Cold. Minus fifty wind chill."

"Minus fifty!" Marcus marveled. "Where were you?"

"Upstate New York. Thirty miles south of the Canadian border. I'll send you pictures. Bye for now, you party animal."

That afternoon, I went to Toys Я Us. I wanted to get Marcus a stuffed animal. This would be a pet he could not kill. I also wanted to buy a book with the story of the Little Mermaid. It was one of my favorite fairy tales. I would hide that and a box of candy in his house until Valentine's Day. Then I would call him and tell him where to find his gifts. At the toy store, I found the perfect gift for Marcus. A mother and two puppies. The puppies barked when their bellies were pressed.

"He should get a kick out of that," I chuckled.

Toys Я Us had the Disney version of the Little Mermaid. It was distorted and the most important point was missing. I had to keep looking. I found what I was looking for at Crown: a faithful rendition of the Little Mermaid by Hans Christian Andersen. I snapped it up, as well as a few more books for my friends' children.

Monday, January 3, I was sitting in my office contemplating my overflowing in-box, when I noticed the corner of a white envelope. I pulled the envelope out of the pile and opened it. It was a letter from Marcus dated December 21. I looked at the postmark: December 23, 1993, Northern Virginia. Obviously, a traveler had brought it to the States and mailed it locally. I smiled as I read the letter. Marcus was starting to open up. He had started with: *"Wow! Your letter was fascinating"* and ended with *"I want to talk, but not on the phone with the KGB listening."*

Buried in the middle was the usual belly aching about the hardships of the post, defensiveness in response to my suggestion to face his pain, and admission that he found it difficult to open up to me. We had a lot to talk about when I got to Tashkent.

I went into Helga's office.

"Guess what Helga? I got a really nice letter from Marcus. He's still belly aching about the hardships of the assignment, but at least he's willing to talk. Finally, we're getting somewhere."

Helga was cynical. "He's trying to get sympathy. From the behavior you've described, there's something wrong with that guy. I'll check with the grapevine and get back to you."

At the end of the day, Helga came back with the verdict from the women's grapevine,

"He's a playboy. He's like a bee that goes from flower to flower. He'll probably end up with a blonde bimbo."

I thanked Helga for the information. I had learned something valuable: not to get my name linked with his.

I called Marcus Friday night, Washington time, to tell him I was thrilled to receive his letter. "I think you're getting there," I said. Subconsciously, you're doing many of the right things. You just have to put it all together by bringing to your consciousness the reasons for your behavior. I think it's very encouraging that you're willing to talk. Good communication is key to every relationship. I'm looking forward to talking when I get to Tashkent later this month."

The days before my departure for Central Asia were a bit stormy. Sean was being a pain, not letting me leave on January 12, as I had planned. I wanted to be in Almaty for the weekend, so I could go skiing. One of my goals on this trip was to ski all three Central Asian republics. He said he could not afford to have me out of the office for three weeks. He, however, took off for three weeks on a regular basis.

"Three weeks in three countries is the absolute minimum for accomplishing anything," I insisted.

He would not budge. He wanted me to leave over the weekend, in violation of his own travel rule: "Never travel on your own time. Always travel on government time."

I had no problem switching my Delta flight to a Saturday departure, but the Lufthansa connecting flight to Almaty the following Monday was fully booked. I was on standby and fuming. I stormed into Sean's office.

"Thanks to you," I said huffily "I'm flying standby coach to the other side of the world. On a holiday weekend yet!"

"You get no sympathy from me," he said. "I've done that."

"Not recently," I retorted icily.

"Before you go," Sean continued "I want you to send this task order to the contractor."

I looked at it. It was about a currency study.

"I don't think this fits into the contract," I said. "The contract is about delivering technical assistance. This is an academic exercise that's guaranteed to get us into trouble with the IMF. Currency introductions are their turf."

"I'm the boss around here," Sean raised his voice. "You do as I tell you."

"Since you're the boss, you can send it over under your signature. I don't want my name linked to this thing," I insisted. "I don't want the IG after me."

Things between Sean and me got even worse a few days later. He called me and the contractor's project manager into his office and demanded an hour by hour description of what we were going to do during the trip. I felt my blood pressure skyrocket.

"What are you trying to do to me?" I demanded to know after the contractor had left. "Do you want me to crack up? I'm under tremendous pressure and you're increasing it. You're treating me like a college freshman, for heaven's sake. I've been around this shitty town longer than you have. I know what I'm doing. Will you cut me some slack?"

Sean was shocked at my outburst.

"I don't want you to crack up," he said quietly.

"You could have fooled me," I continued. "And while we're at it, you're driving everybody else in the office crazy too. You leave Bill in charge, when you're not here and he can't take it. You're killing him. I took care of the shop before you got on the scene and you won't give me the time of day. Then, most of the time, you're leaving us in the dark, as if we were mushrooms. We find out what you've been up to from outsiders."

"Bill is older than you," Sean said. "He should be in charge when I'm not here."

"It's not the age Sean. It's the personality that counts. I think you have a problem with a woman who doesn't fit the Southern belle model," I shot back, alluding to Sean's Southern upbringing.

The only good news that week was getting a seat on the Lufthansa flight to Almaty.

I ran a few last minute errands Saturday morning, then packed. Gerry came over at 4:00 p.m. to drive me to the airport. I suspected he was doing this in order to give me a few more safety tips. "Don't worry," I reassured him. "I'm an old pro at this. This is my fourth trip to the region, remember?"

"Yes, but it's winter. Do these places have deicing equipment?"

"I'll be flying into Almaty and out of Tashkent. It's warmer in Tashkent. For all I know, it'll be sixty degrees. It was pretty warm last December. Quit worrying. Everything will be fine," I said pinching his right cheek as he drove.

As I was waiting to board the flight to Frankfurt, I remembered I had left the banana chips for Marcus on the kitchen counter. Oh well, I thought. He'll live.

The following morning, as I was getting off the plane in Frankfurt, I noticed the IMF's tax advisor to Uzbekistan.

"Rob, what a pleasant surprise. Were you on this flight? I didn't see you. Then again I was in coach," I said.

"I was in Business Class," Rob said. "I'll be flying to Tashkent tomorrow."

"You will?" I said. "Could you do me a favor and take something to Marcus Metamarro at the Embassy? I'll be on the flight too, but I'll be getting off in

Almaty.

"Sure, Janet. Anything for you," Rob said.

"I'll give it to you on the flight," I said. "Where are you spending the night?"

"The airport Sheraton, and you?"

"I'm going to my regular hangout in Wiesbaden," I replied. "I like the small town atmosphere. I do use the Sheraton's pool and sauna, though. That's where I'm headed now."

"Your problem is that you have too much energy," Rob said. "You're a lot like Metamarro."

"It's not a problem if you use it constructively," I responded. "I'll see you tomorrow."

I followed my usual routine in Germany: luggage check, swim and sauna, train to Wiesbaden, nap at the hotel, stroll and dinner after the nap, jogging and shopping the following morning. The first item I purchased was a bunch of bananas for Marcus. I chuckled "I don't think there's been another IMF mission that has delivered bananas in any country. I'm blazing trails again."

I wished I could get off in Tashkent with Rob and deliver the bananas in person to Marcus. But this was not the plan. At the gate, I looked for Rob and could not find him. I looked for him in Business Class after I boarded the plane. No Rob.

"Could he be in First Class?" I wondered. "He could have upgraded from Business."

Sure enough, Rob was in First Class. I handed him the plastic bag with the bananas.

"If you give these to Metamarro," I joked, "he'll be your slave. He's nuts about bananas. And if you want to find me, I'm in coach with the hoi polloi. But I'm not complaining. It was a miracle I got on this flight. I would be happy sitting on the toilet."

My consolation was that my consultant, following U.S. government regulations, was also in coach. I couldn't sit with him, though. He smoked. Before dawn tomorrow, we would be in Almaty, last year's Alma Ata. I wonder how cold it will be, I thought as I relaxed in my seat. Exactly eight months ago, Marcus and I were on this flight. That was the first and only time we had spent the night together.

CHAPTER SEVEN
Blazing Exotic Trails

The arrival in Almaty that cold January morning was quite different from May's arrival. It was cold; very cold. The pilot had said that the air temperature in Almaty was -25 Celcius. I did not exactly know how cold that was in Fahrenheit, but it had to be in the single digits, if that. I could see the lights of the sleepy city reflected on the snow-covered ground. Would there be landing lights at the airport, or just a guy waving a flashlight? This was the first time I would be landing in Central Asia in the dark. I did not know what to expect. As we approached the airport, I saw the blue lights lining the runway. All right! Things were not as bad as they could be. Considering the weather conditions and the rather bad shape of the runway, the landing was surprisingly smooth. I walked from the plane to the arrivals hall, congratulating myself on the foresight of wearing my down coat, hat, and boots.

Waiting for one's luggage was always exciting in Central Asia. The Almaty airport did not have a carousel. The luggage was dumped manually onto the floor of the baggage claim area through a trap door. The passengers rummaged through the pile of luggage, looking for their own. Fortunately, my skis and suitcase appeared safe and sound. The logistics people from the aid mission whisked me and the consultant into a waiting vehicle that took us to the hotel. There was still time to get some sleep before I faced Mr. Wonderful, the mission director, and reported to duty. The contractor's project manager was arriving from Moscow on a different flight.

I had a lot of work to do in the three days I was scheduled to be in Almaty. I got bad vibes from Peter Daniels, the field economist I was introducing to my counterparts. He was a city slicker who was trying to navigate on the icy Almaty streets in Wingtip shoes, a summer blazer and trench coat, and no hat or gloves. I had to hold on to him to make sure he didn't take a spill. Definitely not my kind of guy.

The next stop was Bishkek, Kyrgyzstan. Our delegation was meeting with Kyrgyz officials to arrange the placement of resident advisors. First, we stopped by the Embassy to brief Ambassador Rabinowitz. He had a reputation for being paranoid; seeing plots and conspiracies where none existed. That Embassy had the highest personnel turnover in the region. Then, we made a quick stop at the local U.S. aid office. We had to find a car and driver to take us to Tashkent the following Thursday. In addition, I wanted a car and driver to take me to the mountains Saturday and Sunday. I was determined to go to Ala Archa, where I had hiked with Ned Bennett the previous June, snow or no snow. By the end of the day, I had found a car and driver. Alexei, turned out to be a trainer for the Kyrgyz rowing team. Still no snow, though.

After dinner in Bishkek's only Italian restaurant, Daniels suggested we stop at the hotel bar for a nightcap. I declined, saying I had to get up early to go skiing.

"But there's no snow," Spencer Lewis, one of the resident advisors, observed.

"It's not morning yet," I said.

I bid everyone good night and went upstairs to my room.

The snow gods must have heard my prayers. The following morning, I looked outside my window and it was snowing! It looked like powder and it was sticking. Yes!! I could go skiing after all. Alexei and I set out for Ala Archa in the midst of a snow storm. I was a little worried about the performance of the little Lada Alexei was driving, but there were no problems. Alexei was built like a line backer. I felt confident that he could push the little Lada out of any snow drifts it might get stuck in. I had a fine time skiing the trails I had hiked last summer. I even did a little bushwhacking. On an impulse, I skied along the road to the park entrance, a distance of ten kilometers, while Alexei followed in the car. When we got back to the hotel, I made a date for the following day to go to a place called Shong Tash (Black Boulder).

Shong Tash turned out to be hilly and very popular with the Kyrgyz. Dozens of people climbed to the top of the hills and slid down on plastic bags. Some rode horses, while others picnicked on the snow. I saw only one other X-C skier.

Alexei took me to the Black Boulder after which the area was named. It was covered with names and messages. He explained that this was a magical boulder. It remembered those who touched it. It even cried. He asked me to touch it to see that it was moist. The boulder stood on the snow covered ground. There were no overhangs where melting snow could drip on it. If there was water underneath it, I could not understand how it could reach the top of the boulder. If not magical, the boulder was certainly mysterious. But I had come here to ski.

Things started to unravel the next day. There were difficulties in placing Spencer Lewis in the Finance Ministry due to a reorganization. Then, the aid mission director ordered us to abort the Tashkent portion of the trip and return to Almaty. The Uzbeks had refused, after two days of negotiations, to grant a visa to an American consultant. The mission director wanted to send the Uzbeks a signal. I was furious. He was playing right into the hands of the hardliners. They would like nothing better than to keep all Americans out of the country as long as possible.

"Listen," I told Daniels. "I can't tell you what to do, because he's your boss. My travel orders, however, were issued in Washington. I'm not going to let him jerk me around. He can prevent me from going to Tashkent as a government official, but he can't prevent me from going there as a private citizen. I'll go there and goof off until I catch my flight back to the States."

I called Marcus to inform him of Butcher's orders. Maria, the secretary, answered and said Marcus was at a meeting. I said it was urgent. Marcus came to the phone.

"Carl Butcher ordered us to abort the Tashkent portion of the trip to send the Uzbeks a message."

Marcus was furious. "What does Fister have to do with you? He didn't have a visa, and he was on some kind of black list. You have a visa and you're welcome in this country."

"You're preaching to the choir," I said. "I'm coming no matter what Butcher says. But I'll be coming as a private citizen, so I won't be able to do any business."

"You work for a doozy of an agency," Marcus shouted. "I feel for you. I've got to run now. I'm in a meeting."

I spent a sleepless night. Sean jerked me around in Washington, and Butcher was jerking me around in the field. I believed in the cause and wanted to help the Central Asians, but these guys made it very difficult. They cared more about ego trips than doing some good. I could not take it any longer. I drafted a letter of resignation. I would submit it when I got back. By morning, I had changed my mind. I didn't want to give them the satisfaction of driving me out.

At 8:00 a.m. the following morning, I called Butcher. No answer. I tried again a few minutes later. Still no answer.

"Where the hell are the switchboard people?" I exploded. "Asleep at the switch?"

Finally, I got hold of Butcher shortly before 9:00.

"Hi, Janet. How are you?" Butcher seemed cordial.

"How am I?" I let loose. "I spent a sleepless night. I have reservations to return to Washington from Tashkent. Sean made me change my reservations before I left, so I had to fly standby coach. Now you're asking me to change my plans once more."

"Janet, you don't understand," he protested. "We need to send the Uzbeks a message."

"I understand very well," I interrupted. "You're playing into the hands of the hard liners. Fister knew he was working on a sensitive project. He should have gotten a visa in the States. I don't see why I should abort my mission because he screwed up. It took me weeks to put it together. Our country refuses entry to thousands of people every day. How can you point the finger at the Uzbeks for refusing entry to one American?"

"I have to go," Butcher said. "I have a meeting."

What a coward. I got dressed and went to breakfast. I had to find a way to get to Tashkent on my own. It did not take me long to locate the World Bank representative. He agreed to give me a ride. This important issue settled, I decided to make up for some of my lost sleep by taking a nap. When I got up from my nap, I realized I had missed the 2:00 p.m. meeting with Ambassador Rabinowitz. I wondered if that would be a problem. I found out at dinner time, when I reconnected with my team.

"Janet, I have some good news and some bad news," Daniels said. "Which do you want first?"

"Give me the good news."

"Butcher changed his mind. We have permission to go to Tashkent."

"All right! So what's the bad news?"

"Rabinowitz is pissed at you. He thinks you and Spencer are cutting deals with the Kyrgyz behind his back."

"Whaaaat?" I said. "The man is seriously paranoid. I was taking a nap and overslept. Didn't you cover for me?"

"I did the best I could," Daniels said. "It gets worse; Rabinowitz is trying to get dirt on you. He thinks you took an Embassy car to go skiing. He's asked the motor pool guys for the log."

"The man is out of his mind," I said incredulously. "I did not take an Embassy car. I hired my own and paid for it out of my own pocket. I'll take care of Rabinowitz later. Now, the important thing is to hire a car to take us to Tashkent. A four wheel drive would be ideal. The roads are pretty icy."

I let the World Bank rep know that I would not be riding with him after all. I also had to call Marcus to tell him the good news, although I suspected he had something to do with Butcher changing his mind.

I found Marcus at home that evening.

"Marc, everything is cool. We're coming Thursday. We don't have a car yet, but we should be able to get one tomorrow. I see your hand in this."

"You bet. Didn't you see the cable I sent you?" Marcus asked.

"No, I didn't go by the Embassy today. Rabinowitz is pissed at me, but that's another story."

"Well, I sent cables to Butcher in Almaty, to Washington, and to Bishkek from ambassador Curtis. I copied you on them. I used some pretty strong language."

"Really, Monkey?" I said, delighted. "I know you're potent with a pen when you get fired up! So tell me, how's the snow? I'm determined to ski in Uzbekistan this time. I want to check out Yanyabad."

"Nothing doing," Marcus said. "We've had a warm spell and the snow is melting."

"You're forgetting you're dealing with the snow queen here," I joked. "I have a special pact with the snow gods. It was in the upper forties when we arrived in Bishkek on Friday, and within hours there was a blizzard. I got some great skiing in over the weekend."

"I've already booked you for meetings all day Saturday," Marcus replied.

"Well, what about Sunday?" I said hopefully.

"I'm putting together a road race and I'm sure you'd like to participate," he said.

"A road race, in the middle of Winter? Where?" I asked, surprised.

"In town."

"Marcus!" I protested. "We talked about going skiing before I left Washington. You knew I was bringing my skis. You never said anything about a road race. I didn't bring my running shoes, just hiking boots."

"You could wear those."

I was irritated at the control games Marcus was playing. He had been playing those games ever since I met him. He had merely expanded his repertoire to private activities. I would ski Uzbekistan, or else. I would take a couple of days off if I had to.

"I'd better go, Marc," I said. "I see my delegation is trying to get my attention. I'll see you Thursday. I'll call when I get in. Bye for now."

Early the next day, Peter Daniels, Chris Bellows, the contractor's project manager, and I met in the hotel lobby. It didn't take long to load the van, fill the gas tank, and set off across the icy mountain roads.

At Chris's request, I had to tell the driver to slow down several times during the trip. Apparently, speeding on slick roads without snow tires, was considered normal in that part of the world. Fortunately, the road conditions improved when we descended to a lower altitude.

My excitement was mounting at the prospect of seeing Marcus again. He had said he wanted to talk. That was good news: it showed he was beginning to trust me. We approached Tashkent from the north and I pointed out to my fellow travelers some of the landmarks I had encountered on my previous visits. I noted that the U.S. Ambassador and his deputy also lived nearby.

"Is the deputy married?" Peter asked.

"No, he's not," I responded, surprised at the question. "Why do you ask?"

"I was wondering what the social scene was like around here."

"This is definitely much more of a party town than is Almaty," I explained. "There's a large diplomatic community and lots of things are going on."

At 5:30, we pulled into the parking lot of the Hotel Uzbekistan. The trip had taken ten hours. We had made very good time, considering the weather conditions. I was counting minutes until I could call Marcus.

Once we had checked in at the hotel, I suggested we rest for a while and then have dinner at the Korean restaurant. I would ask Marcus to join us. Peter and Chris agreed. I said I would let them know when Marcus arrived. As soon as I was in my room, I dialed his office number. I knew it by heart.

"Hello?" Marcus sounded testy.

"It's Janet. We've just arrived all in one piece. Do you want to join us for dinner at the Korean restaurant?"

"OK," he agreed. "What time?"

"Seven?"

"Fine. Where do we meet? At the restaurant?"

"Why don't you come to my room?" I said. "I'm in 918. I'll be taking a nap."

"All right. See you then," Marcus replied.

I lay on the bed with my clothes on and closed my eyes. Sleep was out of the question. At least, I could relax for a few minutes. I was still thinking of the questions I would ask Marcus during our talk, when I heard a knock on the door.

"Who is it?" I asked in Russian.

"It's me," a male voice said in English.

"Who's me?" I teased. "I don't know any me."

"Marcus. Quit fooling around."

"Oh, that me." I laughed and opened the door.

Marcus walked in with a dark look on his face. I gave him a hug. He did not hug me back. I didn't ask what was wrong; I was sure he would tell me.

"Boy, are you a sight for sore eyes!" I said. "You don't know what I went through to get this delegation here!"

This was the opening Marcus was waiting for. Actually, any statement would have served his purpose. He sat stiffly on the chair across from my bed, wearing his trench coat over his suit and looking straight ahead.

"What YOU went through!!" he exploded. "This has been the week from hell. All last weekend, I kept shuttling between the airport, the Embassy, and the Ministry of Foreign Affairs to get Fister a visa. As you know, I did not succeed. But that's not the worst thing that happened."

"No?" I asked, curious. "What else happened?"

"This goon from the KGB saw me naked as I was walking from the shower to my bedroom," Marcus said, fuming.

"Really? Where was he?"

"In the neighbor's yard, standing on a chair, and looking over the wall."

I visualized the scene and felt like laughing. It was too funny. Marcus obviously was not amused, so I tried to empathize.

"Did he take any pictures?"

"No, I don't think so," Marcus said. "I threw my sweats on and ran next door. I didn't see a camera."

"Did you moon him?"

"No," Marcus said quietly.

"I would have," I continued. "Then, I would have given him this."

I made a gesture with my left hand grabbing the right arm above the elbow, the right hand in a fist moving upward.

"Do you think he'd understand the meaning? Maybe he could look it up in his obscene gestures manual. Seriously, Marc. I think you're overreacting. Besides, you were partially responsible for the incident."

"Me?" Marcus turned to look at me.

"Of course. You had your blinds up and didn't cover yourself. Why is this such a big deal, anyway? He didn't catch you screwing a hooker, or anything."

Marcus calmed down somewhat, but still looked gloomy.

"It's just that I have no privacy. If I only had a little more privacy," he complained.

I suspected that the privacy issue had its roots in events long ago and far from Tashkent. I tried to reason with Marcus.

"Why do you feel you have no privacy? You live alone in a three bedroom house. How much more privacy do you need?"

"The phone is tapped," Marcus went on "and they're watching me."

"What proof do you have that they're watching you constantly? You just mentioned one incident. My guess is it's related to last weekend's airport drama. Do you have proof of others?"

"No," he responded, hesitating.

"OK, then. Let's talk about something happy. Is San Francisco a done deal?"

"I haven't quite nailed it down yet, but it looks promising. This guy wants me. I'm counting days until I get out of here."

"And what if the Big One hits while you're in San Francisco? That doesn't worry you?"

"This is a chance I'll have to take. It'll be something to tell my grandchildren," Marcus said.

"There are problems everywhere, Marc. You can't control events. But you can control your reaction to the events. Do you think I'm having a ball in Washington? The turf wars are driving me nuts. I'm doing my best not to get caught up in them. You didn't even ask how I was. If you got interested in other people, it would take your mind off your problems. What about the poor Uzbeks? You know how Alisher lives and he's a deputy minister. Can you imagine how the common folk live? Let's go to dinner. You'll feel better after you have your kapamaki and tempura udon."

"I need to wash my hands," Marcus said, still frowning. He walked into the bathroom and shouted out to me, "You can't even find decent soap in this country."

"Here," I said. "Use the soap I brought. It's from Elounda, the place where I saw your initials and freaked out. I'll enlighten you, sooner or later."

"I'm already enlightened," Marcus said in a huff.

"Ready?" I asked after Marcus finished washing his hands. "Let's go round up my delegation."

We went down the hall and I knocked on Peter's door.

"Mr. Metamarro is here from the Embassy," I said. "Are you ready to go to dinner?"

"Mr. Metamarro," Marcus chuckled.

"Shhh. Be quiet," I whispered. "We have to be formal. I don't want them to think we're too familiar."

"Not quite ready," Peter said behind the closed door. "I'll meet you upstairs."

There was no answer at Bellows's room, so I slipped a note under his door. Marcus and I went to the restaurant on the roof and sat side by side at a table by the window. Chris and Peter showed up a few minutes later and I made the introductions. Marcus immediately launched his tirade against Uzbekistan. The two other guys could barely get a word in edgewise. Finally Peter asked Marcus, "How long have you been here?"

"Too long," I responded.

"I didn't say it, you did," Marcus said frowning, then added. "I can't wait to get out of here. My next post is San Francisco, then Washington indefinitely."

Marcus continued to whine to the point where I wished he would leave. As if on cue, he got up. I got up too. He threw his share of the tab on the table and touched my arm.

"I'll see you tomorrow," he said. "I have to go now."

He bid everyone goodnight and marched out of the restaurant.

"Wow!" Peter exclaimed. "This is one bitter guy. Are we going to hear more tomorrow, or is he finished?"

"Marcus is OK, really," I said. "He's just had a tough week."

A few minutes later, I also left. I wanted to check the schedule Marcus had left for me. In my room, I glanced at it and saw it was packed. Sunday was described as a rest day for the delegation, but I knew that Marcus wanted me to participate in the foot race. Afterwards, there would probably be a party. I got the feeling that Marcus was doing his best to avoid his talk with me. In addition, there was no time for skiing. I had to extend my stay. I made a mental note to fax Sean about the change. My first priority, however, was to corner Marcus and have that talk with him. It was apparent that something was wrong with him, and I was determined to find the cause. I called him first thing in the morning.

"Marc, I saw the schedule and I smell a rat," I said firmly.

"What do you mean?" he asked, perplexed.

"The schedule is packed with activities from morning to night. When are we going to have our talk? You wrote me you wanted to talk," I said, a hint of annoyance in my voice.

"How about breakfast at my house Sunday morning?" Marcus suggested.

"Fine," I agreed. "What time does the race start?"

"1:00 p.m., but I have to leave by noon to mark the course," Marcus explained. "Do you want to come over at 9:00?"

"Sounds good. I'll see you in a few. A car is coming for us at 8:30, but I have to put myself together and have breakfast, first."

The first meeting of the day was at the Embassy with Marcus to go over the schedule. It was the beginning of a rather tense week. Marcus was still in a black mood and proceeded to dominate the meetings, frequently showing off his fluent Russian. I took as much wind out of his sails as I could. Chris Bellows was watching the dueling duo with a smile on his face.

"It was interesting watching the two of you go at it," he told me afterward. "Marry the bum, that'll show him."

Fortunately, Marcus left the delegation alone in the afternoon.

That evening, I was chatting with Bellows in the lobby of the hotel when I saw the British Ambassador, Percy Berger, walk by. He stopped to chat. He had served in Athens and liked to practice his Greek with me. After Bellows left, Percy invited me to dinner at his house Saturday night.

"I would love to," I replied. "I must check my schedule, however, to make sure I can. I'll confirm tomorrow morning. What's going on around here? I see a lot of dignitaries going by."

"There's a party for Indian Independence Day," Berger explained.

"Do you think I could crash it?" I asked.

"Why not?" Berger said. "Nobody would turn a beautiful woman away."

At that moment, Jonathan Bond, one of the U.N. people, walked up.

"Come on," he told me. "You can impersonate my wife."

I thought that was an excellent idea. That would make me Mrs. Bond. I walked into the room on Jonathan's arm and shook hands with the Indian ambassador and his wife. Jonathan was telling everyone who would listen that I was his wife.

"Jonathan, will you stop that?" I whispered. "What if your real wife shows up later?"

"Impossible," Jonathan assured me. "I haven't got one."

I looked around the room and saw Marcus chatting with an Uzbek.

"Excuse me, Jonathan," I said. "I need to tell Mr. Metamarro something."

I walked up to Marcus and pulled on his jacket sleeve. He turned around and looked at me, smiling. Then, he told the Uzbek, "Dr. Bradley would love to teach at your university. She's a very good economist."

I smiled at the Uzbek education official and whispered to Marcus, "I need to talk to you."

He couldn't get away from the Uzbek. I took a piece of paper and wrote:

"Dinner tomorrow night at 8:00 at the British Ambassador's residence. Can you make it?"

That caught Marcus's attention.

"He didn't invite me," he said, puzzled.

"He invited me," I said. "I can ask him if I can bring a friend."

"That wouldn't be cool," said Marcus.

"Suit yourself," I said. "See you tomorrow morning."

Before going to sleep, I mentally reviewed the day's events. Marcus was full of vinegar. He seemed pleasant at the Indian party because he was performing. I couldn't wait for the one-on-one on Sunday.

When I went down to the 8:00 a.m. breakfast meeting the following morning, everyone was there except Daniels. The only two available seats around the table were on either side of Marcus. I chose the one on his right. As usual, Marcus and I ordered the same thing: kasha without meat and green tea. The kasha arrived with a pool of grease on top. In perfect synchrony, Marcus and I emptied the extra grease into an empty cup, then took a spoonful of jam and mixed it with the kasha. The other meeting participants watched this ritual with interest.

"Are you sure you two aren't twins separated at birth?" Bellows teased.

"I'm sure," I responded. "We're something else, which is not the subject of this meeting."

When the conversation turned to the previous day's meeting with the Central Bank chairman, Marcus shouted at me, "You asked the Chairman stupid, basic questions. You don't read my cables."

I felt like slapping him. "I'm sorry, Your Excellency, I have twelve countries to worry about and you have one. I've read enough of your cables to know that you misspell the name of the Uzbek currency: it's s-u-m, not s-o-m. The latter is the Kyrgyz currency. See?" I said, tapping his shoulder.

I pulled a Kyrgyz and an Uzbek banknote and stuck them under Marcus's nose.

"Well, then we have to change it," he said, deflated.

The meeting participants were watching the exchange with their mouths hanging open.

"Excuse me," I said. "I have to go see what happened to the missing member of my delegation."

After checking with Daniels, I went back to the dining room and told everyone that he was coming.

"The Finance Ministry is close by," I said. "Anybody want to walk?"

"Not me," Marcus said. "I don't want to get sweaty."

"I don't mind getting sweaty," I said. "I'll see you all there."

It was a clear, crisp morning. Walking the half mile to the Finance Ministry was very pleasant. Marcus behaved himself during the meeting with Alisher, but started acting out again at the Cabinet of Ministers. He had decided to crash that meeting at the last minute. After the last meeting of the day, Marcus asked me if I was still going to Percy's dinner party. When I responded in the affirmative, he revealed he had to attend a party at the French Embassy.

I went to my room and got ready for my evening with Percy. I thought of what to wear and decided against a dress. If I wore my black wool pants, I could wear boots and avoid wearing hose and heels. My cream blouse and pearls would make the outfit dressy. I disliked high heels and hose, and avoided them whenever I could.

At Percy's, I was surprised to find that I was only one of four guests and the only woman. I also noted that Percy's house was not as luxurious as Marcus's, although he had a higher rank. It was a case of first come first served. The dinner conversation was very entertaining. I could have stayed longer than 11:00 p.m., but I needed a good night's sleep. I wanted to be fresh for my big talk with Marcus and the road race the next day. I asked Suhrat to pick me up at 8:30 a.m.

Back in my room, I gathered my gifts for Marcus: the stuffed dogs, the Little Mermaid book, the box of candy, and the Valentine. I intended to hide the last two items somewhere in Marcus's house, then reveal the hiding place on Valentine's Day. Included in the care package, was a diagram of The Quantum Mechanical Body by Deepak Chopra. I planned to continue the discussion on metaphysics I had started with Marcus on the phone. I packed the gifts and a change of clothes in my carry on, took a quick shower, and went to sleep full of anticipation.

The following morning, I grabbed my carry on and ran to the parking lot to meet Suhrat. He was there, smiling as usual. At Marcus's, he asked me when I wanted to be picked up.

"*Eta vsio civodnia*," I said. "This is all today. Tomorrow 9:00 a.m. at the hotel."

I rang the bell by the gate. Marcus opened it shortly. He was in en garde mode: no hug, no smile. He wore jeans and a button-down shirt with the sleeves rolled up.

As soon as I walked into the living room, I noticed the plants were dying. Some of them were sitting on the radiators next to the windows. Obviously, they were getting too much heat, and Marcus had not been watering them enough. First the birds, now the plants.

"Marcus!" I exclaimed. "The plants are dying. You shouldn't put them on the radiators. It's too hot for them. Haven't you been watering them?"

"I don't care," Marcus shrugged.

He ushered me into the kitchen.

"Do you want a cappucino?" he asked. "My sister sent me a machine for Christmas."

"You know I don't drink coffee," I said. "But this is too tempting. I'll make an exception this time. Just a little coffee and a lot of milk please."

"How about pancakes for breakfast?" Marcus asked.

"That would be lovely," I said. "I'll make them."

Marcus wanted to know all about Percy's party. I gave him the rundown on the guests and the dinner conversation. After a healthy helping of pancakes and a couple of cappucinos, we retired to the living room. Marcus assumed his familiar posture of lying on one of the two couches, forcing me to sit on the other.

"Before I forget," I said, pulling out the stuffed dogs and putting them on the couch next to me. I pressed the belly of one to make it bark. "I'm sorry only one is barking," I apologized. "The other one must have been damaged in the suitcase. Other than that, these pets should last indefinitely."

Marcus shook his head from side to side with a pained expression on his face.

"You don't like stuffed animals?" I asked, surprised. "If you don't want them, you can give them to Alisher's kids. I'm sure they'll love them. Now for the business at hand. By the way, do you think your place is bugged?"

"Probably," Marcus said.

"Then let's put some music on and I'll whisper," I suggested.

I pulled out the diagram of Chopra's quantum body and placed it on the coffee table next to Marcus. The diagram was shaped like an up side down isosceles triangle and was divided into segments by horizontal lines. The lowest segment represented the material body. This was followed by the body of energy, the mind, intellect, ego, causal body, and universal consciousness. The last two segments constituted the soul, or higher self. I pointed to the segment representing the material body.

"This is the only part that dies," I explained. "Everything else is energy, therefore indestructible. It simply detaches from the material body at the point of death. It reattaches to another body when the soul, in consultation with its guides, decides the circumstances are right for furthering its progress. We come to Earth to have experiences that further our soul's growth. If we exercise our free will NOT to have these experiences in one life, then we simply reincarnate until we do. When we have had all the experiences we need and balanced all our karma, we cycle off the earth plane. There is no longer a reason to incarnate. We become guides for other souls who have chosen to be on the earth plane."

"It's just a theory," Marcus retorted. "It hasn't been proven."

"Marcus, I have been telling you for over a year that you have triggered an experience of mine that fits this theory. Why can't you at least accept the POSSIBILITY of something like this happening?"

Marcus had dug his heels in and was not about to budge.

"You can't prove it."

"Yes, I can," I shot back. "I read a book by a dentist who hypnotized his patients to ease their anxiety. They lapsed into past lives. I can get hypnotized, too. Why don't you try it yourself and find out?"

"I have enough trouble with this life. I can't be bothered with past lives."

"Past lives can shed light into your problems in this life."

It was useless. He wouldn't budge. Nothing, however, galvanized my resolve to do something like someone telling me that I couldn't. My training had started early during the battles with my father. He had told me that he wouldn't give me a penny to study in America.

"You'll come crawling back when your savings run out, or you'll turn into a whore," he had shouted.

"We'll see about that!" I had shouted back.

I resolved not to go back home until I had a B.A. in hand. I did better than that. I got a B.A. Summa Cum Laude in three and a half years. Not only did I not become a whore, I was still a virgin when I graduated. Now Marcus was daring me to prove that reincarnation was for real. He was so much like my father, it was uncanny. Marcus's reaction steeled my resolve to explore my past lives.

"OK, forget reincarnation for now," I said. "I'm leaving you the diagram, in case you want to rethink the issue. Let's talk about you. Since you're already on the couch, this is an excellent opportunity. Do you want me to sit behind you like a good analyst or do you want to face me?"

"I want to face you."

"Tell me about your earliest childhood memory," I said eagerly.

"I'm trying to remember kindergarten," Marcus revealed.

I perked up. Lack of childhood memories is an indication of psychological trauma.

"Kindergarten? I have memories of holding onto my crib when my teeth were coming in. They hurt and I cried, but nobody came. Finally, I sat down resigned to my fate. I guess the seeds of my independence were sown during that incident," I explained.

Marcus's defensive body language, hypervigilance, and lack of trust and sexual desire, also pointed to psychological trauma. Not to mention that he had been raised Catholic. The plot was definitely thickening. I decided to explore the religion angle.

"Did you go to parochial school?" I asked.

I had heard stories from my Catholic friends of nuns who beat children and threatened them with hell if they disobeyed.

"I went for a while," Marcus said. "They took me out. Thank God. Parochial school is vile."

"Did the nuns hit you?"

"No."

He did not explain why he found parochial school vile and I did not want to press, for fear he might stop talking.

"I went to Catholic church until I was thirteen," I volunteered. "When I was little, the ritual was magical with all the Latin words. They didn't switch to Greek until the 1980s. But the light went on when I was thirteen. I resented the priest for taking wine and bread during communion, while the lay people took wafers. I also resented his special status and the fact that I, as a female, could never attain it. I never went back. When I was sixteen, I joined St. Andrews American church, Protestant non-denominational. Both sides of the family, the Catholics and the Orthodox, were hopping mad."

"I was an altar boy," Marcus volunteered.

Another red flag went up for me.

"An altar boy? Were you molested by priests?" I asked, leaning forward.

"I don't remember," he said. "You block it, you know."

"There are ways of remembering," I said. "You can get hypnotized, for example."

Marcus did not seem thrilled with the idea.

"Do you have any nephews or nieces?" I asked, changing the subject.

"Only two," Marcus said. "Each of my sisters has one child. My oldest sister is pregnant again, so there'll be three. How about you?"

"My brother isn't married," I said. "But the virtual siblings have been busy. Among the three of them, there are seven children. My virtual brother's wife is expecting in May, so there'll be eight."

"I feel tired," Marcus said. "I'm going to take a nap." He closed his eyes.

I was not convinced he was sleepy. It was still early in the day and all he had done was have breakfast. I was convinced, however, that he was playing a pull/push game with me: doing his best to bring me to Tashkent, then giving me the cold shoulder when I got there. That, combined with the mood swings, the intense anger, the black/white thinking, and, most importantly, the lack of trust pointed to severe trauma.

"I'll wake you up when it's time to leave," I said. "In the meantime, I'm going to write the fax I want to send tomorrow."

Marcus's nap did not last long. I was still working on my fax when he opened his eyes.

"What time is it?" he asked.

"11:30," I responded. "Do you feel rested now?"

"I'm OK," he said. "I'm going outside to wash the car. We can leave afterwards."

While Marcus was outside, I hid the Valentine gifts in a little cupboard by the door. I hoped Marcus would not look there for a couple of weeks. He finished washing the car and came inside.

"I'm going to change," he announced, and disappeared into the bedroom.

I took off my bulky sweater and put on my anorak. I stuffed the sweater into my bag. Marcus reappeared wearing his sweats, a scarf, and hat. I noticed that the loose clothing gave no hint of his well toned, fit body. Nobody I knew was running in sweats anymore. Everyone was wearing clingy leggings. The men, perhaps more than the women, were showing off their athletic bodies. Obviously, Marcus did not want to draw attention to his body. I filed that away, then said, "What's with the scarf? It's going to cut down on your speed."

"It's not a serious race," Marcus said. "It's a hash. You're supposed to clown around. You'll see."

We walked outside. Marcus opened the gate and backed the car into the street. I closed the gate, then slid into the passenger seat, tossing my bag in the back. It was a bright, sunny day. Good day for a race. I no longer regretted not being in the mountains. I would go later in the week, I was sure. I looked at Marcus. His mood did not match the weather.

"Nice weather for a race," I said. "Even smoggy Tashkent looks good today."

"It stinks."

"Well, I've smelled fresher air elsewhere," I admitted, "but you have to look on the positive side: you have a beautiful house; you have plenty of food; crime is low; you got a promotion out of this assignment; when you're Charge, you get Ambassador's pay; and last, but not least, the Peace Corps girls adore you."

"It stinks."

"OK, have it your way," I said, irritated. "It stinks."

I was sure that when other people were around, Marcus would put on his happy face. He parked the car. The two other men who would be helping mark the course arrived soon after. I noted they were both wearing black leggings and wind breakers; exactly what I wore. Marcus in his sweats looked like an anachronism. He made the introductions. One man was Ahmet, the number two at the Pakistani embassy. Very sexy, I thought.

The other one was, Paul, an American resident advisor.

"Are you going to run in these?" Paul said, pointing at my hiking boots.

"I'm afraid so," I said. "I thought we would be hiking or skiing in the mountains. His Excellency here made other plans, which he revealed only after I left the States without my running shoes."

"That's what you get when you travel with a diplomat," Paul observed. "Never a straight answer."

"Amen to that," I replied. "What do we do? I'll help."

Marcus explained that part of the plan was to make chalk marks giving misleading cues, then point people in the right direction.

"If I understand you correctly," I observed. "You expect me to do this course in these boots not once, but twice."

"You don't have to," Marcus said. "You could wait at the hotel."

"And do what at the hotel?" I asked.

"Your nails?" Marcus said, then sprinted away.

I ran after him. "Come back, you coward. I'm going to strangle you for that sexist comment."

I caught up with him, took the two ends of his scarf and pulled them in opposite directions. Marcus pretended to be choking.

"Don't do that," Paul teased. "The Peace Corps girls will be very upset."

"If they knew what a male chauvinist pig he is, they would strangle him themselves," I retorted.

Marking the course was not too difficult. I could manage it by walking fast instead of running. Besides, I was wearing my lightweight boots. They were almost like sneakers. During the race, the markers were supposed to bring up the rear so they would not give away the true course. Once we finished marking the course, we returned to the starting point to wait for the runners' arrival. A couple of dozen people from Tashkent's international community showed up: some from the U.S. Embassy, some from other Embassies, the U.N., and the Peace Corps. It was an enjoyable event. At the end, everybody got some shredded paper to throw around. Marcus put some in my turtleneck.

"Marcus," I protested. "This stuff itches and I can't get it out."

"Take it off, take it off," Marcus shouted, referring to my top.

I felt the blood rise to my head. Now you tell me, I felt like saying. How come you didn't ask me to take it off when we were holed up in your pad? I guess you were afraid I might ask you to take off something too.

Not wanting to create a scene in front of a sizeable portion of Tashkent's international community, I kept my mouth shut. The post-race party was at the home of the Peace Corps director. As soon as I arrived, I made a beeline for the bathroom. I took off my sweaty turtleneck and washed the shredded paper off my skin. Then I splashed cologne on my face and upper body and put on my clean turtleneck and bulky sweater. Part of the ritual at the party, was to down pints of beer, while toasting the race participants. Even Marcus made an exception to his no-drinking rule and had a glass of beer.

The party did not last very long. After the snacks and the beer had been consumed, the guests became rather quiet and soon started to depart. I helped Marcus carry his cooler to the car and put it in the trunk. He then drove me to my hotel. He was again his stiff, private self. No hugs, no kisses. Just, "Bye. Don't forget dinner tomorrow."

He was planning a big dinner for my delegation. I was not keen on the idea, especially since there was another big dinner on Tuesday, but I had not been able to talk Marcus out of it.

I ran into Chris and Peter in the lobby.

"Look who's here," Chris teased. "Tashkent's social butterfly. Now I know why you like it here. There's at least one party every night and you're there."

"Sorry I didn't invite you to the race," I said. "I didn't think it was your thing."

"That's all right," Chris said. "We didn't have running clothes, anyway."

"Oh, before I forget," I continued. "Marcus is planning a formal dinner for us tomorrow at 7:00 p.m."

"Tomorrow?" both sounded disappointed. "We wanted to watch the Super Bowl. There's a Super Bowl party tomorrow at the Embassy at 6:00 p.m."

I was encouraged. "Really? I would rather do that than go to a formal dinner with toasts and crap. Maybe Marcus forgot about the Super Bowl. I'll remind him. Maybe he'll change his mind. I'll let you know."

"Do you want to have dinner with us?" Peter asked. "We're going to Tion."

"Sounds tempting," I said, "but I'm full of beer and snacks. I couldn't eat. I'll just take a bath and relax."

I went to my room. I waited a few minutes, then called Marcus.

"Did you know there was a Super Bowl party at the Embassy tomorrow?" I asked.

"Rats, I forgot about the Super Bowl," Marcus admitted.

"Marc, why don't you forget about the dinner and come to the Super Bowl party?" I suggested. "You may have two cooks, but you still have to plan the menu and send invitations. At the Super Bowl party, you can relax and have some fun. The guys really want to watch the game."

"Well, then why should I suffer through a representation function?" Marcus sounded angry.

"That's just the point. I don't want you to suffer through anything. I want you to relax and have fun. You haven't sent out the invitations, so there's no problem. Will you cancel it?"

"I'll think about it."

"If you must have it, could you have it at 8:00 instead of 7:00? This way, we could watch the game a little longer."

"I'll think about it," Marcus repeated.

"Fine," I said. "I'll see you tomorrow, somehow or other. I have a five thirty with the Ambassador. Bye for now."

* * *

The first meeting the following day was with the resident representative of the World Bank. Adrian Cramer from the U.S. Embassy arrived at the World Bank office for the meeting. I asked him about the status of Marcus's dinner.

"The invitations went out this morning," Adrian said, handing me mine.

I looked at the time: 7:30. That was the only compromise he had made and a partial one at that. I hated it when Marcus pulled rank on me. My delegation, the Ambassador, and probably every other American on the guest list would rather watch the Super Bowl. Yet, we had to dress up, go to Marcus's house, and pretend to have fun. If Marcus got any satisfaction out of the event, it would probably be due to a brownie point for representation and the opportunity to control others.

No way in hell am I going to be on time, I thought. I'm not showing up a minute before 8:00. My intention materialized as a result of the car breaking down en route to Marcus's house. Marcus was pacing the floor when we walked in, full of apologies. Soon after, he started the ritual I had become well familiar with. The first step was the house tour, while guests oohed and aahed at the fountain, sauna, and indoor pool. Then came drinks in the living room, while the two cooks shuttled back and forth between the kitchen and the dining room. Finally, dinner was served and Marcus directed everyone to their seats.

"I don't want you near me," he told me. "I've seen too much of you already."

"His Excellency is being witty," I observed.

Everyone laughed. The food was excellent. Marcus had even procured some California wine. The dinner ritual would not have been complete without toasts. Marcus started them. I rated his performance excellent. The Ambassador would certainly remember this when performance appraisal time came.

I'm going to get him for this, I thought. All the more reason to extend my stay.

Chris Bellows left for Moscow the following day, but Peter Daniels and I had two more days of meetings. Without Chris's moderating influence, the friction between us increased. I felt frustrated by his tardiness, disheveled appearance, and insecurity, which manifested in a need to be in control. His one redeeming feature was a sense of humor. Tuesday evening was the European Union (EU) dinner. Daniels had gotten bent out of shape because his name was not on the guest list. He asked me why that was.

"How should I know?" I responded. "At any rate, I'm sure that nobody will throw you out if you show up."

I was in my room getting dressed for dinner when the phone rang. It was Marcus.

"Are you going to the dinner?" he asked.

"Of course I'm going," I replied. "I'm getting ready right now. Then I have to get my baby out of the shower."

"Your baby?" I imagined Marcus arching his eyebrows.

"Peter Daniels. He may have a Ph.D., but he's acting like a baby. He's the last of ten children, you know. He didn't get enough attention as a child, so he's seeking attention now."

"So, you'll be going with him, then." Marcus said, a tone of annoyance in his voice.

"I'm afraid so. Otherwise, he might be an hour late. I'll see you there."

I hung up the phone and pondered what to wear. The little black Liz Claiborne dress would be just the ticket for this occasion. It was one of my favorites. It didn't wrinkle and showed off my small waist and some cleavage. I wanted to observe Marcus's reaction when he saw me.

The EU dinner was at The Gallery. This was one place that had Suhrat stumped. He knew the street, but not the establishment. It must be some new creation. He was driving slowly looking for street numbers. I noticed Marcus's car parked on the right side of the street.

"Stop," I told Suhrat. "There it is."

We had to walk through an alley to get to the entrance. The place was very picturesque. It included a courtyard full of plants and three rooms full of paintings. No wonder it had appealed to the French EU representative; it looked like a French art gallery. Marcus had quite a reaction when he saw me, but not the kind I had hoped for.

"Your fax can't go," he shouted in the middle of the crowded room. "You have to send a confidential cable. You have no sense of security, like when you were talking about Dr. Conrad's mission on the phone. The Uzbeks must think he's a spy."

I took him aside. "If you can't say anything nice to me, keep your mouth shut. This is not the place to talk business. We can do that in your office. What time do you get in, 8:00?"

"8:30," Marcus said quietly.

"Fine. I'll see you then."

I suspected Marcus's outburst was partly a distancing tactic and partly due to jealousy of Daniels who had escorted me to the party. I found his demeanor offensive, however, and had to respond to that. He was glum for the entire evening and left early. I felt sorry for him. I had the urge to follow him and try to soothe him, but I did not want to feed the rumors circulating about us. Marcus was doing an excellent job of that. I would see him in his office the next day.

First thing the following morning, I rewrote my fax to Sean. I left out everything Marcus might consider a breach of security and simply wrote that I would be doing business through February 2 and would take annual leave on February 3-4. I would cable my trip report. New text in hand, I showed up at the Embassy looking for Marcus. He was already typing away in the cable room.

"Could Your Excellency please glance at this and tell me whether it meets with your approval?"

He took a look and scribbled his initials on the bottom.

"Yeah, OK," he mumbled, returning to his typing.

They were the smallest initials I had ever seen.

"Wow! These really jump out at you. Could you make them a little smaller?"

I teased.

"Get out of here before I change my mind," he threatened.

"By all means. But before I go, I want to know whether you and the Ambassador can have dinner at Alisher's tomorrow."

"Tomorrow? I can make it. I'll ask if the Ambassador can. Are you coming by later?"

"Yes," I said. "I have to finish my trip report and write a letter to mental Rabinowitz. I'll be back around 5:00."

I had to finish by 7:00 because I was having dinner with the Deputy U.N. Representative at 7:30. The day's meetings were a success, as judged by the absence of arguments between Daniels and me. Not only that, we both went back to the Embassy and started cranking out our trip report. Daniels was going back to Bishkek the next day and I was going skiing. Around 7:00, Marcus came and looked over my shoulder.

"Are you still working on your report?" he asked.

"Yes. We're almost done," I said, briefly glancing at him.

"Well, I've got to run," he said. "I'm late for a da— dinner," he said.

Good try Marc. Substituting the word dinner for date, but I'm not falling for it, I thought. I know the kinds of dates you have.

"Have a good time," I said without looking up. "Try not to fall asleep in your soup."

* * *

The following morning was clear and above freezing. I wondered about the ski conditions. I was going to a place called Yanyabad that an Embassy Foreign Service national had recommended. At 8:00 Suhrat was already waiting in the hotel parking lot. I asked him to stop by the post office first. I needed to call my friend Claire, who had my car, to let her know of my change in plans. Calling from the post office was much cheaper. I had stopped making personal calls from the hotel. The $10 dollar a minute, four minute minimum rate was outrageous.

With that chore out of the way, I, with Suhrat at the wheel, started my quest for Uzbek snow. Yanyabad, my destination, is about 200 km northeast of Tashkent. No snow was to be seen en route and I asked Suhrat if there would be snow in Yanyabad. He was optimistic.

"*Snyek boudyet*, there will be snow," he assured me.

Indeed there was. Whether it was skiable was a different story. The town itself was perched on the edge of a mountain, and Main Street had been plowed. I estimated the temperature to be just above freezing, but there seemed to be no place suitable for skiing. I asked Suhrat to wait for me, while I took a little hike up the mountain. Lo and behold, the road I took was unplowed and had enough snow. I went back to the car, put my skis on, and skied up the mountain. I sat at the top eating lunch, admiring the scenery, and basking in the sunshine. I had realized my ambition of skiing Uzbekistan, but had not found the powder I was hoping for. At that point, I noticed a little cloud coming over the mountain. Within minutes, the cloud had covered the entire area, visibility went to near zero, the temperature dropped by at least ten degrees, and a frigid wind started to howl. So much for spring conditions. I was lucky to find my way down without taking a spill.

Suhrat was pretty cool about the whole thing, but I was getting nervous about getting back safely. Fog had shrouded the entire area. Visibility stopped at the hood of the car.

Halfway to Tashkent, it started to rain. At the outskirts of Tashkent, the rain turned to snow. Never in my life had I seen such huge flakes! By the time I got back to the hotel, at least an inch of snow was on the ground. I was thrilled. This meant another day of skiing was possible. I asked Suhrat to pick me up at 7:30 the following morning. The destination this time would be elusive Chimgan, the most popular ski area.

I called Marcus as soon as I got to my room.

"Have you looked outside?" I asked, excited.

"You bet I have," he responded laughing. "I'm wearing my summer suit and froze my butt going to lunch."

"I'm going skiing tomorrow, too. Am I blessed, or what?" I said, talking a mile a minute. "What time are you picking me up tonight?"

"Seven," Marcus answered. "We'll be coming in the Ambassador's car."

"OK," I said. "This gives me a couple of hours to spend with Tanya. I have to go to the bazaar to buy some red carnations for Alisher. See you soon, raccoon."

Back in my room after my shopping excursion, I pondered my options for a dinner outfit. Given the weather conditions, I opted again for the outfit I wore at Percy's dinner. My down coat would keep me plenty warm on the way. At 7:00 I was in the lobby. Marcus came within seconds, shivering in his summer suit.

"Do you want to borrow my ski jacket?" I asked. "You could throw it over your shoulders."

"No," he insisted. "I'll be OK."

"Suit yourself," I said.

We went to the parking lot and I got into the back seat with the Ambassador. Marcus sat in the front, next to the driver.

"I'm glad Janet's in town, so I get to go out," the Ambassador remarked. "This guy is a prince," he said of Alisher. "No other Uzbek has invited me to his house."

"And let's not forget who discovered him," I reminded him.

"Of course not, my dear," said the Ambassador patting my thigh.

"Isn't Tashkent lovely in the snow?" I remarked looking at the snow-covered trees lining the wide road.

"It's not lovely when you're freezing," Marcus piped up.

"You chose to freeze," I noted. "I offered you my ski jacket."

Alisher was still at work when we arrived at his apartment. If there was one man who worked longer hours than Marcus, it was Alisher. His new apartment was a little larger and the building was in better shape. No doubt, this move was related to Alisher's move from the Tax Administration to the Finance Ministry. Nodira, Alisher's wife, ushered us to the dining room to wait for him. I excused myself for a few minutes to play with the children. I had brought Houmai a little truck and Nargissa a tablet to write on that could be erased by pulling a lever. I rejoined Marcus and the Ambassador in the dining room.

"May I serve you some tea, Your Excellency?" I asked the Ambassador.

"Excellencies," Marcus corrected me.

"Pardon me. I forgot you're an Excellency too," I said.

"Foot massage?" Marcus asked smiling, while I was pouring him tea.

"Actually, I'm pretty good at massage," I said smiling, "but it's a little hard to do when your foot is in your mouth."

"This guy," the Ambassador said pointing at Marcus, "can find the same thing wonderful one minute and awful the next. I guess you could call him mercurial."

"Tell me about it," I chimed in. "I've been on the receiving end of his dark moods. When he decides that something is black, no amount of logic can make him change his mind."

Alisher finally came in. The children ran up to him, wanting to be held. He gave each a hug, then came into the dining room and shook hands with us. This time he did not cook. It was already past 8:00 p.m. Nodira had been reminded of Marcus's and my vegetarianism, so she had prepared meatless soup and plov. I never tired of eating plov. Marcus was finding it increasingly hard to take. He seemed to be in a good mood. Then again, his boss was there. It would be something to write home about if he acted like this when he was alone with me.

We left at 10:30. The Ambassador would be the first one to get dropped off, then Marcus, then I, since my hotel was in the opposite direction. It was my chance to arrange a ski trip with Marcus. The Ambassador also skied. He would understand the temptation of fresh snow.

"Mr. Ambassador," I ventured, "why don't you declare a snow day tomorrow, so we can all go skiing?"

"I don't think I can do that," he said. "There isn't enough snow."

"Well, I'm going to Chimgan," I continued. "I've arranged for a car to pick me up at 7:30. Do you want to come along Marcus?"

"Could I go, Mr. Ambassador?" he asked. "I have a vacation day coming up and there's nothing urgent tomorrow."

"By all means," the Ambassador replied. "I have no objection to you entertaining Janet. While you're at it, check if the lift at Beldersay is working. I may go skiing Saturday."

"It's settled then," I said with a tone of triumph in my voice. "I'll pick you up at 8:00."

The following morning, I discovered to my horror that 7:30 had come and gone and I was still in bed! I had 15 minutes to get ready and drive over to Marcus's. It was impossible. I called him up.

"Marc, I'm sorry. I just got up. I can't be there before 8:30, at the earliest."

"No sweat. I just got up too," he replied. "This will give me a little more time to get ready."

I threw my coat on top of my night shirt, pulled up my boots, grabbed my skis, and ran to meet Suhrat in the parking lot. If he had left, the probability of the trip taking place would be considerably reduced.

"*Mnye ochin zhal*, I'm very sorry, I'm not ready yet. Fifteen more minutes please."

He nodded and tried his one English phrase on me. "Nooo problem."

I ran back to my room and put my ski clothes on. I threw a change of clothes in my carry on, bottled water, trail mix, and a couple of chocolate bars in my backpack and ran out of the room.

"Marcus's house first," I told Suhrat. "He's coming too."

Suhrat was not nosy, but he had taken me to Marcus's house quite a few times. He couldn't help himself.

"Is Marcus married?" he asked.

"No," I replied.

"And you?"

"Neither am I," I said, wondering what the next question would be.

There were no more questions.

"I understand," he said with a wink. "Handsome man, and you are a pretty woman."

"Thank you."

I was bracing myself for the Marcus deep freeze. Suhrat parked in front of the gate and I rang the bell. Marcus came to the gate carrying downhill and cross country skis.

"You're going downhill too?" I asked, surprised.

"I may do a couple of runs," he replied. "I'll have to see how it goes."

He loaded his skis in the wagon, then went back to the house for his backpack and cooler. When everything was loaded, he locked the front door, slammed the gate shut, and climbed in the back seat next to me. He looked like a man going to a funeral rather than on a ski trip with a shapely blonde.

It's amazing what a little snow can do for the drab Soviet infrastructure. Everything looked beautiful. There was at least a foot of fresh snow on the ground. The old Volga performed admirably, and the road was plowed and sanded, for the most part. Marcus wanted to ski at Beldersay, a few kilometers before Chimgan, but I wanted to ski at Chimgan first and then at Beldersay, so we drove on. It was snowing when we got to Chimgan and the top of the mountain was shrouded in fog. The poor visibility convinced Marcus that downhill skiing would be a bad idea. In addition, we would have to wait half an hour for the lift to start. So, X-C skiing seemed to be the best bet. We put our skis on and headed down an unplowed road toward Chimgan's "zona odiha," a campsite with little cabins. Suhrat waited for us at a restaurant. The main road going through the campsite was plowed, so we couldn't ski on it. Breaking trail on three plus feet of snow did not seem appealing, so we retraced our steps, got into the car and drove to the intersection of the main road with the one leading to Beldersay. The latter had about a foot of snow on it. There was no way the Volga could make it. We saw some downhillers getting dropped off at that intersection, then skiing to the ski area. We figured it would be downhill all the way. As we got out of the car, I offered Marcus some Vaseline for his face.

"It prevents wind burn," I told him.

He shook his head no.

"Where is your water?" I asked.

He pointed at the cooler.

"But what are you going to drink, while you're skiing?" I persisted.

"Nothing," he replied. "We're not going to be gone that long."

"You should drink while you're skiing," I cautioned. "If you get dehydrated, you get tired and may have an accident. Let me see your water bottle."

Marcus's water bottle was a half gallon glass bottle from Ocean Spray cranberry juice.

"I have enough water for both of us," I said. "Let's go."

The tracks the downhillers had just made were disappearing fast. We followed them to the ski area. I noticed that Marcus was doing the diagonal stride going downhill.

"You're working too hard," I shouted as I whizzed by him. "This is supposed to be fun. Double poling is easier going downhill."

I made it to the lift in no time and waited for Marcus to catch up. The lift was running, the ambassador would be happy to know, but hardly anybody was riding it. The operator was trying to drum up some business and asked us to take a ride.

"Do you have any clue how steep this is?" I asked. "We could go up once and ski down the bunny slope. Or, if it's too steep, we could ride the lift up and back. What do you think?"

"Maybe on the way back," said Marcus.

He told the lift operator we were X-C skiing and we would take the lift on our way back. I was glad to see Marcus pull ahead as we started to climb. That indicated he was in good physical shape, if somewhat inconsiderate for not checking whether I was following. I stopped several times to take pictures, so I fell farther behind. Marcus was waiting for me at the end of the road in front of the entrance of another "zona odiha." That campsite must have been for VIPs because it was surrounded by a six foot fence and had warnings to the effect that nobody would be admitted without a pass. That made me want to trespass even more. I told Marcus I could not resist doing something forbidden. What could they do to us anyway? We had diplomatic passports. I started to look for a way in. An eight-foot high turnstile to the right of the locked gate was actually turning. I considered that an invitation to enter. I squeezed in and Marcus soon followed. We sneaked past some guys shoveling snow and headed for the restaurant (closed) at the top of the hill near the ski slope. Visibility was bad because of the fog and continuing snow, but one could imagine how beautiful the view would be on a clear day. I stopped and took pictures of Marcus and of dachas perched near the ski slope and he took pictures of me. I wanted to keep on skiing.

"Look at this snow! Isn't it wonderful?" I gushed.

"I have to be back by six," sourpuss Marcus replied. "I'm giving a dinner party."

"There's been a party every day since last Friday," I remarked. "That makes eight. Why are you giving another party? Aren't you tired of all this socializing?"

"I didn't want to be alone," Marcus explained. "You're welcome to come, if you have nothing else to do."

"And if I did, I would cancel it, so I could spend some more time with you."

Hearing this, Marcus turned around and started skiing toward the exit. We skied back to the lift, but the operator had stopped it for lack of business. We asked about lodging in the area and he took us to a lodge at the bottom of the main downhill trail. Ski-in-and-out facilities in Uzbekistan! Wow! The place looked pretty nice on the outside. The inside, however, was a different story. It was rather basic. So basic indeed that the bathroom was about a hundred yards away. Having sampled quite a few bathroom facilities in Central Asia, I concluded that having the bathroom as far away from the dining room as possible was a sound, albeit inconvenient, decision. Marcus and I put our skis back on and headed up the hill to the intersection with the main road.

"Rest stop," I shouted.

I had been sipping water once in a while, but Marcus had had nothing to drink for the past several hours. If I asked him to drink, he would probably refuse. I took out my bottle and had a couple of sips.

"May I have some water?" Marcus asked.

I wiped the mouth of the bottle and gave it to him. He drank without letting the bottle touch his lips.

"Chocolate?" I offered.

"Just a little piece," he said. "I'm trying to cut down. Fig Newton?"

I took one, noticing they were fat free. We moved on.

"I'm taking the road less traveled," said Marcus smiling for once.

He was breaking a new trail.

"Don't complain if you're alone then," I commented. "I'm taking the path of least resistance."

I continued to ski on the old, barely visible tracks and kept an eye out for a pit stop. There was no way I could hold it all the way back to town. I let Marcus go ahead, skied to the side of the road, and squatted behind a snow bank. I suspected Marcus was doing something similar up ahead.

"If anybody sees me, half the shame is mine and half theirs," I laughed, remembering a Greek proverb.

Suhrat was waiting with the hatch open. He had taken a lunch break in Chimgan and had filled up on shashliks. He asked us if we wanted some.

"*Nyet*," we shook our heads. "We're vegetarians."

I took my skis off and put them and the poles in the car. Marcus had already put his in. I slipped into the back seat next to him and Suhrat started the car.

"That was great," I said. "I wish we could ski some more."

"I'm tired," Marcus said. "I haven't had this much exercise in a long time."

"Really?" I said. "I'm just getting warmed up. What should we do next, swim?"

"You're forgetting my dinner party," he reminded me.

"Yes, of course."

"I also need to go by the Embassy to check a few things," he went on.

"Me too," I said. "I have to make sure the cable with the trip report has been sent. So, first stop is your house, second is the Embassy, and third is my hotel."

At Marcus's house, we startled the two cooks who were chatting in the living room. They did not expect anyone that time of day. Marcus dropped off his gear, while I waited. Then, we both got into the car and headed for the Embassy. This time, Marcus sat in the front, next to Suhrat. A few miles down the road, Suhrat stopped.

"What's the matter?" I asked.

"Flat tire," Suhrat responded.

We got out of the car.

"Good thing it didn't happen in the mountains," I said.

"These guys can change tires anywhere," Marcus commented.

Suhrat pulled one of the two spares out of the trunk, jacked up the car, and replaced the tire in less than 10 minutes. We got back in and Suhrat drove off.

You're treating me as if I have a contagious disease, I wanted to say to Marcus. I've never seen anything like this in my life.

Suhrat stopped the car in front of the Embassy. Marcus and I went inside. The consular officer, Greg Kemper, stopped Marcus.

"Where were you? I've been looking for you all day."

"I went skiing," said Marcus, his smiling face back on.

"You took the day off to go skiing? With whom?" Greg was shocked.

"Janet. She's a serious skier," Marcus replied.

He ran to his office and I went to check on the status of my trip report. It had cleared the Ambassador and was ready to go.

"See you in a few," I shouted at Marcus, and ran out the door.

I had one and a half hours to go to the bazaar, shower and change, then go back to Marcus's. After a quick stop at the bazaar, Suhrat took me back to the hotel. I put on my gray pants, black boots, red turtleneck and multicolor sweater. I grabbed my backpack with the groceries and ran downstairs to meet Suhrat. I made it to Marcus's ahead of the other guests. I told Suhrat not to wait. Somebody would give me a ride back.

Marcus's house felt like my own now. I knew where everything was. The cartoon I had sent him more than a year ago was in the bathroom next to his favorite tile from Crete. Six of the pieces from the chess set I had given him last summer were on the coffee table where he could see them as he lay down. The spider plant I had given him was in the kitchen next to the place he liked to sit. When I was in the States, he inundated me with cables and found reasons for me to visit. Yet, when I was near, he either picked fights, or was cold as ice. What would it take to melt the ice? I was determined to find out. I was a woman with a mission.

The dinner guests were other diplomats of Marcus's rank: The number two at the German embassy and his wife, the number two at the Indian embassy and his wife, the number two at the French embassy and his wife. I knew the German guy, Juergen, and liked him. I could speak German with him, and he was funny.

Marcus told his guests that we had gone skiing, and how great it had been. It was a perfect evening following a perfect day. The perfect night would be for me to stay and make passionate love with Marcus. I knew, however, that this dream was not to be realized that night. The Indian couple offered me a ride back to my hotel. I followed the other guests out the door. Marcus was standing on the steps by the front door saying goodnight to his guests. He hugged me, thanked me for the ski trip, and wished me a good trip home. When others were watching, his body was almost relaxed.

Back in my hotel room, I thought that this was the last night I would be spending in Uzbekistan for a long time. After my defiance of Butcher and my problems with Ambassador Rabinowitz, I was a persona non grata in the region. I didn't really care. Marcus would be leaving in a few months. I would try to get a leave of absence to be with him in California. That was the number one item on my agenda. I went to my room and looked around. I wanted to remember that room well. Marcus had been there, if only to complain bitterly about how awful life in Uzbekistan was. I undressed and put my flannel night shirt on. After a day of skiing, the tiny bed felt almost luxurious. I quickly fell asleep.

The following morning, I debated whether I should go jogging. I decided against it. I had a couple of hours for breakfast and packing, before I had to leave for the airport. I had just returned from breakfast, when I heard a knock on the door.

"Who is it?" I asked in Russian.

"Azim," a male voice answered.

The logistics guy? What was he doing here at 9:00 a.m.? I opened the door.

"We have to leave for the airport," he explained.

"Three and half hours ahead of time? That's ridiculous," I said. "Besides, I'm not even packed."

"We must," he insisted. "In case there are problems."

"I'm not expecting any problems," I replied. "The airport is only twenty minutes away."

"Please." Obviously, he had his orders.

"Wait for me by the dezhournaya," I said. "I'll call you when I'm ready."

During the Soviet era, the dezhournayas kept tabs on hotel guests. They also provided services, such as keeping keys, providing tea and towels, and picking up and delivering laundry. Many of the hotels in Kazakhstan and Kyrgyzstan no longer had dezhournayas. Uzbekistan still followed the old system.

As soon as Azim left, I called Marcus.

"I'm calling to say goodbye," I said. "I don't know if I'll be back. I'm PNG with Butcher and Rabinowitz. I'll see you back in the States, I'm sure."

"Bye, Janet," he responded. "Have a good trip."

I hung up the phone. I had so much to tell him, but held back. I was sure he couldn't handle what I had to say, anyway. I packed quickly and called Azim to help me with the luggage. Downstairs, I checked out and got into Suhrat's car, perhaps for the last time.

There were problems at the airport, as Azim had predicted. Suhrat, for one, fussed that the $100 bill I had given him was too old. I told him the Embassy cashier could exchange it. The luggage people insisted on weighing my carry on and wanted me to pay $100 for 10 kilos of excess baggage. I refused, saying carry on luggage was not weighed in any other part of the world. I negotiated the excess baggage charge to $40 and paid it, fuming. The best way to get in and out of Uzbekistan hassle free is by car. Unfortunately, that way one could not go very far.

I glanced at snowy Tashkent as the plane took off, and took a picture. I wished I didn't have to go. The answer to the Marcus puzzle, however, was not in Tashkent. It was in the United States. Of this, I was certain.

CHAPTER EIGHT
Quito: Key to the Inner Journey

As soon as I got back to Washington, I started my research on Marcus in earnest. The first book I turned to was the Merck Manual of Diagnosis and Therapy. I had started consulting it since I first noticed Marcus's depression and mood swings. After he contracted hepatitis, I read several times the section on Hepatic and Biliary Disorders. Now, I turned to the sections dealing with Psychiatric and Genitourinary Disorders. I glanced at the latter section. Marcus was young and had healthy habits. The probability of a sexual problem with physical origins was low. I turned to the section on Psychiatric Disorders, and started with the chapter on personality disorders. I paid special attention to the definition of personality traits versus personality disorders. "Personality traits are patterns of perceiving and relating to the environment and oneself; but the disorders are rigid and maladaptive, and damage social, interpersonal, and work relationships." Marcus fit the profile of someone with a personality disorder.

I then read about mental coping mechanisms. "Dissociation (neurotic denial) effects temporary but drastic modification of one's personality or sense of personal identity. These modifications include...short-term denial of responsibility for one's acts or feelings." I recalled at least three incidents where Marcus had denied responsibility for events in his life. He routinely answered questions regarding his feelings using "it" or "things" as subjects instead of "I." He also "spaced out" when alone with me, giving the impression that his consciousness was somewhere else. "Projection is the act of attributing one's own unacknowledged feelings to others; it leads to prejudice, rejection of intimacy through paranoid suspicion, overvigilance to external danger, and injustice-collecting." Marcus used projection on a regular basis. His body language was unambiguous in showing overvigilance to external danger, in fact, he perceived danger where none existed. "Splitting allows the user to divide people..... into all good, idealized saviors, and all bad, devalued malefactors." Marcus did that often, as well.

Next, I read descriptions of personality disorders, paying special attention to the criteria for the borderline and avoidant personality disorders. Characteristics of the borderline personality are frequent mood shifts, impulsivity, inappropriate and frequently uncontrolled intense anger, and uncertainty concerning identity. The Merck Manual has this to say about borderline and avoidant personalities: "These persons are extremists for whom the world is either black or white, hated or loved, never neutral. Interpersonal relationships are far more dramatic and intense, there is greater expression of overt anger and greater confusion over sexual identity. Borderline personalities are commonly seen in primary care medical practices, where they tend to appear frequently with vague somatic complaints, often do not comply with therapeutic recommendations and tend to be very frustrating to their physicians. They respond to rejection with temper tantrums.......Those with avoidant personalities are unwilling to get involved with people unless certain of being liked; they are restrained within intimate relationships due to fear of being shamed or ridiculed; they are inhibited in new interpersonal situations because of feelings of inadequacy; they believe they are socially inept, personally unappealing, or inferior to others."

The avoidant and borderline traits fit Marcus like a glove. He had admitted that his childhood had been awful, without elaborating. He had said that he had not been beaten, but there was no question that he had sustained severe trauma. He was unable to trust anyone, including himself. Given his damaged sexuality, I strongly suspected sexual trauma. Abuse early in life is consistent with a borderline personality organization.

In addition to understanding Marcus, I set out to discover why, despite my childhood trauma, I was emotionally much healthier than Marcus. My father had verbally and physically abused me on a routine basis. Relatives and other men had sexually abused me, yet I had overcome my aversion to being touched and my hatred of men. I had also overcome my resentment of my mother for not protecting me. Why had I outpaced Marcus in my healing process?

The most obvious difference was gender: I was female and Marcus was male. Thus, it was easier for me to get in touch with my feelings about the abuse. Another difference was that I had rebelled against my abusive father, while Marcus had continued to comply with parental directives in an effort to gain approval. I also had the fortune of having substitute parents, who were kind and loving. Having defied my father and survived, I had gained a sense of empowerment and accomplishment. I could not explain, and doubted anybody else could, why I had rebelled, while Marcus had continued to comply. I had always felt, however, that I was more than a little battered body. I did not know exactly what, but I was determined to find out.

More importantly, why was I attracted to yet another man with emotional problems? My former fiance, Chester, had been obsessed with winning the lottery. He had driven hundreds of miles non-stop to buy lottery tickets in states with large jackpots. After suffering a bout of deep depression, he had been fired from his job. At my insistence, he had agreed to get tested and was eventually diagnosed with bipolar disorder. Then there was Gerry - an obsessive-compulsive man with frequent depressions, i.e., another fixer-upper.

I had come close to marrying two men with mental problems. Now, I found out that Marcus also had symptoms of a psychiatric disorder.

"What does this say about me?" I wondered. "Why am I a magnet for mental cases? Am I a mental case myself?"

I went over the Merck Manual's section on psychiatric disorders once more. I did not think I fit any of the criteria for personality disorders. I also did not have any problems with sexual function. It was true, however, that I had never had sex with someone I loved. My primary motivation was lust. This had worked for me, albeit imperfectly, until Marcus came along. Now it no longer worked. I wanted sex as part of a loving relationship with Marcus. It seemed impossible. He was like a fortress. My intuition told me, however, that inside that fortress there was a tender, loving man who wanted to love and be loved. I just had to be patient;

something new for me. It did not escape me that Marcus was teaching me lessons in a negative way. He was teaching me to be patient, although he was impatient himself. He was teaching me to love, although he was too traumatized himself to be able to love. He was also teaching me to be compassionate, something I used to think was for sissies. I felt more comfortable charging into battle waving a sword.

I turned to the section on disorders of sexual function in the Merck Manual. It divided dysfunctions into primary (lifelong, with normal function never having been achieved due to intrapsychic conflict) and secondary (acquired after a period of normal function). I suspected that Marcus's disorder was primary. Among the psychological factors of dysfunction were: fear of intimacy (Marcus had admitted that), guilt following a pleasurable experience (he felt guilty about receiving gifts, imagine how he would feel about pleasure during sex), depression and anxiety due to stressful life situations (these were also present). Possible causes of anxiety were fear of failure and demand for performance. Marcus measured his worth by how well he performed. I suspected he suffered from tremendous performance anxiety. I also suspected that he was sexually less experienced than me, which added to his anxiety. Other inhibiting factors included traumatic events in childhood (he had described his as awful), feelings of inadequacy, religious training, and excessive modesty. These also applied to Marcus.

Something had happened to Marcus that made him connect sex with fear. But what? He had said that he did not remember being molested by priests, but had symptoms of having been sexually abused. He was aware that he could have blocked the trauma. The additional problem was his fear of remembering. These were at least two fears he had to deal with. In addition, there were the blocked feelings toward the parents. People learn how men and women interact by observing their parents. Marcus's mother was overwhelmed with the demands of raising seven children, while her husband worked long hours and offered no help. Instead of standing up to her husband, either by limiting the number of children, or by demanding help, she had enlisted Marcus as a helper. Thus, he had gotten three negative messages: to be a man means to work long hours, to be a woman means to slave at home, and sex is bad because it produces unwanted children.

I had also gotten negative messages about men and women from my parents. My father was a controlling, abusive autocrat and my mother compliant and passive aggressive. I stood up to my father ever since I was a little girl and urged my mother to do the same. My mother, having been trained to be a good girl, was incapable of it. She also suffered from many stress-related ailments, including two nervous breakdowns. My maternal grandmother provided a more attractive model for me. She was a suffragist who had supported herself from an early age. She and her husband were a love match, and had a happy and much more equitable relationship. My mother had married my father because he and her parents had pressured her. Her only rebellious act was to co-sign my passport application and a statement to the effect she would support me while I was in college.

"Go live your life the way you want," she had told me. "Don't be like me."

That incident had improved my opinion of my mother. Thus, one crucial difference between Marcus and me was that, although I had been abused, I did not see myself as a victim. I had always fought to defend myself and to do what I wanted. The bottom line was that Marcus had serious problems to overcome. I had known this since our first hike in the mountains. Now, I had names for the problems. I could walk away from Marcus, as I had walked away from Chester and was planning to do with Gerry. That was no solution. Chances were that the next guy I would be drawn to would also have similar problems. The only way to attract a different type of man was to be different myself. Maybe I had not healed from my own childhood trauma, although, as far as I knew, I had not repressed anything. But if I was fine, why did I always get involved with men who resembled my abusive father? Marcus was the best match yet. In addition to a Mediterranean heritage, he shared with my father mood swings, uncontrollable anger, extreme modesty, phobias, need to be in control, stubbornness, and a perception of women as servants of men. Marcus was most appreciative of me when I flattered him and did what he wanted, and was annoyed when I asserted myself. I had fought with my father like cats and dogs and he had died before we could reconcile. Maybe Divine Providence had arranged for me to meet Marcus in order to finish my unfinished business with my father. Sean was another reminder. Like my father, he was a controlling micromanager. I had to get a break from my hectic job and concentrate on myself. I would ask for a year's sabbatical and teach at a college away from Washington.

I contacted Dorothy Barnes, a woman I had met a year earlier. Barnes was in charge of research grants at Alaska Pacific University (APU) in Anchorage. In addition, I wrote to ten colleges and think tanks on the West Coast. I wanted to be as far away from Washington as possible and still be in the country. Dorothy was enthusiastic about my teaching at APU for a year and invited me to visit. I said I would plan to be there the last week in March. Then, I got a call from professor Greg Liu at San Francisco State University. He said he really wanted me to go there.

"I read the letter you sent to Stuart Trimble," he said. "He died two months ago."

"He did? I'm sorry to hear that," I said, shocked. "This is the first time I get a job offer by writing to a dead man."

"When can you come visit?" Liu asked.

"Well, I don't know. I'm going to Anchorage the last week in March."

"Great," Liu said. "You can stop here on your way to Anchorage. You'll love San Francisco, I'm sure. Everybody does."

"You talked me into it," I said. "I'll change my reservation and let you know when I'll be arriving."

I hung up the phone and chuckled. The only two positive responses I had gotten were from those places where Marcus had gotten offers, as well. In due time, I would let him know of the most recent "coincidences." After I made my travel plans, I called up Marcus.

"During your medevac wanderings," I teased, "you must have become an expert on Bay Area hotels. I want something cute, preferably near the ocean. The Marriott doesn't turn me on."

"Try the Miyako Hotel on Post street," Marcus suggested. "It has a sauna and Japanese garden."

"It sounds nice, but pricey," I said. "I'm paying my way out there, so I don't want to be extravagant."

"What are you doing in San Fran?" Marcus asked.

"I'm checking out San Francisco State University (SFSU)," I replied. "Then, I'm going to Anchorage to check out Alaska Pacific University."

"Janet," Marcus protested, "you're going where I'm going."

"For your information," I said, "I met Dorothy Barnes, my Anchorage contact, before I met you. This professor at SFSU is really hot for me. He persuaded me to stop in San Francisco on my way to Anchorage. Don't worry. San Francisco is a big city. If we both end up there, you won't have to see me if you don't want to."

I hung up the phone wondering why Marcus was so irked at the thought of my getting an assignment in San Francisco. It did not make sense. Actually, if I had to choose between San Francisco and Anchorage, I would pick the latter. Dorothy had said that there were X-C ski trails right on the APU campus. If I went to SFSU, I would have to drive three hours to get to the Sierras. On the other hand, there were other sports I could do in California. I was not ready to make a decision yet. I would have to wait until I inspected both places.

Gerry seemed none too happy at the prospect of my being away for a year. I planned to take Barney with me, as well. For me, being away from Gerry would be the litmus test. If I missed him, I would return to Washington and marry him. Ours had never been a torrid love affair, but we got along reasonably well. And Gerry could function sexually. There was no guarantee that Marcus's many problems could be solved. He did not even want to talk about them. I could love Marcus platonically and still be married to Gerry, or so I thought.

On March 23, I got on the plane to San Francisco, skis in tow. Greg Liu was meeting my flight. At the airport, I found out that the department chairman and his wife were part of the welcoming committee too. Liu, a former Foreign Service Officer, had put together a busy schedule for me, starting with lunch at a Japanese restaurant in San Mateo. He was so eager to please me, I became suspicious. I left San Francisco without making a commitment. I told Liu and the Department Chairman, Edgar Derber, that I would make a decision after I visited APU.

I was excited at the prospect of going to Alaska, the last frontier. Dorothy had told me that she would not be able to meet me at the airport, but would meet me the following morning at my hotel for breakfast. She had also made arrangements for a X-C ski trip for me, which included the coach of the Alaska X-C ski team. I took a cab to the Sheraton Anchorage and tried to see as much as I could in the dark. There were not many high rises in Anchorage, so the Sheraton stood out. In fact, I got the impression that the whole town was put up in one weekend with prefab buildings. It definitely had the flavor of a frontier town. I checked into a room with a view of the snow-capped Chugach mountains.

Dorothy came over the following morning in her yellow Toyota. Actually, you could barely see the yellow. The car was almost completely rusted out. Dorothy was short and heavy, but quite a bundle of energy. She went a mile a minute.

"I hope you don't mind my little rust bucket," she told me. "It's very reliable."

"And that's what counts. Especially around here," I observed.

Dorothy took me to the Cafe Amsterdam for breakfast. As soon as we sat down, she said, "APU had a $1 million budget deficit last year. The President wants to lay off a lot of faculty members. I may lose my job too. I didn't tell you earlier because I was afraid you wouldn't come."

This clinches it, I thought. I'm going to San Francisco.

The job in Anchorage had fallen through for me as it had for Marcus. He had been considered as an advisor to the mayor of Anchorage. There were elections in April, however, so the mayor didn't want to hire someone his successor might not like. I marveled at the new twist of what I now believed to be a Divine Plan. There was a reason for me to be in San Francisco, but I would make the most of my visit to Anchorage.

I had lunch with APU faculty members, met the APU President at a reception in Dorothy's honor, and had dinner with Dorothy in Anchorage and at the Alyeska Resort in Girdwood. I spent the weekend skiing in the Alaskan wilderness with coach Fred, Edna Thomas, an Austrian friend of Dorothy's, and Edna's husband Tim. The latter was a cartographer who had mapped most of Alaska. We stayed at a lodge in Denali State Park, owned by another Austrian who led wilderness trips. Tim and Edna paid my share and refused to be compensated. On my last day in Anchorage, Dorothy and I promised to stay in touch. Before I got on the plane the following morning, I mailed my postcards, including one for Marcus. I wanted an Anchorage postmark on it.

I waited until noon my first day back at the office to call Greg Liu.

"I have made my decision," I told him. "I'd like to come to San Francisco."

"That's wonderful!" Liu sounded thrilled. "What do I have to do to make it happen?"

"You need to send a letter to my supervisor inviting me to teach at SFSU. We can take it from there."

Liu said that he would ask the dean of the business school to send the letter right away.

I wanted to tell Marcus about all this, but I waited until April 6, the anniversary of his medevac. I wanted to ask him if he planned any more medevacs during his tour. On the appointed day, I tried calling him several times, but there was no answer. I tried him early on April 7. Again no answer. I started to worry again about the volatile Italian.

On April 8, my secretary handed me an envelope. I recognized Marcus's handwriting on it. I opened it and saw an invitation to a conference scheduled in Tashkent in mid-May. Marcus had included a letter saying he would be in New Delhi on April 2-9 to have a broken tooth repaired. I could not believe it! On the anniversary of his medevec Marcus was on a dentevac! Spring must not agree with that man, I thought.

I decided to call him on April 10. We had a lot to talk about. It was 9:00 p.m. in Tashkent when I called.

"Hi Marc, how did the dentevac go?"

"How did you know I was on a dentevac?" he asked, puzzled.

"You wrote to me. I got your letter in the pouch Friday," I said.

"I wrote to you?" Marcus sounded surprised. "I don't remember. My memory is going."

"Since your memory is shot, I don't suppose you remembered that April 6 was the anniversary of your medevac. I called you and there was no answer."

"It was?!" Marcus laughed. "I was on a dentevac on the anniversary of my medevac? How do you like that?"

"Another 'coincidence' no doubt," I remarked. "So what happened? Did a jealous husband punch you in the mouth?"

"No, I bit on a rock in lentil stew. How was Alaska?"

"FANTASTIC! I've never seen so much snow in my life. There were nine FEET of snow on the ground! We stayed at this lodge that was buried under the snow. The grounds keeper dug out the third floor windows so we could see outside. We had to go through a tunnel to get to the lodge and the outhouse. Needless to say, the skiing was great. I sent you a postcard. How was New Delhi? Was the poverty depressing?"

"I wouldn't know about that," Marcus laughed. "I spent most of my time lying by the pool at the Holiday Inn."

"Sean is driving me nuts, Marc, but the end is near. The letter from the university is coming."

"What letter? What university?" Marcus shouted. "I want to know what you're doing."

"Calm down, will you?" I said. "When things get firmed up, you will be the first to know. Oh by the way, I keep forgetting to tell you. There was a story in Der Stern about Felix Bloch. Remember him?"

"Yeah, what about him?" Marcus sounded curious.

"A call girl named Tina surfaced in Vienna. She said that Bloch used to go to her every Saturday to be humbled. She would have him kneel up to half an hour, then walk on all fours and fetch her payment in his mouth. There's a picture of Tina in a low cut, black leather teddy and over the knee boots, holding a whip."

"Why are you telling me this?" Marcus was shouting again. I imagined he was knitting his eyebrows.

"Don't you see?" I went on. "If this story is true, it supports the spy theory. If the KGB had pictures of Bloch at Tina's, it could blackmail him into spying. After the Department kicked him out, he worked as a cashier in a supermarket in North Carolina and got arrested for shoplifting. Fine show for our former Charge in Vienna. I always thought he was weird."

"I've got to go," said Marcus. "I want to get to bed early. It will be tough going to work tomorrow."

Interesting reaction, I thought. Was it Bloch's alleged perversion, or spying that set Marcus off? And he's awfully worried about me getting assigned to his new post.

On April 22, I called Marcus to let him know that Richard Nixon had died.

"That was to be expected," Marcus said without emotion.

"He was one of our best presidents in the foreign affairs area," I observed.

"He was a crook," Marcus said emphatically.

"He was devoted to his wife," I continued. "Did you see how he cried at her funeral? He passed away a few months after she did."

"He was a crook."

"Right," I said, "and smokers should be shot, and Tashkent stinks. To change the subject, my story on X-C skiing in Central Asia was published. Do you want a copy?"

"Really?" Marcus seemed pleased. "Yeah, send me one."

"On the issue of my escape from Sean, the university that invited me is by the ocean and three hours away from the mountains."

"Stanford," Marcus guessed.

"Close," I said with glee. "San Francisco State."

Marcus's mood shifted again.

"Janet, I sent you a letter," he said sternly.

"Yes, and in the same letter you said you wanted to talk. We can't do it on the phone because it's bugged. When I'm in Tashkent, you book me solid and there's no time. On the rare occasions we're alone together, you space out. I don't believe anything you say or write."

I would have kept going, bugs or no bugs, but Marcus ended the conversation. He said he had to get up.

Later, I wrote Marcus asking him not to talk about my being assigned at the same post as he. The deal might fall through and the rumor mongers would have a field day for nothing. I also wrote Marcus that Barney was ill and that I was taking him from specialist to specialist. I was hoping that Barney would improve by mid-May so I could go to Tashkent for the tax conference. Peter Daniels and Carl Butcher, however, were doing their best to keep me out of there. I was the one who had set up the tax project in Uzbekistan almost two years earlier and they would not do me the courtesy of allowing me to accept the Uzbeks' invitation. Apparently, courtesy had nothing to do with it. The name of the game was power and control. I found the game more and more distasteful. I also suspected they wanted to prevent me from seeing Marcus. I called him and told him that.

"Don't send any angry cables," I cautioned. "That would add fuel to the fire. Besides, I'd rather be here. I want to do the MS 100 mile bike ride. Will you sponsor me?"

"I will give you $100," Marcus said.

"You will?!!" I was surprised at his generous contribution.

"My father has MS," Marcus explained.

I knew that. I had seen a Metamarro family picture from Marcus's sister's wedding and had asked Marcus why his father used a cane. The $100 contribution made Marcus my biggest sponsor. I left Barney at the animal hospital and did the MS 100 mile ride on May 14-15. On May 16, I called Marcus to tell him I had completed the ride and that I needed his check.

"I knew it was you, before I picked up the phone," he said, laughing.

"I'm glad your ESP has improved," I commented. "I assume you also know why I'm calling."

"Yeah, yeah, I know. The check is in the mail," Marcus said.

"The check is in the mail?" I joked. "Now I'm really worried. This is one of the oldest lies, along with I'll respect you in the morning. Besides, the mail is unreliable."

"Don't worry. You'll have the check soon," Marcus assured me. "Now, about San Francisco. I haven't been talking about it, but I don't want you to do it for me."

"May I do it for me?" I asked. "I told you I need to get out of Washington for a while."

"You're endangering your career."

"This is a risk I have to take."

"Well, I said my piece," Marcus said, sounding defeated.

"Thanks very much for your opinion and especially for your contribution. You're my biggest sponsor."

I thought that had settled the issue, but the worst was yet to come. Despite my TLC, two operations, and the efforts of many dedicated veterinarians, Barney's condition worsened. His cancer spread to his lungs and he was put to sleep on May 23. I was devastated. Gerry and I had visited him in the hospital in Annapolis the day before. I hoped he would recover. But the vet had called Monday morning to say that Barney had difficulty breathing. An X-ray showed his lungs were full of tumors. There was nothing else he could do. I gave the OK to put him to sleep. Then, I closed my office door and dissolved into tears. I felt like a coward for not being able to hold Barney's paw while the vet gave him the fatal shot. Barney was always so full of life, I could not bear to see him dead. I went home early and gathered all of Barney's pictures. I would frame a few and make an album of the rest.

After I calmed down somewhat, I thought about my life at that point in time. Barney, my anchor and source of unconditional love was gone, my relationship with Gerry was terminally ill, and my job provided less and less satisfaction. I was definitely in a period of transition, but transition into what? I wasn't sure. I did not expect to waltz into Marcus's arms and live happily ever after. I considered Marcus a walking tinder box, long overdue for bursting. I also knew that Marcus was linked to the work I needed to do on myself.

The following day, May 24, I woke up and started crying. Never again would Barney wake me up again by licking my face. I would not walk him, or take him to the creek for a swim. He would never again fetch tennis balls, or lie in the yard to chew on them. More than ever I needed to get to San Francisco. At the office, I spent most of the day tracking down my memo on the sabbatical. The bureau's personnel officer could not move it along unless certain questions were answered. I made a list of the questions and went in search of answers.

I went home that day feeling defeated. Maybe I should just give up like the rest of them. Go in, do my job, collect my paycheck. Quit asking questions about the meaning of life and whether my job was consistent with the reason I was on the planet. Why should I care if Marcus had been abused as a child and was afraid of intimacy? I had more than enough projects to keep me busy. I did not need a mammoth problem like Marcus. As I was going through the mail, I noticed what looked like a card with his handwriting on it.

"That must be the check," I thought. "I didn't expect it so soon. But why the card?"

I opened the envelope. It was indeed a card with an abstract painting on the front and a $100 check inside. I read the message.

"Dear Janet: As promised, I am enclosing a $100 check payable to the National Multiple Sclerosis Society. Congratulations on finishing the 100K tour. It is certainly a worthwhile cause. Now regarding San Francisco, it is a free country and you may do whatever you want. However, it is misguided and crazy for you to leave your job, and come to San Francisco to be with me. If you think our relationship will "develop," you are wrong. If you want a shred of friendship to remain out of this relationship, your pursuit must end. You can have togetherness and bliss with the right man, but not with me. Marcus."

I read Marcus's message several times to make sure I understood it correctly. How could he be so certain he was the wrong man for me? He thought I was going to San Francisco just to be with him and tried to blackmail me. His failure to mention Barney's illness showed lack of empathy. I let out a scream.

"What an arrogant jerk! Who does he think he is? I'll show him."

I took the check, tore the card into little pieces, and threw it in the trash. That did it. It was San Francisco or bust. I was jolted out of my grief and started mapping a strategy for reaching my goal. First, I had to respond to Marcus. I took a piece of paper and wrote:

"Dear Mr. Metamarro:"

That sounded too contrived. I threw the paper away and started over.

"Dear Marcus: This is to acknowledge receipt of your very generous contribution of $100. Please be informed that the tour was 100 miles, not 100 kilometers. The second part of your message betrays total ignorance of myself and my motives. I thought you were someone to whom I could relate at a level above that of a simple mortal. Apparently, I was wrong. I regret any distress I might have caused. Have a nice life. Sincerely, Janet Bradley."

Marcus was out of line and I let him know. From now on, communication would be through official channels only. I would ignore his cables, unless instructed otherwise. As I put my note in an envelope and sealed it, I marveled at Marcus's ability to push my buttons. Of course I did the same to him, otherwise he would not blow up at me like he often did. He was so much like my father, it was uncanny.

In early June, Bernice Tucker responded to Sean's memo regarding my sabbatical by scribbling underneath the text: "No objection to the sabbatical, but we can't hold the position." What kind of answer was that? How could I go on sabbatical if there was no slot for me to come back to? I had worked extremely hard on the Former Soviet Union program and had not been promoted. Now, they didn't even want to hold my slot, so I could take some time off. I called Liu.

"I don't know Greg. I don't think this is ever going to work. I'm ready to give up."

"Never say never," Greg replied. "We'll figure something out."

I spent most of June talking to personnel and canvassing the agency for an empty slot I could occupy when I got back.

"I don't care if anybody reserves a slot for me," I told personnel. "Just let me go."

That was illegal, I was told.

I often thought of Marcus and missed talking to him, despite his mood swings and blow ups. I was determined, however, not to talk to him. He was the one who had been rude, he should apologize. I had mailed him a book for his birthday, before I got his nasty note. It was about a bicycle trip in Tibet, a place I intended to visit some day. I wondered if Marcus would take the opportunity to thank me for the book and apologize for his nasty note. In the meantime, people who saw Marcus in Tashkent were telling me that he was very unhappy. I made some feeble excuse for him. The truth was, however, that Marcus would be unhappy anywhere, unless he found the courage to look inside himself and clean out the garbage he had been hauling around for decades. With his avoidant personality, that was no easy task.

I could not throw stones at him. I was hauling my own garbage around. In June 1994, I learned the meaning of the word depression. I could not find a good reason to get out of bed. Barney was gone, Sean drove me to distraction, Gerry was frequently depressed himself, and Marcus was flipping out. I felt as if my body were made out of lead and that thick walls were closing in on me. I ached all over. What should I do? Go to the doctor and get doped up? I did not believe in that. My body reflected the state of my mind. I had to pull myself out of this. I could not die without exploring the flashbacks Marcus had triggered. I had no energy to exercise, but I could do yoga. I did the stretches for depression and insomnia every day. I survived June.

In early July, Sean came into my office.

"I have a plan to rehabilitate you," he said.

"I beg your pardon?" I said, puzzled.

"Patch things up with Butcher," Sean explained.

"I don't really care," I said. "I'm resigned to being banned from Central Asia. Besides, you said yourself that he's around the bend. If I don't get along with him it proves I'm not."

"Don't be such a pessimist," Sean said. "I talked to Butcher. He agreed to let you go to Almaty, but you're not allowed to travel in the region."

"So what am I supposed to do? Stay in Almaty and lick his boots for a couple of weeks? Would that make good use of the taxpayers' money?"

"Oh come on, Janet. Play ball. It took a lot of effort to broker this deal."

"OK, I'll go. It'll give me a break from banging my head against personnel's wall. No more than two weeks though. I'm NOT doing last year's five week stint."

I made plans to go to Almaty the last two weeks in July. I asked Gerry if he would like to go on a trip the middle of August. He said he was taking off the first week in August to go to his family reunion. Then, he had to prepare for a big meeting in mid-August. I was surprised.

Nothing significant happens in Washington in August. Gerry wanted to postpone our trip until September; perhaps a bike tour in Maine.

"I have to go in August," I said. "If I don't have plans for August, that lunatic Butcher may keep me there the whole month."

Once more, it was separate vacations. I called up Mountain Travel-Sobek to ask if there were any vacancies on a trip to the Galapagos in mid-August. The woman laughed.

"You want to go to the Galapagos in August and you're calling in July? People make plans months, maybe years ahead of time."

"I don't have that kind of life," I said. "Could you please check into what trips are available? Maybe somebody has canceled."

The woman agreed to check and call me back.

"I can't believe this," she said when she called back, "but there's one space available on Beagle III. This boat has space for only ten passengers and gets booked a year in advance. The cruise is August 16-22. The group arrives in Quito the day before, then flies to the Galapagos and boards the boat on the 16th. There will be interpreters to assist you in Quito."

"I don't need an interpreter," I said. "I speak Spanish. In addition, I have a friend who works at the U.S. Embassy there. I would like to arrive on the 13th and leave on the 27th."

With my vacation plans out of the way, I prepared for my Almaty assignment. I arrived feeling like Butcher's prisoner. This guy must think that the Foreign Service is the equivalent of the army. He was full of himself, expected people to obey without question, and to slave away like he did. People who knew him when he first joined the service said he used to be a decent fellow. He had changed after his wife died in a plane crash. I was not so sure. Personalities are formed in childhood. If Butcher could not recover from his wife's death, that said something too. I would use this assignment to research His Excellency, Mr. Butcher.

I felt sad as I landed in Almaty. During previous trips, I would call Marcus to ask about the plans for the Tashkent portion of my trip. Now, there was no Tashkent portion and no talking to Marcus. I knew he was unhappy. I also knew that I could not save him from himself. Only he could do that. My head told me I was better off without him, but my heart ached for Marcus. Maybe I would feel better after a nap. Also, I had Arasan, the public bath, to look forward to. At the office, there would probably be the usual artificial crisis. It would keep my mind off things.

The first thing I had to deal with was not quite a crisis and not at all artificial. Jeff Curran, one of the advisors in Kyrgyzstan was in trouble. His mother was terminally ill and he was drinking heavily. I had specifically asked him during the interview whether his mother's illness would hamper his performance. He had assured me that it would not. His coping mechanism pointed to a drinking problem. I had to decide whether to pull him out and I had to do that long distance. Mental Rabinowitz and Chicken Butcher would not even let me know why I was banned from Kyrgyzstan. I had to rely on Spencer Lewis for help in making my decision. The latter had pulled all the stops to help Curran, he even located a Catholic priest to counsel him. It was hopeless. Curran would have to ship out.

The rest of my assignment was routine, except for two helicopter trips, one to lake Issyk Kul in Kyrgyzstan and the other to Kazakhstan's Cherin canyon near the Chinese border. The helicopters were old ones from the Soviet air force. The airport where they were parked used to be off-limits to foreigners, as well as most locals. Now, Russian pilots were flying Americans to tourist destinations.

The most exciting part of these trips was flying through canyons. The helicopter's blades came very close to the walls of the canyons. One false move and we would be history. Better to die like this than in a hospital bed, I thought.

The views were fantastic. The mountains were initially green. Then, as we flew over the tree line, they turned into gray rock and eventually into glaciers and snow. Great place for heliskiing. We opened the windows and took really sharp pictures.

As I had expected, Butcher tried to keep me in Almaty longer. I told him I had plans I could not change and left as scheduled. In the car taking me to the airport, I thought that this mission had gone better than I had expected. For one thing, the Almaty per diem was the highest in the region. My vegetarian meals were very frugal, thus, I would be making money on this trip that would go toward my Galapagos adventure. But first, I planned to rendezvous with my mother in Athens and go to a Greek island for a couple of days.

Turkish Airways was on time. I was surprised to see that open seating was in force. This was something the local airlines usually did. Once on the plane, I pondered where to sit. I spotted a young man sitting by a port side window and asked in English if the seat next to him was taken.

"No, it's not," he responded.

I sat down and asked where the plane was coming from. I had assumed that the route was Almaty, Tashkent, Istanbul.

"No," the young man said. "It's Tashkent, Almaty, Istanbul."

"Were you passing through Tashkent?" I asked.

"No," the man replied. "I spent two months working at the American Embassy as an intern. My name is Kemal Kolan, by the way."

"Janet Bradley. I work on the U.S. aid program for Central Asia."

"So, you're Janet Bradley. We knew you were in the area and wondered whether you'd be coming to Tashkent."

"Not this time. I've been there many times before. It's a tough post, but not as tough as Dushanbe or Ashkhabad."

"Yes, but most people from Tashkent got real plum assignments afterwards. Paris, Rome, London. Marcus Metamarro got assigned to San Francisco, his hometown. If you can believe that. You must know Marcus," Kemal guessed.

"Yes, I have worked pretty closely with him in the past two years," I confirmed. "He used to be in charge of the aid programs for Uzbekistan before he became DCM."

"He was unhappy the last two months, very unhappy," Kemal remarked.

He spent almost the entire flight talking about Tashkent and Marcus. When I told him I had received an invitation to teach in San Francisco, he blurted out,

"You should go live with Marcus. You'd be good for him."

"I think not," I replied icily. "Marcus and I are not on very good terms at the moment."

Kemal wrote his U.S. address and phone number on an Uzbek banknote and gave it to me. I gave him my card, although I knew I would probably never see him again.

In Greece, my mother and I spent a couple of pleasant days on the island of Hydra. Then, it was back to the States for a week before I left for Quito and the Galapagos.

I arrived at Dulles airport on the familiar flight Delta 61 and breezed through passport control, baggage claim, and customs. On the cab ride home, I thought of my Foreign Service colleagues who, under normal circumstances, spent their careers living overseas and moving every two years. I couldn't do that. I loved exploring, but needed a place to call home. In my travels around the world, I had not found a country I would rather live in than the United States. I was becoming increasingly disenchanted with Washington, however. I was no longer fascinated by the power mongers, power groupies, and spin doctors. They seemed to be so shallow and immature. Most of the career civil servants, on the other hand, seemed bland and boring. Marcus was the exception, but I shuddered at the reason why. He was working incredibly hard at a career his father had chosen for him. He claimed to want to know himself, but avoided every opportunity at introspection. Marcus did not know who he was and was afraid to find out. He was increasingly angry at me for pushing him to look inside himself.

I called Gerry as soon as I got home. I wanted to tell him that I had arrived safely. If Barney were alive, I would have gone straight to Gerry's.

"If you want to have dinner, better hurry up," I warned. "I've been up since 4:00 a.m. Athens time and I'm fading fast."

Gerry came over and we went to dinner at Vicino's, our favorite Italian hangout. We discussed our respective vacation plans. I didn't really care how Gerry was going to spend his vacation, but felt I should show some interest. Sadly, I thought we were like so many married couples. There was no magic and no sparks, we were hostages of habit. Physically, Gerry was every woman's dream, tall, blond, handsome, former life guard and football player. But his pessimism hung over him like a dark cloud. Like Gerry's former wife and girl friends, I had been unable to dissolve it. He made even less effort than Marcus to understand himself. I had to get to California, not only for mental health reasons, but to break the Gerry habit.

At the office the following day, I phoned Rob Neider, the personnel guy who talked straight and was sympathetic to my cause. He advised me to forget the IPA approach, as this was too bureaucratic. It would require approval by a committee and the head of management. They could string me along for ever by postponing the committee meeting. I should press for an answer on the IPA request. If that was denied, I should follow plan B.

"Thanks, Rob," I said. "I will get on this as soon as I come back from my vacation."

I E-mailed Peter Simmons, my friend at the American Embassy in Quito, my arrival date and time and hotel number. In the meantime, Sean seemed to be managing by memo from outer space. He was hardly ever around. Maybe he had taken seriously my suggestion to retire, and was looking for post-retirement employment. Helga was also looking to get out, as was Bill. The whole place was falling apart.

The week passed in a flash. Saturday, I was on my way to National Airport and then Quito via Miami. All of a sudden, I was seized with excitement. I was going to the Galapagos! Two dreams come true this year. First, I skied Alaska and now I would tour the Galapagos. What I did not know at the time I was waiting for my flight, was that Quito would be the gateway to a far more fascinating destination than the Galapagos Islands.

At the hotel Alameda, I found a message from Peter. Was I free for lunch tomorrow? It was too late to call him back. It would have to wait until morning. I took a quick bath and hopped into bed. I was still in bed when Peter called.

"Good morning. Did I wake you up?" he asked.

"No, not really. I was just lying here thinking about getting up. I got in late last night. The plane was late leaving Washington and I missed my connection in Miami," I explained.

"How are you feeling?" Peter asked. "Any altitude problems?"

"Well, I do have a slight headache," I admitted. "Other than that, I'm fine. Don't worry, I know the drill: Drink lots of water, avoid alcohol, get plenty of rest."

"I was thinking of going out of town for lunch," Peter said. "Is that O.K. with you?"

"Fine," I responded. "I have all day tomorrow to see the town."

"I'll pick you up at 11:30," he said.

Peter drove up in a green Jeep Cherokee, his baby daughter in the back seat. He drove about half an hour outside of town to a restaurant that looked like a hacienda.

"This place has great steaks," he explained.

"There is something I should tell you," I interrupted. "I'm vegetarian, but I'm sure they can come up with something for me."

Peter was surprised. "You are?! Since when?"

"Since August 4, 1992. I got violently ill during a trip to Uzbekistan and swore meat off for good. I wasn't eating much of it anyway."

We caught up with each other's news, while keeping an eye on toddler Caitlin. Peter had been in Quito for two years and had applied for a one-year extension. Next, he wanted an assignment in Jerusalem. I told him all about the craziness of the Soviet aid program, then asked about the local economy. We spent at least two hours talking and walking outside. Peter regretted that he would be in the States when I came back from the Galapagos.

"When I get back from the cruise, I don't want to stay at the Alameda," I said. "It's too much like the Sheraton. Do you know of a funky place that's clean?"

Peter suggested Cafe Cultura, a Bed and Breakfast around the corner from the

Alameda. He took me there and showed me what it looked like. Then, he was off to a diplomatic reception.

I walked around for a few minutes to familiarize myself with the center of Quito. I was looking for a bookstore to buy a tourist guide. There were a lot of shops in the Roca and Amazonas area, but most of them were closed. I noted the location of a couple of bookstores with the intention of returning the following day to look for my guide. I also noted the location of a couple of food markets, where I could buy fruit and snacks. I had a light supper at the hotel and retired to my room.

After breakfast at the hotel, I headed to the bank around the corner to exchange some dollars for sucres, the local currency. Then, I walked to the nearest bookstore. One thing I noticed right away was that books were expensive. I looked at the tourist guides carefully to determine which one would serve my needs best. Once I chose one, I browsed some more. A book caught my eye. The title was _Muchas Vidas, Muchos Sabios_ by Brian Weiss, M.D. The book was about a patient of Dr. Weiss's who was plagued by many phobias. She was cured when Dr. Weiss hypnotized her and she recalled events from this and previous lives that had caused those phobias. I was stunned. I had suggested that Marcus get hypnotized to recall traumatic events from his childhood. I, of course, wanted to get hypnotized to explore the flashbacks that Marcus had triggered. And here was a respectable psychiatrist, who had studied at Yale, writing about hypnotic regression and past lives. I thought of buying the book, but decided against it. It was silly to buy the Spanish version of a book that had originally been written in English. I would wait until I got back to the States.

The rest of the Galapagos group was due to arrive that day. Some were coming from the States and some from the jungle and the mountains. We would fly to the Galapagos the following day. I walked to the Cafe Cultura and reserved a room from the 24th to the 26th. I walked around Quito some more noting shops I might like to visit before returning to the U.S. Having adequately exhausted myself, I retired to my room to read about Equador and the Galapagos.

Early next morning, I had breakfast at the hotel restaurant and put my bag close to the exit. I would identify my fellow adventurers by their bright red Mountain Travel-Sobek luggage tags. Sure enough, in a few minutes two sunburned men deposited luggage with the tell tale tags near mine. They must be the mountain people. I approached them and introduced myself. They were Rob and Dan from California. Soon, two women walked up. They were Gail and Janice from Florida. A couple from Wisconsin, Rita and Walter, came up next. Finally, Claire and her children Betsy and Craig, also from California, introduced themselves.

If I had not read about the Galapagos beforehand, I would have been disappointed. Baltra, the entry point, was a barren volcanic rock. The rest of the islands were the same for the most part. The exception was the islands, like Santa Cruz, with considerable elevation that stops the rain clouds. The highest point on Santa Cruz is 864 meters above sea level and abounds in vegetation. Our guide, Jorge, met us at the airport and directed us to a bus that took us to the port. There, dinghies took us on board the Beagle III, named after Darwin's boat. The Beagle had a crew of five, including captain Arturo Cruz. The first thing that caught my eye was a big bunch of bananas hanging over the stern. Marcus, the banana addict, would have been happy here. We took our gear to the cabins located on the aft section of the boat. I shared the last cabin on the port side with Claire. Back on deck, Jorge outlined the rules and regulations to be observed when visiting the islands, and the day's itinerary. This would become a daily ritual. Then, the Beagle III headed for Las Bachas, a pristine beach on Santa Cruz island. Jorge had told us that this would be a wet landing. Tevas were recommended. The dinghy dropped us off near a white beach surrounded by black volcanic rocks. It was a good introduction to the islands' fauna: marine iguanas, pelicans, red sally crabs, and starfish. The next stop was a mangrove lagoon. Moishe, the designated dinghy captain, turned off the engine and Jorge pointed out a wide variety of species: blue footed boobies standing on the black rocks, yellow warblers in the trees, huge turtles and rays under water. Shy reef sharks, white and black tip, also made a brief appearance.

Back on Beagle III, it was tea time. No doubt a custom brought to that part of the world by the captain's English wife. At dinner, my vegetarianism again became an issue. Winter, one of the crew, took it upon himself to give me double portions of everything else. After dinner, Jorge discussed the following day's itinerary. We would travel overnight and anchor near our next stop: South Plaza island. After breakfast, we would board the dinghy, make a wet landing, and hike around the island. The plan for the rest of the week was essentially the same: travel overnight, anchor near our destination, have breakfast, and explore the island via hikes or snorkeling. The only thing we were allowed to leave on the islands was footprints. The only thing we could take was photographs. I thought of the trash I had seen while snorkeling on Hydra. The Ecuadorans could give the Greeks a lesson in ecology. If another group was on the island, we had to wait until it left. When we were preceded on land by the ninety passengers of the Galapagos Explorer (Exploiter according to Jorge), the waiting was considerable. Thereafter, when the Explorer was sighted in the vicinity, we raced through breakfast to land first.

The Beagle III itinerary was fixed. No changes were allowed afterwards. The cruise started in Baltra and stops were made at Santa Cruz-Las Bachas, South Plaza, Santa Fe, Hood, Floreana, Santa Cruz-Puerto Ayora, Jervis, James, Bartolome, and back to Baltra. For me, it was a healing journey. The Galapagos were the perfect place to observe the miracle of creation and the development of the species. For the first time in my life, I felt part of a bigger, Divine Whole. I no longer felt like a misfit whose life was an accident. Intuitively, I knew there was a reason I was on the earth. I just had to find out what that was. I was certain that my trip to Equador provided a piece of the puzzle.

Valuable lessons in psychology and sociology could be learned by observing the Galapagos animals. With the exception of the giant tortoises, they had never been hunted. As a result, they were not afraid of humans. Blue footed boobies nested on the hiking trails, confident that the human visitors would step around them. The iguanas and sea lions would lie on the trails and would not budge, despite hand clapping and shouting by the humans. I was especially taken with the sea lions. They would nudge me with their noses as I was snorkeling and then speed away in torpedo fashion, daring me to follow. Mothers would leave newborns on the beach, umbilical cords still attached, and go fishing. That was the epitome of trust.

I thought of Marcus. He was the opposite of the Galapagos animals. He could not trust and was afraid of people, especially women. I knew he had been hurt at an early age, but so had I. He said he obeyed as a means of getting love and attention. I, however, felt that being loved when you're good was nothing. True love was unconditional. I broke every rule hoping to hear, "You're behaving like a brat, but we love you anyway." I never heard it. But I never gave up. Unconditional love was what I was after. Gerry had told me he loved me, but I had not believed him. First, he did not love himself. Someone who does not love himself cannot love another. Second, he did not accept me as I was. He was always trying to make me into his ideal version of the feminine. He thought if he tried long and hard enough, he would succeed. If Gerry was in love at all, it was with a fantasy. Maybe I was in love with a fantasy too: a Marcus free of fear. My head told me to forget Marcus and stick with Gerry. But my heart told me the opposite. I had to go with my heart.

The idyllic cruise came to an end all too soon. On August 23, the Beagle III anchored once more off the coast of Baltra and waited for the next group of travelers. Jorge rode with us to the airport to pick them up. Gail, Janice, and I were staying longer and made plans to get together. The rest of the group was returning to the States the following day. Gail and Janice stopped by my hotel and admired my spacious room and balcony. Afterwards, we went to dinner at a nearby restaurant.

Back in my hotel after dinner, I noticed a fire burning in the fireplace in the sitting room to the left of the lobby. I went in and sat on the sofa. I noticed a large wicker basket full of magazines next to the sofa and went through them. I pulled out an issue of Natural Health and looked at the table of contents. The title "Hypnotic Regression: A Way of Curing Phobias?" caught my eye. The Weiss book last week, and now this. I plunged into the article. A man plagued by phobias used hypnotic regression to recall traumatic events from his current and previous lives. He was cured as a result. The author referred the reader to the Association for Past Life Research and Therapy (APRT) in Riverside, California for further information. No question about it: California and hypnosis were on the path to self awareness. I took the magazine to my room and wrote down APRT's address and phone number.

Lying in bed, I recalled the chain of remarkable events in my life over the past two years: being pulled to Central Asia; deciding to marry Gerry on my first flight to Tashkent and asking God for guidance; meeting Marcus a couple of hours later; the feeling of deja vu and the flashbacks after first seeing him; finding out I shared childhood trauma with Marcus; the numerous times our cables and letters had crossed; all the times we had thought the same thing and finished each other's sentences; the dreams I had about Marcus asking for my help; going to Crete to avoid him and seeing his initials there; my Anchorage assignment falling through and getting an offer in San Francisco like Marcus had; finding a place on the

Galapagos cruise on short notice; seeing the Weiss book in a Quito bookstore; Peter directing me to Cafe Cultura; the feeling of oneness in the Galapagos; the magazine with the APRT address. Wherever my path led, Marcus, hypnosis, and California were on it. Suddenly, I felt I had fulfilled my mission in Ecuador. I had the urge to change my reservation and fly home the next day, but I decided to stay in order to climb an Ecuadoran mountain. I couldn't summit in my sneakers and cotton pants, but I could go as far as the snow.

The following morning, I called up Gail and Janice and asked them if they wanted to go to Cotopaxi. It was only 50 kilometers from Quito. We could probably go by taxi. They agreed and said they would arrange for transportation. In the end, they did much better than a cab. They hired a whole van. Departure was set for 8:00 a.m. the following day from the hotel Alameda. The van pulled up a couple of minutes after 8:00 a.m. and we climbed in. The driver spoke English. Thus, I was spared the role of interpreter. I asked the other women if they had any problem with the altitude. Quito was at 8,400 feet and we were going higher. Gail said she was OK if she did not exert herself that much. Janice said she was fine. We reached the entrance of Cotopaxi National Park in an hour and took a few pictures at the entrance. While Quito with its palm trees had a tropical flavor, Cotopaxi looked Alpine. There were lots of pine trees and the temperatures were considerably lower than in Quito. We rode through the park, stopping briefly at the visitors' center. Then we continued on toward the mountain top, stopping a couple of times to take pictures of Cotopaxi's snow capped peak.

"Can you believe this?" I exclaimed. "We're at the equator in August on a snow capped mountain. Is this unbelievable or what?"

We were above the tree line and the wind was picking up. The driver followed the dirt road as far as possible, then stopped.

"I'd like to hike up to the snow," I told the two other women. "Anybody coming?"

Gail decided to stay in the van, but Janice agreed to go for a while. Soon, the road was blocked by snow. We took each other's picture in the snow. At that point, Janice said she would go back. I said I would go a little higher and walked between the patches of snow.

Naturally, I thought of Marcus. He would have loved it here. The strong wind reminded me of our first hike in Uzbekistan's Tien Shan mountains. I looked at the top of the mountain. I could see the lodge that served as base camp for the final ascent. I would like to reach the top of that mountain some day. Warren, my geologist friend, had said that, at 19,437 feet, Cotopaxi was the highest point on earth, if measured from the bottom of the ocean. It was also the highest active volcano. At any rate, I was not too far from the top. I felt exhilarated and on the verge of an exciting discovery. Suddenly, Washington's petty bureaucrats seemed quite unimportant.

I looked at the van a few hundred feet below. Gail and Janice were there waiting for me. I quickly descended and apologized for keeping them waiting.

"I have this thing about mountains," I said. "As far as addictions go, it's not a bad one."

By the time we got back to Quito, it was almost dinner time. I asked my two companions if they would like to come to Cafe Cultura for tea. They declined. If they had tea, they would not be able to have dinner. They wanted to rest for a few minutes, then go out to dinner and sample the local fare. I met them at the Alameda and we took a cab to the restaurant.

That was the last meal we shared in Quito. I was leaving the following morning, but the other two were staying a few more days. Gail invited me to Florida. I said I would like to go diving there some day, but did not know when. It looked like I would be in California most of next year. Then it was time to say goodbye. We hugged and wished each other a good trip home. I wished them a pleasant stay in Ecuador and left to walk back to my hotel. Lying in bed in my room, I was so excited I had trouble falling asleep. When I finally did, I had the following dream:

Marcus and I stood in front of a big, heavy door. Suddenly, the door opened of its own accord and a beam of light shone through the darkness behind it. I took Marcus by the hand and said, "Come on. Let's go see what's in there."

"No," Marcus said, pulling his hand out of mine.

He did not say why, but I sensed he was afraid. I left him standing in front of the door and walked through it, toward the light.

CHAPTER NINE
The Inner Journey Begins

After the Galapagos magic, Washington seemed superficial and dull. I dreaded going back to my office. I had to go back, however, to continue my battle for the sabbatical. The day after my return, Gerry suggested we have dinner at an Indian restaurant in Bethesda, MD. I agreed. A vegetarian could eat well there.

"Why don't you invite Helga?" Gerry suggested. "She lives around the corner."

"If I invite her," I responded, "we would talk shop and I couldn't stand it. I want to spend one more day before I deal with Foggy Bottom."

As luck would have it, Barry, another one of my colleagues, was at the restaurant with his wife.

"Oh no," I whispered to Gerry. "If I talk to him, he'll probably tell me about some office stuff. If I ignore him, it would be rude. OK, I'll talk to him. If he tries to talk shop, I'll say I don't wanna hear it."

Gerry and I approached the couple.

"Oh hi, Janet." Barry was all smiles. "How was your vacation?"

"Totally awesome. I hate to be back."

"I have news for you," Barry said, with a sly smile.

"I DON'T wanna hear it," I said emphatically. "I'll hear it at the office tomorrow."

"Fine, fine," Barry made a gesture of surrender. "It's good news, but since you don't wanna hear it, I won't tell you."

My curiosity was aroused.

"Good news? What is it?"

"You said you didn't wanna hear it," Barry reminded me.

"I want to hear it, if it's good news. Tell me."

"Sean is retiring," Barry said, triumphantly.

"He is? You mean he took my suggestion? I can't believe it. When?"

"Mid-September."

"In two weeks? I knew he'd been cooking something. He's been invisible the past couple of months."

Sean, my major frustration in Washington, was retiring. This changed things considerably. Should I still try to go to San Francisco? Something told me I should go: the same something that had told me I should go to Philadelphia when I was eight, and to Central Asia two years ago. I got the feeling that I would meet someone important in San Francisco. I decided to continue my battle for the sabbatical the following day.

The first thing I noticed as I walked into my office was a package lying in my chair. I looked at the handwriting. It was Marcus's. I opened the package and found a letter and three of the video tapes I had lent him.

"I am sorry you reacted as you did to my last letter," he wrote. *"I felt the need to send an unambiguous message. I, too, wish you the best in your life. Hope to cross paths again when both of us are maybe healthier and happier, and more*

together."

I was not fully satisfied. He was sorry about my reaction, but not about what he had written. Furthermore, he still did not reveal why he did not want me to go to San Francisco. Did that man ever level with anybody?

"Speak for yourself," I said, when I saw the reference to being 'healthier and happier and more together.' "I've had it with being played like a yo-yo. I'm going to haunt you until you level with me." His getting back in touch gave me the opportunity to do the same. I wrote to him at his parents' address, telling him about my Galapagos trip and the status of my San Francisco assignment. I waited until noon, then called Greg Liu.

"The IPA is out," I said. "Do you have any bright ideas? I don't think this is going to work."

"Never say never," responded Liu. "There's one more thing we haven't tried. I'll ask Pelosi to intervene."

"You're going to ask a member of Congress to get involved in a mid-level bureaucrat's sabbatical? Greg, you're crazier that I am," I chuckled.

"What do we have to lose?" Greg asked. "Pelosi can do it. I know she can. I know someone in her San Francisco office."

"Why not?" I relented. "If I go out, I might as well go out with a bang."

The very same day, Liu called Congresswoman Pelosi's office. He told his contact that he would fax a letter asking for help in getting Dr. Bradley assigned to SFSU during the Spring 1995 semester. Upon receipt of the letter, Congresswoman Pelosi's staffer, Sandi Maruyama, called my personnel office. Within days, a letter by the Congresswoman herself was faxed to the head of my agency. Procedure dictated that my office draft a response. Bill, acting for Sean, gave me the letter to answer.

"Let me get this straight," I said. "You want me to draft a response to a Congressional letter asking that I be assigned to SFSU."

"I don't know what else to do with it," Bill said lamely.

I E-mailed Rob, my ally in personnel, and asked for advice.

"I'll tell you over lunch," he said. "Are you free today?"

"For you, I certainly am," I said.

"Twelve thirty OK?"

"Fine."

We went to the State Plaza Cafe across the street from the State Department.

"Rob, this is insane," I remarked. "I don't see why my wanting to take some time off is such a big deal. I'm asking for leave without pay for Christ's sake. I'm actually going to save Uncle Sam money with this. If all else fails, I'll go AWOL."

"Don't do that," Rob pleaded. "You'll ruin your career. I'll tell you what. Send me an E-mail saying you're burned out and want time off. If you can do that with a straight face, I'll approve it. If you ask for ninety days or less, only office director has to approve."

I was stunned.

"An E-mail! I've been writing memos cleared by half a dozen people for six months and you can do this via E-mail?!!"

"For ninety days or less."

"This might just do it. I'll have to count the days in the semester. What's my share of the lunch?"

"Lunch is on me," Rob said. "It's the least I can do for an upstanding public servant."

"Rob, you're a jewel," I said beaming. "I'll send you a postcard from California. It's the least I can do."

I rushed back to my office and pulled out my appointment calendar. I circled the beginning and end day of the semester and counted the business days in between: eighty four!! YES! YES! This would work. I E-mailed Rob my request for eighty four days of leave without pay. The same day Rob E-mailed back: "Subject: 84 days. Leave without pay approved."

I was ecstatic. After the memos and dozens of E-mails, I got my approval in a four word E-mail. Now I could draft a response to Congresswoman Pelosi in the affirmative. I called Liu.

"We're in business Greggie. I'm coming over in early October to nail things down. I want to design a couple of new courses, so they have to be advertised."

Liu said he would take care of it.

Most people go to bars or restaurants to celebrate. I went to bookstores or outdoors. I went to Olsson's at Metro Center to look for Dr. Weiss's book, and a book about fathers and daughters. I needed to understand how my relationship with my father was affecting my current relationships with men. I headed for the psychology section and started checking titles. A title jumped out at me: _Mothers, Sons, and Lovers: How a Man's Relationship with his Mother Affects the Rest of his Life_ by Michael Gurian. This would be useful in preparing for my next encounter with Marcus. I pulled it off the shelf. Farther down, another title. _The Wounded Woman: Healing the Father-Daughter Relationship_ by Linda Schierse Leonard. Bingo. It was exactly what I was looking for. Finally the Weiss book. The English title was: _Many Lives Many Masters_. Three birds with one stone. Was this synchronicity or what? I bought all three books and started reading the Gurian book on the metro. I would send it to Marcus ahead of my arrival in San Francisco. If he read it, we would have something to talk about. I finished the book the following day.

On September 13, I copied Marcus's July 29 letter, marked the text where he had written:

"Hope to cross paths again," and wrote in the lower margin, _"Our paths will cross sooner than you think. I'll be in SF in early October. Looking forward to seeing you on a level playing field."_

I put the letter in the book and mailed it to Marcus's office. I smiled to myself.

"Things are moving. Yes, siree!"

With the leave all squared away, my thoughts turned to the Association of Past Life Research and Therapy (APRT). This was far out stuff and I was a U.S. government employee with Top Secret clearance. What if word got around that I was even talking to such people? I would probably be branded a nut and my clearance would be pulled, or at least downgraded. Then, I thought of Dr. Weiss, who had risked getting his license revoked by publishing that book on past lives. In the end, he had an international best seller and a long patient waiting list. I decided to call APRT after business hours and leave a message asking for a list of therapists in my area. That way, I would not have to talk to anybody.

The list arrived within a week, along with information on the APRT Journal and a list of publications by APRT members. I went over the list of members and checked those with at least five years' experience. I decided against a man. I would not be comfortable with a man, given my father issues. So it had to be a woman, but which one? I looked over the list of publications. A title caught my eye: _Caution: Soulmate Ahead_ by Janice Cummings. I looked for the author's address in the list of members. It was in suburban Maryland. She was the one. I planned to call Janice, as soon as I got back from San Francisco.

I boarded United flight 57 to San Francisco in an upbeat mood. It seemed incredible that the leave had been approved, after all. It just goes to show you that perseverance conquers. Greg was meeting me at the airport. He had bought a red Porsche and told me I could borrow it. I asked for a bicycle instead, saying that driving a Porsche was not my style. As luck would have it, Greg had recently bought a ten-speed bicycle at a garage sale. He told me I could use it during my stay. Greg met me at the gate and could not wait to show me the Porsche.

"You're like a kid with a new toy. You know that?" I remarked.

I didn't want to rain on Greg's parade, but thought that the Porsche was a white elephant. All that horsepower, and it could carry only two passengers and minimal luggage. It was definitely not my style. It did look good, however, and I told Greg that.

"You should see how it drives," Greg said. "You want to get something to eat?"

"Actually, yes," I consented. "I forgot to order the vegetarian meal and had very little to eat on the plane."

Greg drove like a maniac to Serramonte shopping center.

"Very impressive," I assured him, "but don't forget our near miss last time I was here."

"Don't worry, don't worry," Greg said coolly, "our work is not done, so our time has not come."

After a mediocre Chinese meal at Serramonte, and a quick stop at Greg's favorite driving range, we drove to the Holiday Inn Express in San Mateo. The following day, I would relocate to Roberts At-the-Beach Motel in San Francisco, a block from the bike path and close to SFSU.

Thanks to the jet lag, I was up at 5:00. By 6:30, I was outside jogging toward the Bay. The jet lag and the clear weather gave me the opportunity to watch the sunrise over the Bay. I found a trail and followed it to a marina I had seen in the distance. I stopped for a few minutes to watch the sunrise. It was beautiful. I closed my eyes and breathed in the crisp, salty air. I smelled eucalyptus and ran in that direction. A sign informed me that I was in Coyote Point State Park. I ran past the yacht club and up the eucalyptus hill. I could see the airport in the distance and San Francisco farther away. To the right of the trail there was a man facing east and doing Tai Chi. I smiled. I had come to the right place. I felt the urge to do the Sun Salutation, a series of yoga postures, but did not follow through, for fear I might look silly to a passerby.

"Bradley," I told myself, "you think like an uptight Washington bureaucrat. Six months around here should help loosen you up."

It was close to 8:30 and Greg was picking me up at 10:00. I ran back to the hotel to get ready. Greg was on time, but I discovered I had missed the breakfast buffet.

"Don't worry," Greg said. "We'll go to my place. It's only ten minutes from here. You can have breakfast there. Besides, I want you to meet Cindy, my little sweetheart."

Greg had five children. Cindy, the youngest, was four.

Cindy, Greg, and I went to the back yard to pick fruit for breakfast.

"We have a full schedule today," Greg announced. "First, there's a lunch and talk about China sponsored by the World Affairs Council. Then there's a reception at the St. Francis to celebrate Taiwan's National Day."

My heart skipped a beat. Marcus worked at the World Affairs Council. Maybe he would be at the talk.

"And when am I checking into the motel?" I asked. "I can't do it in the morning."

"Call them up and tell them you'll check in late," Greg suggested.

I changed into a jacket dress for the two events. The talk on China was in Woodside. On the way over, I told Greg a little about Marcus and the coincidences between us.

"There are no coincidences," Greg said firmly. "You have karma with this guy. You must be soul mates."

I smiled. "I'm new to metaphysics, but what I've read so far points in that direction. There's this feeling that I've known him for ever. I felt it right away, when I first saw him."

The talk was in some millionaire's house and was preceded by a buffet lunch. Guests ate in the garden at tables around the pool and under the trees. The sun was pretty hot. I asked a couple sitting at a shady table whether Greg and I could share it. The couple readily agreed and revealed they regularly attended WAC events. They had just returned from a WAC-sponsored trip to Washington.

"Really?" I perked up.

"Great trip," the woman said. "Of course, our leader was someone who knew his way around. I can't remember his name. It starts with an M."

"Marcus Metamarro?"

"Yes, that's it. You know him?" The woman seemed surprised.

Greg and I exchanged glances. "I've run into him a few times," I said vaguely. "We're in the same line of work. When were you in Washington?"

"Last week in September," the woman replied.

Marcus was in Washington and in the State Department the previous week, and he had not contacted me. Apparently, he was not ready for a path crossing. I decided to call him later. If his home number were listed, he couldn't be too serious about avoiding me.

After the reception downtown, Greg and I went souvenir shopping. I was also looking for the Sunday paper: I had to find a place to live. Finally, around 9:00 Greg dropped me off at the motel. He said he would bring the bike over the next morning, after our meetings at the university. I thanked him for a lovely time and locked the door. I dialed San Francisco directory assistance and asked for a listing under Marcus Metamarro. His number was listed. I quickly thought of how to approach him. I had to cut him some slack. After revealing to me some of his secrets, he obviously felt I was too close for comfort. I took a deep breath and dialed his number.

"Hello?" Marcus answered right away.

"So, your number is listed," I said brightly. "Pretty risky, don't you think?"

He laughed. "Where are you?"

"In San Francisco. I arrived yesterday. Today I was at a talk in Woodside sponsored by your outfit, then went to a reception at the St. Francis. I met the mayor. We parked at the Sutter-Stockton garage. Is your office in the WAC building next door?"

"Yes, that's right," he replied, cautiously.

"Where are my skis?" I asked.

"I left them in Tashkent," Marcus responded. "I thought you didn't want them."

"I see. And you couldn't pick up the phone to ask? How about my Chopra tapes? Where are they?"

"They're in my shipment and I don't have a clue where that is," Marcus responded.

"I see. Do you have the Sunday paper?" I went on. "I'm looking for a place to live, and I can't find the paper. I went to several hotels downtown, but they were all sold out. The street boxes were either empty, or had Saturday's paper."

What came out of Marcus's mouth after that could only be described as babbling. "What do you mean you couldn't find the paper?" he shouted. "There are papers everywhere. I can't see you. I don't believe in the stars. There are too many coincidences. This is no coincidence. I'm not the way I was in Tashkent. I'm happy. I'm involved since last month. This is where I am now. It's going well. I'm happy. This past life stuff makes me very uncomfortable. I'm reading your book, but I got my own copy. I don't like your underlinings."

I was shocked at how agitated he sounded. I tried to calm him down.

"I underlined what was important to me," I explained. "Are you sure you want to do this over the phone?"

"Yes, this is the way it has to be," he said in a huff.

"Marcus, you said we were friends," I reminded him. "At the end of July you said you wanted to cross paths when we were healthier and happier. Now, you're telling me you're happy and don't want to see me. Why are you so negative toward me? I'm curious, if nothing else."

"You'll have to stay curious for now."

"I hope to talk to you sometime when you're calmer," I said. "Bye for now."

I sat on my bed, shocked at Marcus's reaction.

One thing is for sure, I thought. I hit the bull's eye with that book. His mother is definitely part of his problems with intimacy. Let's see what he does next.

Maybe that book had triggered painful memories he had repressed. Obviously, he was unable to deal with them. I was certain I triggered him, as well. He did it to me. He was the primary reason I had to take time off to deal with my issues. I liked to confront, however, and he did not. This trait made his case tougher, because his first line of defense was to run away. I had learned that running away did not work. As an eight-year-old battered child I believed that, if I went to the City of Brotherly Love, everything would be all right. Of course, it had not been. By running away, I had removed myself from the abusive situation, but had taken the wounds and the pain with me. To heal, I not only needed to remember everything that had happened, but to experience the feelings that came with the memories. I was certain I could recover repressed memories through hypnosis.

Marcus's fearful reaction told me that he was not ready to deal with his trauma. He was terrified of me getting near him. The involvement he mentioned was probably a last desperate attempt to keep me at bay. In fact, I had been wondering when he would spring the "other woman" tactic on me. Everything else he had tried, so far, had failed. And why did he say he believed me when I said I was here for my own reasons? Why else would I be here? I had decided to ignore his vacillation and go by my gut feeling. I had a ton of things in common with Marcus and knew he was attracted to me. Yet, he was running from me as if I were Count Dracula. And I was dying to find out why. Was there a sexual problem, or some other, sinister reason, or both? My search for answers would have to wait. I had other fish to fry. Tomorrow, I would find out what courses I would teach and how much I would get paid. I took a bath and went to bed.

I started my day by jogging on the beach and stuffing the pockets of my wind breaker with sand dollars. They were the largest I had ever seen. Afterwards, I went to the market near the motel and bought fruit, crackers, muffins, and herbal tea. I was set for breakfast and snacks for the next couple of days. Greg came at 10:00 and brought the bicycle, then took me to the faculty club at SFSU. I found out I would be teaching courses in two different departments, so I met with two department chairs. The money they offered me was less than my salary, but I could afford a pay cut, especially with my expected rental income. Everything was set. I was very tempted to drop by Marcus's office, but he had clearly said he did not want to see me. Then again, he had written that he wanted to cross paths again. One thing was certain. Marcus was like a feather in the wind. One could not rely on what he said, or even wrote. What messed him up so badly? If he could only let it out, he would be on his way to recovery.

With the university meetings out of the way, I returned to the motel and put on my biking clothes. I would do a biking tour of San Francisco. I took the trail by the ocean and rode to Cliff House, then rode around Golden Gate Park. I got back to the beach near the motel in time to watch the sunset.

The following day, near the Civic Center, I saw some boxes with publications containing information on housing and adult education classes. The Learning Annex catalogue had Brian Weiss's picture on the cover. He was giving a lecture in San Francisco the following week. Common Ground had an ad on the Whole Life

Expo. It would be in town during the coming weekend. I took copies of both publications. I wanted to mail the information to Marcus.

That night at the motel, I wrote him a long letter. I wrote about how meeting him had changed me, why I had to get out of Washington for a while, how I had overcome the fear of looking inside myself, and that I was confident he could do it too.

The day before my return to Washington, I rode Greg's bike to the closest post office and had the mailing for Marcus weighed. When the market across the street opened, I bought some manila envelopes and enclosed my letter, and the information on the Expo and the Weiss lecture. Marcus would get it after I was gone, but hopefully before the weekend. With this chore out of the way, I took a ride around lake Merced. If I could find a house in the Sunset area, I could ride my bike to work. Greg was coming for the bike that afternoon; I wanted to put in as many miles as I could before then. After the bike ride, I went back to the motel, showered, and changed. Greg came over after his class, and we went to dinner at a Chinese restaurant in the neighborhood.

The following morning, Greg came to drive me to the airport. Once there, we had lunch while waiting for my flight to board. I picked up the tab as a token of appreciation for everything Greg had done for me.

"See you in January," I called out, as I ran to get on board after the last call.

On the flight, I thought about Marcus and Greg. I had met Greg a few months ago and he had done so much for me that I questioned his motives. The one time Marcus had given something, the $100 pledge to the MS Society, he had included a virulent message. I felt that the official dinners he ostensibly gave for me in Tashkent were really for self-promotion. He wouldn't even give me the Sunday paper. Then again, I also felt he was trying to protect me from a secret danger. He didn't have to tell me that he had had an awful childhood; I could tell by his behavior.

"What's the matter with me?" I wondered. "Why can't I just write him off as hopeless and move on?"

The connection I felt was to Marcus's inner core, the part of his he was afraid to discover. It was a first for me. Exciting, but scary. I leaned back in my seat and closed my eyes.

Back in Washington, I called Janice Cummings.

"So what do you want, hypnosis for an addiction or a past life regression?"

"It's not about an addiction," I protested.

"Past life regression then." Janice was trying to pin me down. "How about October 30?"

I looked at my calendar. "You want to do it on a Sunday? It's not inconvenient?"

"If it were, I wouldn't be suggesting it," Janice said. "4:00 p.m. OK?"

"Fine," I agreed. "The day before Halloween is quite appropriate for doing spooky things."

"Bring a 90 minute tape, if you want to tape the session," Janice advised.

"I certainly will," I said.

I hung up the phone with butterflies in my stomach. I had an appointment.

Now, would I have the guts to keep it? This remained to be seen.

My phone rang again. It was Jon Wisner, a colleague who worked on the Former Soviet Union.

"I'm thinking of bidding on a job in Tashkent," he said. "You've been there many times. Can you tell me what it's like?"

"Sure, come on down," I said. "You can look at some pictures from Uzbekistan I have in my office."

Jon was in my office within minutes.

"When are you thinking of going to Tashkent?" I asked. "This year's bidding cycle is over."

"1996. I'm thinking ahead," Jon explained.

"I'd rather be in San Francisco," I said. "I'm moving there in January."

Jon looked at my pictures and zeroed in on the one with Marcus, Diane, me, and a group of Uzbek women and children.

"Who's that?" he asked, pointing at Marcus.

"Marcus Metamarro, the DCM."

Jon looked at me. "Marcus is in San Francisco," he said quickly. "You're moving there to be with him, aren't you?"

I gave him the pat bureaucratic response for outsiders. "I can neither confirm nor deny that my assignment in San Francisco is related to Marcus being there."

"Marcus was seeing a woman from the World Bank," Jon volunteered.

And I bet her name is Sylvana Vargas, I thought. And if you could believe that Superman and Minnie Mouse made a lovely couple, you could believe Marcus and Sylvana as a couple. In addition, I thought Vargas was a crook. Her positive story on Uzbekistan contradicted everybody else's. In fact, one IMF staffer had urged the IMF to sue the World Bank for fraud after Vargas omitted his factual contribution to a joint Bank-Fund mission report.

In February, I had gone to lunch with Vargas to size her up. She was petite and homely and did a lousy job of covering the gray in her black hair. She was dressed in black, spoke in a soft whiny voice, and frequently looked at the floor, when talking to me.

Inhibited, passive aggressive with low self esteem, was my verdict. I wouldn't trust her as far as I could throw her. I wonder if she's ever gotten laid. And why in the world doesn't she get a better dye job? She makes six figures, for sure.

I had to continue to tolerate Vargas because of her position and had to be alert to more irregularities on her part. Whatever the nature of Marcus's involvement with her, it was bad news. Was Vargas after a green card so she could bring her mother to the States, or were bigger things at stake? I wasn't about to discuss my suspicions about Vargas with Jon, so I changed the subject.

"As far as social life is concerned, Tashkent is the best party town in Central Asia," I continued. "But, if you want anything deep and meaningful, you'd better get married before you go."

Jon Wisner was a tall, handsome fellow. If I were emotionally unattached, I would be definitely interested in checking him out.

On October 15, I finished the Weiss book on past life regression and sent it to

Marcus. I included a little note:

"I think it's time for you to read this book. I am going to try past life regression in two weeks. Will report on the results. Funny you should mention the stars. I had a compatibility chart done on us. The enclosed excerpts are for your amusement. Our story is better than Sleepless in Seattle and When Harry Met Sally. I'll write it up and laugh all the way to the bank, while you're sitting there talking about beliefs. Those who look gift horses in the mouth are doomed to ride jackasses (I just made this up.) Ciao, J."

Five days later, I woke up at 1:30 a.m. with a strong sense that there was something wrong with Marcus. I felt this incredible sadness as I thought of him. I was tempted to call. It was only 10:30 p.m. in San Francisco, but I decided against it. First, he would get spooked. Second, I could do nothing about whatever was bothering him. San Francisco was turning into Tashkent. The feeling that something was going on with Marcus stayed with me for two whole days, but I resisted the urge to call. I could not stand to hear another tale of woe. On October 25, I had my first nice dream about Marcus.

We had gone to see a play. During intermission, we hid behind the curtain and hugged and kissed. The only word we said was: "finally, finally."

The Friday before my appointment with Janice, I came home to find a message from Greg on my recorder. He was in Washington and wanted to have dinner. He had lost my office number. I looked at the time: 8:00 p.m. Too late now. Besides, I was getting a sore throat and wanted to turn in early. Greg called the following morning while I was still in bed. Without Barney around, staying in bed until 9:00 was possible.

"I wish you had given me a little more notice," I said. "I'm afraid I can't see you before you go. I don't feel that well and I'm taking it easy today."

Greg was not crushed. "Any news from your buddy?"

"Not a thing. I hope no news is good news."

There was news from Marcus later that day, however. I got a package in the mail with his handwriting on it. I opened it. It was the book about mothers and sons I had lent him. The letter that came with it was undated. I looked at the postmark: October 20. He was probably writing that letter when I woke up thinking about him and feeling anxious. It was the most thoughtful letter he had ever written me.

"I feel the need to discover who I am and where I am going. A year in San Francisco will assist me in this effort. Even more important, is the nurturance, support, and love of another person who is also seeking self awareness. This, I have found—finally."

I got goose bumps when I saw the word he had used. This was the word Marcus and I had used in my dream. I had the dream, while the letter was on its way. Marcus was ambiguous about who this other person was. The description fit me, but he could have met someone new in San Francisco. Man or woman? Also, he did not write he was in love. He wrote someone loved him and made a few mistakes while he wrote this. As usual, he sent an ambiguous message.

Nevertheless, I felt very encouraged by Marcus's need to look inside himself. Even more encouraging was the fact that he was reading Dr. Weiss's book. Things were looking up.

I got increasingly excited as my hypnosis appointment approached. I left half an hour ahead of time to leave plenty of time for getting lost, car breakdowns, or whatever. I got there early and noticed another car in the parking lot. Since it had New York plates, I did not think it belonged to Janice. A few minutes before 4:00, I noticed a woman sitting in the lobby of the building, and walked toward the door.

It was Janice. I had seen her picture in the APRT publications list. She opened the door for me.

"I came early to do some paperwork," she explained. "Please come in."

She led me into a small windowless office and asked me to sit in a brown recliner.

"So tell me. What brings you here?" Janice asked.

I told the story of Marcus, including the nightmares. Their theme was always the same: he was in danger and was asking me for help. I felt tortured by him, yet I was drawn to him like a moth to a flame. First, I wanted the nightmares to stop. Second, I wanted to find out what it all meant. Janice listened with rapt attention. She nodded from time to time.

"You look as if you've heard all this before," I remarked.

"I've written a book about soul mates," Janice reminded me.

"Yes, I know," I said. "I saw it on the APRT publications catalogue. That's why I chose you. A friend of mine told me almost two years ago that this man and I are soul mates. You think so too?"

"Let's see what we can find out," Janice said. "Have you been hypnotized before?"

"No and I doubt I can be," I said. "I'm too high strung."

"Let's try," said Janice. "Did you bring a tape?"

I gave it to her and Janice put it in her recorder. She put on some soft music, lit a candle, and turned out the lights. She asked me to look at the flame of the candle and take a few deep breaths. Then, she asked me to close my eyes and relax. She had me feel the muscles in my feet and then relax them. Then, she moved up to the lower and upper legs, arms, back, neck, and face.

"You are completely relaxed," she told me. "Completely relaxed. Now, go to the life that is most relevant for you now. Take all the time you need to recall images, sounds, smells. Start speaking when you're ready."

I felt as if I were in a black hole.

"I get nothing," I whispered.

"Be patient. Just allow the memories to come."

I tried, but still felt I was in a black hole.

"Just relax and go deeper. Deeper and deeper. Allow the memory to come," Janice repeated.

I took a few deep breaths. Still nothing. A few minutes later, I said, "My hands feel cold."

"Tell me about it," Janice prodded. "Why are your hands cold?"

"I don't know," I said. "They just feel cold."

"May I put my hand on your forehead?" Janice asked.

I nodded. Janice placed the index and middle finger of her right hand in the middle of my forehead. She's playing with my third eye, I thought.

"Feel yourself walking in another place, in another time," Janice said soothingly. "Relax, let the memory come. Tell me if you're walking slowly or rapidly."

Much to my surprise, I began to speak:

"I'm walking rapidly on a beach with pebbles. The air and water are cool. It feels like spring. I'm barefoot. I'm wearing a garment made out of a fabric that looks like burlap. It comes just below my knees. I'm wearing a belt that looks like a rope. My body is young and lean. I'm a little older than thirty. My skin, hair, and eyes are brown. I'm male! My name is Hector."

My tone betrayed my surprise at my last statement.

"How are you feeling inside?" Janice asked.

"I feel anxious," Hector/Janet responded. "I'm walking home. My house is near the beach. It has fat, round columns. Curtains made of white gauze are blowing in the breeze. It looks like a house in ancient Crete. Nobody's home. I feel abandoned, but not too sad. My wife, Helen, has taken our three-year-old son Ajax and left. I'll miss my son, but not her. She's a beautiful, shapely, blue-eyed blonde, but she nags me constantly. We had a big fight just before I went for my walk on the beach. It's always the same thing. She wants me to change jobs and spend more time with our son. I'm a sponge diver and I'm away at sea a lot. She wants me to become a farmer or a merchant. I love the sea. When I'm not diving, I'm sailing. I want to explore as much of my world as I can. I've asked Helen to sail with me, but she's not interested. I'm very unhappy with her. She's a beautiful woman, but I don't feel like making love to her. At night, I lie awake next to her and wonder why I ever married her. I'm afraid it was an ego thing. She was pursued by many men and I was pursued by many women. I'm the best diver around. She was my trophy."

"What happens next?" Janice prodded.

"I don't look for her," Hector/Janet went on. "I take the next boat out. It's a long, wide boat with a big, off-white sail in the center. As usual, we're headed for Egypt. We don't get too close, however, the Egyptians get mad, if we do. We dive with nets in our belts and a big knife between our teeth. We stay under water as long as we can and collect as many sponges as we can. We get paid by the piece. I can hold my breath longer than anyone else, so I get most of the sponges. I guess the other divers envy me. We're not friends; we just work together. This time we didn't get to our diving spot. We hit a reef and the boat starts to take in water. There's a big hole on the fore starboard side. We bail as fast as we can, but the boat continues to take in water. I jump off when I think the boat will sink. Some of my colleagues do the same, but others go down with the boat. I don't help anybody. I just want to save myself. I swim faster than anybody else. Pretty soon, I reach the shore and walk out of the water. I'm not that tired, but I'm thirsty. A woman comes and sees me. An orange scarf keeps her brown hair away from her face. She's wearing a long, off-white toga tied above the waist. She's carrying water in a pointed clay vessel resting on her right shoulder. She gives me some water and I ask what her name is. 'Patricia,' she says."

I started to sob.

"What is it? What's happening?" Janice asked, anxiously.

"Patricia...... is Marcus," I explained in between sobs.

"Let the feelings come. Don't hold anything back," Janice said soothingly. "What happens next?"

I wiped my tears and continued in a soft voice.

"Patricia tells me I can stay in her house as long as I want. Her house is in an olive grove. It looks different from mine. It is white and has small windows with green shutters. She prepares a meal for me. Then I rest. In a couple of days, I feel strong enough to leave. I go to the beach and look at the sea. Patricia comes and stands next to me.

"'Thinking of leaving?' she asks.

"'Just the opposite,' I say. 'I was thinking of staying. I want to be with you. Is it OK?'

"She nods yes. I carry her to the bedroom and deposit her on the bed. I caress her face and hair. She says it's all right to make love to her. She takes off her dress and I my toga. I kiss her full, sensuous mouth and cup her firm, round breasts with my hands. Then, my lips move to her neck and nipples. I bury my head in her breasts, then between her thighs, savoring the aroma of her young, swarthy body. Her soft moans excite me tremendously. My penis is throbbing with desire. I enter her gently and thrust as slowly as I can. I want this to last forever. I have never felt such bliss inside a woman before. I feel transported to a different dimension. As if in a dream, I hear her cry out. I speed up my thrusting and allow myself to come. I stay inside her for the longest time, burying my face in her thick brown hair. She runs her fingers through my hair and along the length of my back. Finally, her hands rest on my buttocks. I feel the passion rising inside me once more. I start thrusting again. Our bodies dissolve into a liquid love energy. I am one with her and the universe. When I snap back into my body, I try to understand what happened. I haven't felt like this before. Patricia, although less beautiful than Helen, moves me in ways I never dreamed possible. She tells me I am free to leave any time I want. But I don't want to leave. I love her."

"Can you describe to me your relationship with Patricia?" Janice asked.

"I'm totally different. I'm not selfish anymore. Patricia is very patient with me and kind. I feel she's part of me. When she's away, something is missing, I feel I'm not whole. I was a warrior, authoritarian. She made me kind, by being kind. We live in the middle of an olive grove. We grow olives. We have two children, a boy called Aeschylus and a girl called Calliope. I become a good father. I play hide and seek with the children in the olive grove. They laugh as they run through the olive trees. Patricia comes and watches us. She tells me I'm like a child, too. There is a lemon tree outside our bedroom window. I put lemon flowers in Patricia's hair. I lift her up and swing her around. She laughs. I put her down and kiss her long and hard in the mouth. I can't wait for the night to come so I can make love to her. My passion for her is growing stronger over time."

"I understand," Janice said. "Now go to the next significant event. One, two, three. You are there. Tell me what is happening."

"We're old. In our seventies," Hector/Janet continued in a soft voice. "I'm home. I'm taking care of Patricia. She has dysentery. I give her herbal medicines, but they don't seem to work."

Hector/Janet started to sob. "I don't want her to die," he/she said in between sobs.

When the sobs subsided somewhat, Hector/Janet continued. "She...she died. I don't want to live. I stop eating. The children come and try to make me eat. I refuse. They're very upset. They say I'm abandoning them on purpose. I get very weak. I'm in bed. The children are sitting on either side of the bed and ask me not to leave them. I'm barely aware of them. I close my eyes. I feel my spirit leave my body. I see the children with their heads on my body, crying. I love them, but not as much as I love Patricia. I can't go back."

"How do you feel about the life you've lived?" Janice asked.

"In the beginning, I was cruel and selfish. Then, I became good and responsible," Hector/Janet responded.

"Now I want you to go to the point just after death," Janice continued. "Sense and feel your spirit move away from your body. Higher and higher, into higher levels of love energy. How do you feel?"

"I'm happy. Patricia is there waiting," Hector/Janet said in a quivering voice. "I want to hold her, but I can't. We're spirits."

"Are you able to join in any way?" Janice asked softly.

"We become one spirit," Hector/Janet responded.

"I want you to feel the united spirits moving higher and higher," Janice continued. "I want you to tell me the effect of that lifetime on you now."

"I'm becoming kinder, but Marcus doesn't love me like he did then," I replied, a tone of frustration in my voice. "I don't know why. I thought he'd remember me, but he doesn't. He's saying he's trying to find his way and I'm there pointing for him, but he doesn't want to go. I want my life to be the way it was then. With Marcus. I don't know if it's possible."

I revealed that Helen, Hector's first wife, is now Gerry. Ajax, Hector's son with Helen, is now Melanie, my ersatz sister. Aeschylus and Calliope, Hector's and Patricia's children, are Melanie's current siblings Jason and Hester.

"Before I bring you back into the room," Janice said "can you look back at that lifetime and tell me what is the greatest lesson you've learned?"

"To be kind," I said without hesitation.

"Slowly, slowly to the count of five I will bring you back into the room," Janice continued. "You will remember everything that has transpired and feel comfortable with it. If there is additional insight, understanding, and information, it will come to you in the hours, days, and weeks ahead in a way that will be comfortable to you. All your past has programmed you to be the person you are today, to erase karma, and to give unconditional love to yourself and others. Number one, slowly coming back totally and completely in October 1994; number two, beginning to feel as if a great weight has been lifted off your shoulders, your heart, and your mind; number three, feeling more at peace with your world and with everyone in it; number four, up and up and up; number five open your eyes whenever you're ready Janet. You're back in the room feeling very, very good."

"Do you think this was real?" I asked, as soon as I opened my eyes.

"What do you think?" Janice retorted.

Maybe," I said skeptically. "I didn't expect him to be a woman and me to be a man. It seems I'm repeating the same pattern with Gerry and Marcus."

"Gerry was the man you were going to marry, but felt something was not right?" Janice asked.

"Yes," I replied. "On the surface, it was right. Everyone was saying he was the perfect man, but something, something did not feel right. It's the opposite with Marcus. Almost everything I know and hear about him is wrong, but it feels right."

"It seems to me, from what you said," Janice commented, "that in that lifetime you were authoritarian and Patricia brought you the balance. In this life, Marcus is authoritarian and you're offering him the balance."

"I'm still pretty bossy and headstrong, but I'm more patient when I'm with him," I explained.

"And this may be beneficial to both of you," Janice remarked. "So he's bringing out your feminine, nurturing side, as he did in that lifetime. But it's his personality now that's the problem."

"I think deep down he's kind," I said. "But he's been hurt. He said his childhood was awful, but didn't give me any details."

"For people who don't believe in past lives, it's beneficial to go back to childhood and try to understand on the basis of that who they are," Janice commented. "Marcus could go to a regression therapist in California and retrieve childhood memories. You should continue to do what feels right and loving to you, and in the relationship, regardless of which way it goes. As you continue to study and grow and work on yourself, there will be a benefit to the other person. From the research I've done, I know that whenever there's a strong soul connection between two people, whenever one improves, there's an energy benefit to the other person. You help the soul of the other person. This doesn't mean that they'll be who you want them to be, or that they'll do what you want them to do. You just nurture for the sake of nurturing."

"Do you think I should tell him about this regression, or will he freak out?" I asked.

"Sometimes, there's a benefit to telling someone what you've discovered," Janice said. "If he's reading Dr. Weiss's book, there must be an opening in his consciousness. Emotions are energy. If you remember anything else in the days and months ahead, let it out. If you're driving the car and feel like crying, cry. Or rent some funny videos and laugh; just let it out. Things you keep inside have more power over you."

I bought Janice's book on soul mates and made an appointment for November 7. The current session had revealed something totally unexpected and unrelated to the flashbacks Marcus had triggered. Alone in the car, I got overwhelmed by the memories I had just uncovered. I mourned the loss of my ancient love and the absence of such a love in my current life. I cried about the pain and fear in Marcus's eyes and his explosive anger. What was this awful wound he was hiding? Did he know, or had he suppressed it? I could barely see the road and the other cars through my tears. I was gratified my instinct had been proven right, but I could not rejoice. I felt like stopping the car and calling Marcus. I had memorized his number instantly; the digits in his number were a combination of my birth month, the year I graduated from high school and the year I got my Ph.D. But I couldn't talk. I was sobbing too hard. It was a miracle I got home without having an accident. After I stopped crying, I felt the need to talk to someone. But to whom? Who would understand? Gerry was out of the question. What could I say? "We had an awful marriage in a past life. Then, you took the kid and left."

Ashley would understand, but I would talk to her in person next weekend. I decided to write to Marcus. After all, he was one of the protagonists in the drama I had just uncovered. I wrote him a tear-stained letter describing the findings of the regression and said I would send him a copy of the tape later.

The following week was really tough. I was flooded with memories from that lifetime and the emotions associated with them. Reliving Patricia's death was agony. I sobbed uncontrollably at that memory. Reliving Hector and Patricia's passionate lovemaking was ecstasy. I was particularly haunted by the memory of Hector making love to Patricia on a moonlit night, while smelling lemon flowers. Their bed was made of a wood frame and leather slats with sheepskins on top. A small, square window was open and the white cotton curtain was blowing in the breeze. A lemon tree stood outside and the moonlight came in through the window. His orgasm was like communion with the Divine. I sobbed at that memory, as well. I was crying because I realized what I was missing in this life. I was crying because I missed making love like a man. Most of all, I was crying because Patricia was gone forever.

I knew beyond the shadow of a doubt that Patricia's soul was in Marcus. I recognized the energy the moment I saw him. I had read somewhere that love at first sight was the remembrance of an old love. My experience had proven this to be true. But even if Marcus were healed and I made love with him, it would not be the same. I wanted to be Hector once more, and I wanted Marcus to be Patricia. It was impossible, and I was inconsolable. I did my work in a fog, then went home and cried until I was exhausted. Sometimes I fell asleep with my clothes on. Sometimes I skipped dinner. No outer journey I had ever taken was as exhausting as this inner journey. I thought about rescheduling the next appointment. There was only so much catharsis I could tolerate at any point in time.

I told Gerry that I could not see him for a few days. I was going through some heavy stuff. I could not even begin to describe to him what I was experiencing. I felt as if someone had inserted a wedge into the core of my being, had torn me apart, and put me back together in a different way. I knew that the experience had changed me forever. I tried to pull myself together. Another regression was coming up, just a week after the first one. Fortunately, I had planned to visit my psychologist friend, Ashley, in Philadelphia just before the second regression. Victor, Ashley's husband, was battling cancer and I had a feeling he would not be alive when I got back from California. In addition, I wanted to meet Roger, a man Ashley had told me about, who could sense the human energy field (aura). He was the one who had said that Marcus and I were soul mates. Roger worked with Ashley as a human lie detector. Ashley would ask a patient how he felt and if the answer did not match the emotion shown in the client's aura, Roger would intervene.

I arrived in Philadelphia Saturday. Victor came to meet me on the driveway. He did not seem too different from his usual self, except he was thinner. Ashley came out, too, and gave me a hug. I watched Victor. He had a distant look on his face. I had seen the same look in my foster father a week before he died. I got a knot in my stomach. I knew Victor would not be around much longer. Ashley knew it too, yet she was so serene. After lunch, Victor took a nap, while I told Ashley about the regression and its effects on me. Ashley did not bat an eyelash. It was as if she heard stuff like that all the time. Now that I had been introduced to past lives, I wondered how many times Ashley and I had crossed paths. In this life, we had met when I came to Philadelphia as a poor, runaway teenager. I had stayed a week with Ashley and Victor as part of a new student hospitality program. It was Ashley who had found the wealthy Chestnut Hill family that took me in. Now, the regression revealed that the children in that family had been Hector's children in ancient Crete. No wonder we had hit it off right away.

Ashley drove me to her office. We were meeting Roger there. He was a medium size, stocky man with warm brown eyes and short, grey hair. He came into Ashley's office and set up a padded folding table to the right of the couch. I sat on the couch with Ashley, while Roger sat opposite us in a chair. Before meeting me, Roger had told Ashley that they had to get me out of my head and into my heart. I felt like a fly under a microscope. I tried to determine what Roger perceived.

"Can you see my aura?" I asked. "I want to know what color it is."

"I can feel it, I can't see it," Roger replied.

"How do you feel?" Ashley asked me.

"Fine," I responded.

"I sense anxiety," Roger butted in.

I admitted I was nervous because I didn't know what to expect.

"What's the table for?" I asked.

"Why don't you lie on it and find out?" Roger suggested.

I lay on my back and closed my eyes. Roger put his hands under my head on either side of the neck. Within seconds, I felt something like an electric current go down the left side of my body and come up on the right side. Roger was injecting energy into me.

"I can feel that," I whispered. "It feels wonderful."

A few minutes later, I was sitting again on the couch listening to Roger's diagnosis. I was astounded to hear him tell me about my troubled childhood and to add valuable insights. He had gleaned that information from my energy field. I felt again like a fly under a microscope.

"When did you start doing that?" Roger asked.

"Doing what?" I asked, puzzled.

"Closing your heart. Just now, your heart chakra shut down."

"I guess when I was a child," I said. "I wanted to be open and loving, but the message I got from my father was that an open heart meant weakness. He shut his own heart down to play his macho role."

"Can you think of someone in your childhood who had an open heart, but was also strong?" Ashley asked.

"My aunt. She was my ersatz mother and lived with us until I was six, or so. I followed her everywhere and she never told me to go away. When she moved out to get married, I was crushed. I think that was the moment I shut down."

Ashley told me to go back, feel my pain, and mourn my loss. I had to understand that my aunt had to fulfill her mission as a woman by getting married and having children of her own. I could build a museum and keep my pain and suffering there. That would be my holocaust museum. I could visit, but I was not allowed to live there. Roger observed that although I considered my father the big villain in my life, my anger was mainly directed at my mother.

"It never occurred to me before," I admitted "but it's true. He beat me brutally until I left home, and she didn't protect me. I remember being about five years old and lying on my side on the dirt, under a pine tree, while he hit me with a bunch of locust branches. The thorns were piercing my legs and I was bleeding. My mother stood next to my father saying, 'that's enough,' but she didn't shield me from the blows. Also, she potty trained me by burning my bottom with the electric iron. She envied her childless friends."

I fell silent, pondering my new insights.

"I'm tired of talking," I said shortly. "May I get back on the table?"

"As you wish," Ashley said.

This time, Roger directed his energy into my head. I felt a buzz.

"What are you trying to do, cook my brain?" I said, laughing.

"No, I'm just trying to rewire it," Roger replied. "I'm enjoying this. You have a lot of energy."

"That's what everybody says," I admitted. "I strike fear into men's hearts. They think I might incinerate them."

At the end of the session, Roger collected his check and gave me a hug.

"When are you coming back?" he asked. "I want to work on you again."

"I can't tell you. I'll be in California most of next year," I replied.

After Roger left, I told Ashley how energized I felt.

"It's as if he recharged my batteries. He has quite a gift. How did he discover it?"

"His father was in the hospital dying. Roger went to visit him and held his hand. In a few minutes, his father said he felt fine and that he wanted to get out of there. They checked him out, but he died at home a few days later," Ashley explained.

"I have a nickname for Roger," I said. "Goldfinger."

"What did you get out of the session, besides recharging your batteries?" Ashley asked.

"I was astounded that he picked up all that stuff about my childhood by plugging into my energy field. I now realize that I've been carrying around a lot more baggage than I thought. And he's absolutely right about my mother. My resentment toward her was buried so deeply, I wasn't even aware of it. I have a better understanding of how emotions affect the body. Negative thoughts and emotions sap our cells of energy, causing illness and eventually death. I need to get busy cleaning out my emotional garbage."

"If you need any help, Roger and I are only a phone call away," Ashley said, approvingly.

"Thanks for the offer," I said. "I have a feeling my stay in California will help a lot. I will have time to remember and think. In Washington, I run around like a chicken with its head cut off, then I collapse. There's no time for introspection."

Back at Ashley's house, we got busy cooking dinner. Victor was in the study working on his computer.

"You know," I told Ashley. "I don't understand how Victor can be a nuclear physicist and be unable to visualize the human body in terms of subatomic particles. Did he read Chopra's book _Quantum Healing_ that I sent him? I thought the title would appeal to him."

"No, he didn't," Ashley said. "He's not open to new ideas. There was a point where he could have turned the cancer around, but he didn't want to do the work."

"That's amazing," I exclaimed. "And you, being a psychologist, could have helped him so much."

"He told me he didn't believe in chakras," Ashley said.

"And what did you say?"

"I don't believe in neutrinos," Ashley replied.

We burst out laughing.

"Has he tried a Goldfinger treatment?"

"He's no longer interested in that, either," Ashley explained.

It was incomprehensible to me that a brilliant scientist like Victor would choose to die, rather than explore alternative ways of healing. Modern medicine had done its thing and it had not worked. The root of his problem was in his emotions, not in his body.

After dinner, we watched a video of Yanni at the Acropolis. I was impressed. The man was truly charismatic, and the music spectacular. One of his closing remarks, stuck in my mind.

"If you look at the Earth from space," Yanni said. "You see no boundaries. We are one. The lines on the map are man-made."

I went to bed peaceful and content. The feeling evaporated in the pre-dawn hours. I woke up from a dream about Hector's soul merging with Patricia's. Was it a dream or a reenactment of that ancient event? Did I have a soul union with Marcus? Janice's book on soul mates said that choice was possible in a spiritually advanced society. Ancient Crete was such a society. Hector had made such a choice. Was his soul linked forever with Patricia's soul? I valued my freedom and independence above all else. The thought of my soul being linked to someone else's suffocated me. I took a few deep breaths and got into a meditative state.

"God, I want a divorce," I thought.

A question came to my mind.

"Did you, as Hector, ask for your soul to be joined to Patricia's soul?"

"I did."

"Your request was granted. Those whom God has joined together, no human can put asunder."

I came out of the meditation shaken. I tossed and turned a few more hours, then got dressed and went downstairs. Ashley was in the kitchen. She took one look at me and sensed something was wrong.

"You were so happy and relaxed yesterday. What happened?"

"It's Marcus. I'm getting bad vibes from him. Maybe he had a bad reaction to the letter I sent him about the regression. I have to go. Tomorrow, I have another session with the hypnotherapist."

I left right after breakfast, although I had planned to leave in the afternoon. Driving back to Washington, I thought of canceling my appointment with Janice. I could not stand another gut wrenching experience. Then again, maybe I could do something different. Maybe Janice could help relieve my anxiety. I could also discuss some telling dreams and the book on soul mates. I wanted a second opinion on a dream I had almost a year ago.

Marcus had disappeared. I went around asking people who knew him if they've heard anything. Somebody said that he lived on a boat somewhere. I thought the boat might be in San Francisco, so I flew out there. I went to the Marina and was wandering around. I saw a group of people in party clothes and asked where they were going. They told me there was a party on a boat and pointed it out. I crashed the party and asked who the host was.

"It's Marcus Metamarro," a man said. "I'll take you to him."

He took me to a jovial, swarthy man, about 5'10", dressed in nautical garb. The man joked and laughed with his guests.

"This is not Marcus," I said.

"Sure, it is," the guest insisted.

I left the party room and started wandering around the boat. By the galley, I heard a man's voice on the p.a. system,

"Please bring upstairs a mug of peppermint tea and my pet rock."

The voice belonged to Marcus. I intercepted the waiter and took a tray with the tea and the pet rock up a spiral staircase. Marcus was sitting in a deck chair, his head resting on his hands. He was alone. I could only see his right side.

"There you are," I said cheerfully.

Marcus looked up somberly.

"So you found me. How clever of you. I suppose you want to know who I really am."

"Yes, I do," I said confidently. "And I'm not afraid to find out."

"Take a good look then."

He turned around. The left part of his face was burned beyond recognition. It was a red, scarred mess.

I had woken up terrified and looked in Freud's interpretation of dreams. I did not like what I saw under left and fire: sin, perversion, homosexuality, purification. That evening I had called Ashley.

"We've made progress since Freud's time," Ashley had said. "The left side represents the yin, the feminine side. His nurturing side is undeveloped."

"I know that much," I had said. "He cringed at the sight of stuffed animals. That's why in my dream he had a pet rock instead of something cuddly and fuzzy. He pretends to be happy, while he's emotionally scarred."

Perhaps Janice would have additional insights into the dream. That evening, I wrote to Marcus about the after effects of the regression. I described my feelings and the memories that triggered them, in case he wanted to try the same procedure. I wrote that making love to Patricia was pure ecstasy. It was much better than the love energy of the spirit world. I wrote about missing being a man and especially making love like a man. I also described my visit to Philadelphia and the session with Roger and Ashley. I ended by writing that I would call him when I stopped crying. I stuck the letter in the book about soul mates and placed the latter in the same envelope Marcus had used to return the book on mothers and sons. The following morning, I mailed the book from the State Department post office. I wondered what Marcus's reaction would be to all this. Five weeks later, I would discover that my regressions had a much bigger impact than I could ever imagine.

My appointment with Janice was at 7:00 p.m. By the afternoon, I had calmed down enough to feel that I could handle another regression.

"How do you feel?" Janice asked as soon as I walked in the door.

"Actually, I feel pretty good right now. But the past week has been really tough. I was regressing spontaneously and reliving the most thrilling and most agonizing memories. I went to pieces and then put myself back together again."

"What do you want to do tonight?" Janice asked.

"First, I want to discuss some dreams," I replied. "Then, I'd like to go back to the first life I lived with Marcus."

I related to Janice three of my most terrifying dreams about Marcus.

"Oh wow," Janice said, about the disfigured face dream. "It speaks volumes. Your unconscious is telling you that he's not who he appears to be."

"I sensed that right away," I said. "I felt he was wearing a mask. About a year ago, I sent him a tape by Deepak Chopra about intimacy. In it, Chopra spoke about dropping the masks."

Janice went through the familiar, by now, steps of relaxing my body and told me to recall walking in another place and another time. She gave me the suggestion to allow the memory to come and to start speaking when I was ready.

"My feet are cold," I said in a few minutes. "I'm walking on snow. I'm wearing moccasins and snow shoes. My body is covered with a tunic made of animal skins. I'm female. I'm young. Mid-twenties, maybe. I have brown skin and black hair braided into two braids that rest on my back. My name is Chaka. I'm a member of the Sioux tribe. I'm in the Dakota territory. The year is 1750. I carry a load of wood on my back. My pet wolf is walking on my left. I'm walking back to my village. I'm relieved to reach it. People wrapped in blankets are sitting around fires built among the tipis. I go into my parents' tipi and leave the wood to the right of the fire. My father is sitting by the fire opposite the entrance, smoking a pipe. He's wrapped in a blanket. He has black, shoulder length hair streaked with gray. He has a feather on the left side of his head. My mother is kneeling on his right, washing dishes. She has gray hair, braided like mine. I don't live with them. My mate and I have a tipi on the other side of the village. His name is Chomka. I like him. He's kind to me and protects me. He's out with the men, hunting."

"Go to the next significant event and tell me what's happening," Janice prompted.

"Our village is being raided," Chaka/Janet continued, a tone of apprehension in her voice. "Chomka and I are lying on the floor of our tipi, under animal skins. He's lying on top of me. I'm worried that he may be killed. We hear the raiders' cries and know they're Cherokee. They came to steal our food and animals. They set fire to our village. We hear the cries of the wounded villagers. We smell tipis burning. By some miracle, our tipi is spared. When all is quiet, we venture outside. Our village has been burned to the ground. Everyone is dead. We are the only two survivors. We don't feel safe there. We gather whatever supplies we can find and escape to the mountains. We don't know how we're going to survive. In addition, I'm pregnant. This worries us even more. There's barely enough food for the two of us, how can we take care of a little baby? We build shelter using tree branches, blankets, and animal skins. In late winter, the time comes for me to give birth. I'm in pain. Chomka is pacing nervously. He has to help me and he doesn't know how. I hope I can survive. Everything goes smoothly. I give birth to a little girl. She's chubby and healthy. We call her Lobka. We're very happy. Soon, it will be spring and more food will be available. When spring comes, we decide to stay in the mountains. We don't try to find another Sioux village. I go to the forest to gather nuts and berries. Lobka is sleeping tied to my back. Chomka traps small animals. When Lobka is two, we have another baby. He's a boy. We call him Gulu. Chomka is fascinated with him. He spends hours playing with, and talking to him.

"We're very happy in the mountains. When Lobka turns thirteen, however, she becomes increasingly restless and wants to see other people. Reluctantly, we gather some supplies and start walking north. Chomka is leading the way, I'm bringing up the rear, and the children are walking between us. After walking for several days, we spot a village in the valley below. It must have at least a hundred tipis. The children watch wide eyed. They've never seen so many people, tipis, and fires. They run ahead, excited. The villagers spot us coming down from the mountains and gather around us. They cannot believe we have spent thirteen years alone in the mountains. They are Navajo. They allow us to stay with them. The only difference in our routine is that I do my chores with other women and Chomka does his with other men. Chomka and I are not certain we can trust the Navajos and they us. The children are very happy to be with other children, however. We look for an opportunity to return to the mountains. The opportunity comes when the Navajo village is raided. The raiders are Sioux. We escape the massacre by hiding in some bushes on the edge of the village. Since the raiders are Sioux, we're afraid that the Navajo will retaliate against us. As soon as the raid is over, we pack a few supplies and head back to the mountains. We find a peaceful valley and build a tipi. We're happy, but the children aren't. They're both teenagers now, and want to be with other people. Chomka and I understand. We ask them to understand why we don't want to go with them. They understand also. We send them on their way, telling them to find a Sioux village."

"So he and you stay behind in the mountains. What is your life like?" Janet asked.

"It's very peaceful in our valley. Chomka and I watch the sunrise and sunset, whenever we can. Chomka traps animals for food and I gather seeds, nuts, and berries. We try to learn as much as possible about our world by observing the animals, plants, and stars. We know the winter will be cold if the animals' coats become thick in the fall. We treat injuries and illnesses with herbs. On clear nights, we build a fire near our tipi and sit next to it. We look at the stars, and share the day's observations. We make love next to the fire. Chomka is very tender. Our marriage was arranged, but I started loving him after we escaped to the mountains. Our love grows stronger over time. I feel complete with him. Once, he was bitten in his right ankle by a poisonous snake. I made an incision and sucked out as much poison as I could. Then, I applied a poultice of herbs on the wound. He was in terrible pain and wished he could die. His entire leg was swollen. I prayed that he not die. I didn't want to be left alone. The herbs worked. Chomka didn't die, but it took him a long time to regain full use of his leg. I took over his job of trapping animals for food. I don't like to kill the animals, but we have to eat."

"Go now to the last day of that lifetime," Janice instructed. "Where are you and what is happening?"

"We're in a cave," Chaka/Janet said, surprised. "Chomka and I. Bears came to steal our food and we hid in the cave. He's holding me in his arms."

"As you are in the experience, I want you to be aware of how death occurs," Janice said.

"There was an earthquake and the cave collapsed."

"I want you to become aware of the last thoughts that you had at the point of death, and to tell me what they were," Janice instructed.

"I'm happy I was with Chomka."

"Feel your spirit move away from your body at that time and place," Janice said. "And as your spirit moves up and up, be aware of another spirit near you."

"Yeah. It's Chomka," Chaka/Janet whispered.

"Feel the energy of the lifting of the two spirits together higher and higher, into higher levels of love energy. Higher levels of light and consciousness. From that perspective, I want you to take an overview of that lifetime and tell me about the effects of that lifetime on you now."

"Love of nature, mountains, and Chomka."

"I want you to look at the soul of your mate. Feel and sense the energy and essence of that soul, and tell me if it is anyone you recognize in this life."

"It's Marcus," I said softly.

"I want you to take a look at your two children, your daughter and your son. Sense and feel the energy and essence of each one individually, and tell me if you recognize them as anyone you know in this life."

"I don't know them," I said, a tone of frustration in my voice.

"Now I want you to feel and sense your spirit go higher and higher," Janice prompted. "I want you to feel your consciousness expand. Allow your mind to be free to receive the first thought that flows through it in response to this question: 'How many lifetimes have you and Marcus lived together?'"

"Eighty six," I answered without hesitation.

After obtaining this astounding answer to her question, Janice brought me back into the room. "This was nice," I said, as soon as I opened my eyes. "But the date, 1750, does not compute. This was supposed to be before Crete and Crete was 2,000 B.C. Also, as far as I know, the Navajo were not that far north."

"Of course in that time and space, time may not be as we know it. The Native Americans did not keep time as we do. I've regressed others into Native American lifetimes, and they couldn't give me any date at all. There is also the theory that past, present, and future are taking place right now, which is not an easy concept for us on the earth plane to understand," Janice explained.

I noted that this regression was not as traumatic as the first one. There was a natural rhythm to it. Chomka and I were part of nature, as were birth and death. In addition, I was spared the trauma of witnessing Chomka's death.

"Although you don't have to explore eighty six lives, this gives you a sense of the pattern of the relationship and your own individuality. Little pieces of who you are. This may be of value to you," Janice commented.

"Yes," I agreed. "It explains why we like mountains and nature, in general. Boy, I will be on the road a lot, if I'm going to explore eighty six lives. So what's new? I AM on the road a lot, as it is. And did you notice something? The memory started by the sensations in my feet. My feet felt cold. In the first one, I had said that my hands were cold. What I didn't say was that my feet were wet from walking on the wet beach."

"This is one way of retrieving memories. Through the cellular level," Janice explained.

I made another appointment for November 17. I had yet to explore the Tashkent flashbacks. On the drive home, I went over the regression in my mind.

"Eighty six lives!" I repeated incredulously. "No wonder I recognized his energy immediately. Maybe, I made it up. But why did I say eighty six and not ninety six or a hundred and six? Why aren't I tired of this soul after all these lives we've spent together?"

I had more questions than answers. And these were questions mortals could not answer. The snake incident explained my dislike of snakes. I did not understand, however, why I was not claustrophobic and afraid of earthquakes, since a cave had collapsed on me during an earthquake. Maybe it was because Chaka and Chomka had died peacefully in each other's arms. In the Cretan life, Hector was actually looking forward to death. He saw it as a way of reuniting with his beloved Patricia. One's feelings at the moment of death seemed to determine how death would be experienced and recalled.

"Eighty six lives!" I repeated over and over. "So how come I recognized him and he didn't?"

I remembered what I had written him once, "You're like a radio sending a distress signal. I'm getting your signal loud and clear, but you have to switch to

163

receive mode to get mine."

Marcus was constantly ejecting pain. Thus, he was unable to receive anything, including comfort and love. The first step toward enlightenment was coming to terms with one's childhood.

Marcus was nowhere near that. He hung onto the fear and anger, obscuring his eternal self. I could not wait until the next regression. I would explore one of the two flashbacks then.

In addition to undertaking my inner journeys, I was busy preparing for my outer journey to California. One thing I had to do was rent my house while I was gone. The other was to find a place to live in San Francisco. Obviously, Marcus was not going to help me. I got the feeling that the Higher Powers really wanted me to go to California, when the residence problem was easily solved on both coasts. Leah, a friend and former colleague of mine, had recently returned from spending two years in Europe. She was only too glad to move into my house. Thanks to Roommate Express, I found a house near the ocean south of San Francisco. The owner, Grace, and I hit it off right away. In fact, Grace offered me her bedroom, instead of the unfurnished room she had listed. I had marveled at my good luck. I sent a deposit right away.

I was trying to wrap things up at work and allocate my portfolio between the two colleagues, who would be taking over in my absence, when the phone rang.

"Hi. My name is Stewart Morris and I'm a member of the Bosnia Task Force. We're sending a team at the end of the month to assess the situation. You've been nominated to participate."

"What? I thought they were still fighting over there," I remarked, surprised. "What would you do with an economist?"

"There's a cease fire. We need someone to do an assessment of the economy," Morris explained.

"But the place is a shambles. There wouldn't be any data on which to base an assessment," I observed.

"I'm told you're very innovative and can work in adverse conditions," Morris persisted.

I got the picture. Someone had blabbed about my exploits in Central Asia and Alaska. They were looking for a combat economist.

"How long?"

"No more than four weeks," Morris assured me.

"OK, I'll do it," I relented. "I can't do a follow up, though. I'm all set to teach in California in January."

How does one do travel orders to a war zone? There were no civilian flights to Sarajevo. The team would have to catch a military flight from Zagreb. I had three weeks to learn everything I could about Bosnia. Once my name was put on the Bosnia team list, the phone started to ring and people started to drop by my office.

"Are you crazy? The place is full of mines," Bill said. "You could get killed. We don't want to see your name on the plaque by the Dip Entrance. And right before you're scheduled to leave for California."

"Relax. Will you?" I told him. "Maybe they'll start shooting again and the

164

trip will get canceled. If you want to worry, wait until I get there."

I became weary at the thought of Gerry's reaction to my announcement that I would be going to Bosnia right after Thanksgiving. He was a worry wart and my adventurous nature added to his worries. Breaking up with him would be the humane thing to do. The best time to tell him about Bosnia would be Sunday night. This way, his weekend would not be ruined. It was going to be an eventful weekend. I would have to do my Christmas shopping early. Everything would have to be mailed the day after Thanksgiving, at the latest.

"One thing I can say about my life," I mused. "It's never boring."

After dinner Sunday night, I brought up Bosnia.

"I have something to tell you," I said, bracing myself for Gerry's reaction.

He put down his coffee cup and raised his eyebrows.

"What now?" he asked.

"The Saturday after Thanksgiving I'm leaving for Bosnia," I said quickly.

"What the hell are you talking about?" Gerry exploded. "I thought you were going to California."

"I am," I assured him. "After Bosnia."

"You must have lost your mind," Gerry opined. "Bosnia is a battlefield. Why do they need an economist in a battlefield?"

"It will not be a battlefield for ever," I explained. "The Bosnia Task Force needs an economic assessment of the place and I was nominated for several reasons."

"The main reason being that you're crazy," Gerry opined. "Which explains why you're working for an agency that is run by idiots and lunatics."

"I prefer to think of myself as adventurous," I said calmly. "Will you please calm down? We're watching the codes. They've been alternating between green and orange. If it's code red on the 26th, we won't go."

This was poor consolation for nervous Gerry. He looked awfully glum. I got up, stood behind him, and put my arms around him. I kissed him on the right cheek.

"Cheer up, Grumpy," I whispered in his ear. "Everything will be all right. You'll see. My lifeline is very long. I'll live to a ripe old age."

"Do what you want," Gerry said, disentangling himself from my embrace.

He got up and planted himself in front of the television in the bedroom.

That wasn't so bad, I thought as I cleared the table. I sensed that I had met Gerry and Marcus in this life to help them release their fear. Gerry hid his fear by withdrawing, while Marcus alternated between withdrawal and explosive anger.

CHAPTER TEN
A Cord Made of Light

I felt quite calm on November 17, 1994, the day of my third appointment with the hypnotherapist. The previous two sessions had caused a shift in my world view and in my reactions to events in my life. For example, the usual chaos at the office did not rattle me any longer. Having discovered past lives where I had been shipwrecked, starved myself to death, given birth to two children in the wilderness with only the help of my mate, survived two Indian raids, and died in an earthquake, I couldn't get excited about the wrong format in a memo. When things got really crazy, I closed my door, turned out the light, closed my eyes, and concentrated on my breathing. All tension left my body. I assumed the vantage point of someone above the Earth. Things that got Earthlings really excited were as transitory as their personalities. The only lasting thing about humans, their spirit, would shed and assume personalities as needed for the lessons it sought to learn.

I was smiling to myself, as I drove to Janice's office. I had stories to tell at Thanksgiving. My three virtual siblings in this life were my children in the Cretan life. I couldn't wait to see their reaction when I told them. Jason and Hester really liked black olives. Maybe this went back to ancient Crete, when they lived in an olive grove. Their sister Melanie, on the other hand, did not care for olives that much. She had not lived in an olive grove in Crete. My thoughts then turned to the two flashbacks. Which one should I explore? The one of the two teenagers in the chariot, or the one of the naked Asian couple? The second one intrigued me tremendously because the man was kissing the woman's neck. My neck was one of my most sensitive points. I decided to explore the second one.

As usual, Janice was waiting in the lobby to let me into the deserted building.

"How are you feeling?" she asked as soon as I sat in the recliner.

"Fine," I assured her. "I have recovered from the Cretan regression. The Indian one was not as wrenching. In general, I'm much calmer than I used to be. I don't feel I have to rush and do certain things before I die. I now know that death is not the end. It's a transition to another state of being. If I don't accomplish everything I set to accomplish in this life, I will come back and finish the task. It's OK if I don't marry Marcus and we don't have any children in this life. We were married and had children before. If we need this experience again, we can have it in one of our future lives."

"Sounds like the regressions have benefitted you," Janice commented.

"Definitely," I concurred. "My life is starting to make sense. I have bursts of intense joy. This is in sharp contrast with how I felt in the past. I hit bottom in May when my dog died and Marcus sent me that nasty note. Seven years ago, I had a thrilling job, a hunk of a boyfriend, and all the material goods I wanted. Yet, I was inexplicably depressed. I would cry and ask myself: 'Who am I? Why am I here? If my life is meaningless, I don't want it to last much longer.' I thought I needed something new, so I got another hectic job in another agency. That career move, however, did bring me closer to Marcus. He and I were in the same building in 1990 and part of 1991, yet we never met. We had to meet on the other side of the planet in 1992."

"You did not meet earlier because the time wasn't right. Everything happens for a reason," Janice explained.

"I'm convinced of this now," I commented. "I had to break my leg in 1990, so I could become more patient and introspective. I knew it instantly. I told Gerry that the accident happened so I could learn to be patient. He, on the other hand, needed the experience of taking care of me so he would stop believing that he was an SOB. If I had met Marcus at the State Department, I would probably have thought that he was just another boring bureaucrat and would not have given him another thought. Seeing him in exotic Tashkent brought back the memories. Sparks flew. Everybody else seemed to fade in the background. This was a once in a lifetime encounter."

"Maybe, once in this lifetime," Janice observed, laughing. "During your last hypnosis, you said you had lived 86 lives with Marcus. Which one of these lives would you like to explore tonight?"

"I want to do the life in Asia," I said. "We like Asian food and eat with chopsticks. I bet that life is the reason."

Janice went through the paces of relaxing my body and told me to go back to the life in Asia and the time I remembered spontaneously.

"I get the name Huang-Chong," I said. "He's my husband. He's young, twenty maybe. He's slim but strong. Not very tall. He has straight, black hair. Chin length. I'm a couple of years younger. Eighteen maybe. My name is Sou-Lin. I'm also slim with straight black hair down to my mid-back."

Sou-Lin/Janet started to laugh. "It's our honeymoon," she explained. "We're a couple of kids. We don't know what we're doing. We're kneeling naked on this bed, trying to figure it out. I've known him all my life. We grew up together. We're cousins. We got engaged when I was five years old. I guess you could say it was arranged. It was expected we would marry when we grew up. But I'm a little nervous. I haven't done this before. It's difficult to relate to him as a husband when all my life I've related to him as a cousin and a friend. But I like his kissing my neck and breasts. I think I'm going to like this marriage thing."

Janice asked Sou-Lin/Janet to go to the next significant event.

"We moved in with his parents, as is customary," Sou-Lin/Janet continued. "We live in a house in the country. It has a row of rooms with mud walls. Our room is at the end of the row. In front of the house, there's a pond with ducks swimming in it and weeping willows around it. We're in China. The year is 1430. Our clothing is pretty much unisex: a long tunic with trousers underneath. I help my mother-in-law with the household chores and Huang-Chong works with his father in the fields. Neither I nor Huang-Chong like his mother. She runs the household like an army general and nags us constantly about growing up. Neither one of us wants to do chores, but we don't know what we want to do. Huang-Chong is upset that his father does not stand up to his mother. We put up with his nasty mother for two years. Then, we run away to a nearby town. We're not quite sure how we're going to live. We don't have that many skills. I know how to weave baskets, however. So I start doing this to earn money. Huang-Chong found a job in an herb shop. He starts to get interested in herbs. I bring my baskets to the shop to sell and I start learning about herbs, too."

"What happens next?"

"I'm at home weaving a basket," Sou-Lin/Janet continued. "I'm very pregnant. I'm waiting to give birth any day now. I feel OK about it, although the added responsibility makes us both nervous. Parenthood will force us to grow up. It's a very long labor. Some women from the neighborhood are helping me. Huang-Chong is pacing nervously outside. I tell the women to hit me over the head if I get the idea to go through this again. Finally, I give birth to a baby boy. We name him Sou-Kong.

We like having him around. He's a good baby. It becomes apparent very early that he's very smart. The bad news is that Huang-Chong's mother tracked us down and raked us over the coals about breaking tradition and running away. She says now that we have a baby we'll have to grow up. She wants us to move back to her house. Huang-Chong and I talk about what we should do. We could move again, but unless we move really far away, his mother could track us down again. Running away is no solution. We decide to stay put and ignore his mother.

"We teach Sou-Kong at home, but soon we realize that he needs a tutor. He's asking questions we cannot answer. We search for the answers, however. Our son is teaching us, while we're trying to teach him. To be able to afford a tutor, Huang-Chong opens his own herb shop in another part of town. I start helping him with the shop. We go to the countryside and collect herbs. We dry them at home and study their properties. We experiment with new mixtures. Apparently, they're effective. Pretty soon, people from faraway places come to buy our herbs. Our entire lives revolve around the shop. We don't have time to socialize. By the time our son is ten, he decides to become a doctor. He's studying really hard and we're very proud of him. Huang-Chong's mother dies at this time. We feel relieved. We won't have to worry about her intrusions any longer. We ask his father to come live with us. Our son leaves home when he's eighteen to study medicine in another city. We're sad to see him go, but hope he will return one day to set up his practice in our town. It would compliment our business. People come to our shop every day to ask for advice. Huang-Chong's father falls ill during his nineties. We give him herbal medications, but feel his immune system is too weak for him to survive. He dies in a few days. We're sad, but satisfied that he outlived his shrewish wife by quite a few years.

"Shortly after my father-in-law's death, our son comes back to town. He has finished his medical studies and wants to practice in our town. We're overjoyed. This is what we had hoped for. We stay up all night discussing the latest advances in medicine. He tells us about a new technique to treat the body, using needles inserted in specific points. He calls it acupuncture. We're very interested in this procedure and ask him many questions about how it works. We all decide that Sou-Kong should open a clinic next to our herbal shop. He will treat patients with acupuncture and we will prescribe herbs to complement his treatments. We continue working until we're in our seventies. We're at peace and completely content. We have a profession we love and that benefits people. In addition, we have raised a good son who's also helping heal the sick. We couldn't ask for anything more."

"Go to the last day of that lifetime," Janice instructed. "One, two, three, you're there. Where are you and what's happening?"

"We're at home," Sou-Lin/Janet continued in a calm voice. "It's night and it's raining very hard. There's a huge flood. Our house is close to an irrigation ditch. The ditch overflows and our house is washed away. We're washed away with it. We're in the water. We're holding onto each other. The water covers us."

"How do you feel?" Janice asked, anxiously.

"We're pretty old, we had a good life. I guess we're ready to die. We're not fighting it," Sou-Lin/Janet explained.

"Can you tell me what your last thoughts were at the point of death?"

"I'm happy that I had the opportunity to help all these people with the herbal medicines. And... I had a good husband and a good son," Sou-Lin/Janet said, her voice breaking, tears streaming down her face.

"Don't hold the tears back," Janice said. "Let them come. When you look back on the life you've lived, how do you feel?"

"I feel good about it. We were more fortunate than most people. We did what we liked to do."

"Now allow your spirit to move higher and higher. Higher and higher, to higher levels of consciousness. From that perspective tell me the effects of that lifetime on you now."

"Interest in health and herbal medicines," I said.

"OK. I want you to take a look at the energy and essence of the person who was your mother-in-law in that lifetime. Do you recognize that person in this life?"

"I think it's my mother!" I said, surprised at my discovery.

"Take a look at your father-in-law in that life and tell me if you recognize him as someone you have known in this life."

"My father?" I was even more surprised.

"Take a look at your son and tell me if you recognize that soul in this life."

"It's my brother," I said immediately.

"Take a look at your husband and tell me if you recognize him in this life."

"It's Marcus, again," I said without hesitation.

"Take a deep breath and relax," Janice instructed. "I want you to go higher and higher and tell me any additional effects of that lifetime on you now."

"Interest in Oriental medicine, Oriental philosophy, and the Orient in general."

"Before I bring you back into the room," Janice said. "I want you to look at that lifetime and tell me the greatest soul lesson you've learned."

"To help others."

My first remark, when I came out of the hypnosis was, "That was totally different again. I can't believe how every time the feelings are different. And the thing about my mother! In this life she's the one who's meek and mild and my father was the one who was screaming and hollering. But I think they were playing roles. They were the opposite, inside. The other thing is that all these people are my relatives. What about Marcus's relatives? They never show up. If they did, I wouldn't know, I guess. I'm telling you what I know."

"They could have been there. We don't know," Janice opined.

"But this is really uncanny about the health stuff and the herbs!" I observed. "Both of us are health freaks. We're reading all these health books. We're both vegetarians."

"In this life, have you had acupuncture done or taken herbs?"

"I used to make my own herbal mixtures," I replied. "I have herb books and used to buy herbs and mix them. But I've gotten lazy. Now, I buy the ayurvedic mixtures. And you should see Marcus's cupboards. They're full of herbal teas. When I was helping him unpack, I got the feeling I was unpacking my own kitchen."

"How interesting. Now, obviously you had a very joyful experience. You liked what you were doing," Janice commented.

"Yes," I confirmed. "But it was not the intense, passionate love affair we had as Hector and Patricia. We had a partnership, a common goal, and a business to run. I guess it was because we were cousins and had grown up together. That's why it was so funny during the honeymoon. All of a sudden, we had to act like honeymooners, and it didn't seem like the thing to do. It was more like: 'Where's the manual? We have to look up what to do here.' And the thing about China! When Marcus was stationed in Tashkent, he kept saying: 'I have to get to China, I have to get to China.' And I don't mean Beijing. He wanted to go to Western China. And I'm sitting there thinking we've lived in China before. He tried to go last year, but there were floods in Pakistan and the roads got washed out. He finally made it this year, the week after Memorial Day."

"How do you feel?" Janice asked.

"I feel fine," I assured her. "I'm getting the hang of it now. But I already forgot the names I mentioned. What did I say? Huang-Chong? Sou-Lin?"

"They come out of your unconscious," Janice explained. "That's why we're taping the session. You could forget at the conscious level."

"And did you notice that, this time, the memory came in a different way?" I remarked, excited. "First, I got the picture from the honeymoon and then the name Huang-Chong. Now all that's left, is to check out the first flashback. It felt nice. I want to know more about that. But I might leave for Bosnia next week. If I do, I won't be back until the end of December and shortly thereafter, I'm leaving for California. I have to check this out before California."

I made a tentative appointment for Tuesday, December 13. During the drive home, I reviewed my sessions. Three lives in three different parts of the globe, and I had been married to Marcus. And every time the marriage was good, but the feelings different. They ranged from burning passion to tenderness and affection. I wished I could confirm that I had lived with Marcus eighty six times. If that were true, we must have had every gender combination and relationship imaginable: spouses, siblings, friends, parent/child. But why did we meet in this life? There had to be some unfinished business. This was not apparent from these three sessions. I hoped that the next session might provide a clue to my unfinished business with Marcus. I was sure it had something to do with my nightmares about him being in danger and asking for my help. My unconscious was sending me a message.

This research is getting kind of expensive, I thought. Enlightenment doesn't come cheap. I'm very lucky to be able to afford these sessions. People who live hand to mouth can't afford such luxuries. Of course, I could learn to hypnotize myself, but Janice's input was helpful.

I had a busy weekend finishing Christmas shopping. I would know by Wednesday if I was going to Bosnia or not. I had to be ready, just in case. I bought several blank audio tapes and made copies of the hypnosis sessions for Marcus and me. I planned to put the originals in a safety deposit box. On Sunday, I placed all the things I wanted Marcus to have in case I died in Bosnia into a box: the remainder of Deepak Chopra's tapes on the Higher Self, copies of the hypnosis tapes, pictures from the Galapagos and Kazakhstan, and several books, including one on Crete. I wrote a letter explaining I was headed for Bosnia and was not sure I would be back. I advised Marcus against listening to the tapes by himself. Ideally, he should listen to them with a regression therapist. If I came out of Bosnia alive, he should wait so we could listen to them together. I mailed the box first thing Monday morning. I got the news on Bosnia as soon as I walked into my office. There was a Code Red over the weekend. The trip was off.

Thanksgiving morning, Gerry and I started the one and a half hour drive to the Eastern Shore of Maryland. The crowd was smaller this year, so everybody was staying at the house. I could not wait to tell my virtual siblings of my discoveries. I would have to take them aside and tell them. I did not want Gerry to know yet. I probably would have to wait until the next day, when things would be calmer. Gerry interrupted my thoughts.

"When are we coming back?" he asked.

I got miffed. We were only half way to our destination and Gerry was already thinking about getting back.

"When do you want to come back?" I asked.

"Tomorrow at the latest."

"I want to stay a little longer now that Bosnia's off. You may leave any time you want. I'll get a ride with Jason and Claire."

Gerry, whom I used to think of as my anchor in a stormy sea, now felt like a weight pulling me to the bottom.

As soon as we got to the house, I was very tempted to blurt out everything about my regressions. Thanksgiving was a time when everyone in the family gave a status report. As in any organization, there were the official and the unofficial reports. The official reports were usually made at the table, and the unofficial ones during conversations in different rooms, floors, or outdoors. I decided that mine would be an unofficial report. Most of those present were uninitiated. In addition, it would be awkward to reveal to everybody that I had a lousy marriage in a past life with the current Gerry, and three wonderful marriages with the current Marcus. The family had seen pictures and slides of Marcus and wanted to meet him. After this revelation, they would want to meet him even more. I took the virtual siblings aside and asked them to stand by. I had something important to tell them, but the time had to be right.

171

After Gerry's departure the following day, I asked the family to gather in the living room. I started by saying that the story I was about to tell them was unusual, to say the least. If at any time they wanted me to stop, they should speak up.

"You were abducted by aliens and are carrying Elvis's baby," Jason interrupted.

I burst out laughing. Humor ran in the family.

"I guess you could say it's in the same category," I said.

After everyone was quiet, I told them about life in ancient Crete.

"After this discovery," I commented, "I believe that our meeting in Philadelphia was no accident. In fact, I believe there are no accidents, in general. Everything happens for a reason. When Ajax disappeared from my life in ancient Crete, he was three years old. When we met in this life, Melanie was two and a half. She used to follow me around everywhere. She got in bed with me every morning. It seems we were both making up for lost time. This also explains why Jason and Hester like olives. Having once lived happily in an olive grove, they ate tons of olives and associate them with happy feelings."

"Great explanation, Dr. Freud," Jason joked.

"It works for me," I retorted. "I'm open to other suggestions. At any rate, you can't comprehend these things intellectually. You have to experience the feelings. If you listen to the tape, you'll know that I couldn't possibly have faked anything. The feelings were too real."

"So my name was Ajax?" Melanie interjected. "Should I start cleaning something?"

Everyone laughed.

"When are we going to meet the man who was our mother then?" Hester asked.

"This may not be possible in the near future," I explained. "He's now in California and feels very threatened by me and my explorations. When I was there last month, he refused to see me. I wrote to him about this three weeks ago, but I haven't heard from him. His primary coping mechanism is avoidance, and here I am, opening the can of worms."

"As usual," Jason observed.

"I'm not surprised to hear you were a man," Hester commented.

I laughed. "That masculine energy is pretty obvious, huh? I feel it too. I have been telling people for years that I'm 50% male and they laugh. Gerry thinks I'm 100% woman. When he told me that, I knew he had no sense of my true essence. If he hasn't gotten it in nine years, it's unlikely he'll ever get it."

Fred was silent.

"Pretty freaky, huh Freddie?" Hester teased. "I bet in your wildest dreams you never imagined that your wife had lived in ancient Crete and her name was Calliope."

"I must admit, it never crossed my mind," Fred laughed.

My revelations made for lively conversation on our way to Annapolis for lunch. After lunch at Pusser's, I hugged everyone goodbye. I would spend Christmas with Gerry and his family and would not see Hester and Melanie until I got back from California.

I counted days until my next appointment with Janice. The flashback I wanted to explore seemed to be from ancient Greece. By exploring it, I hoped to gain valuable insights into my dislike of that country. Memories of my painful childhood there were partly responsible. But I had always felt that there was something more. One of my first words had been "out." As long as I could remember, I wanted to get out of that country. Every time I went back, I got a knot in my stomach as soon as the plane entered Greek air space. I could never relax there and was always relieved to come back to the States.

Finally, December 13 came. I left the office early to make sure I would be on time for my appointment. I had to drive there during rush hour, and allowed time for traffic jams. I arrived at Janice's office in good spirits and told her about my Thanksgiving revelations. Now all the relevant parties knew, except for Gerry. I would tell him before I left for California.

"How are things between the two of you?" Janice asked.

"We're drifting further apart," I said. "He came back from the Eastern Shore before me. I have a feeling this will be the last Christmas I'll spend with him."

"Any news from Marcus?"

"Not a thing," I replied. "At this point, no news is good news. I can't handle my stuff and his too. Recently, though, I got good vibes from him. Once on December 7, I remember because it was Pearl Harbor day, and also this past Sunday. I was tempted to call him, but decided against it."

"Let's see what we can find out today. Are you ready?" Janice asked.

"As ready as I can be," I said, stretching out in the recliner.

Janice put me through the relaxation routine once more and asked me to go to the time and place of the chariot ride.

"And whenever you're ready, tell me anything you're sensing or feeling. Take all the time you need," Janice said softly.

"I've got the name Aesop," I said almost immediately. "And also Kyllini, but I'm not sure if this is the name of a person or a place."

"OK," Janice said. "Let's follow these names for a few minutes and see where they carry you. Aesop going back, back. Going back to the memory of Aesop, to the memory of Kyllini. Allow the perceptions to come and feel yourself in another time and place."

I took a few deep breaths.

"I think he's my brother," I continued. "It's springtime and we're outside. We're riding in this chariot. We're really young. Teenagers. Aesop is maybe sixteen and I'm fourteen. We're both wearing white togas and blue diadems around our heads. Our hair is light brown, or dark blond. Our skin is light. The chariot belongs to my father. We just sneaked away, got on it, and are riding in this field. Jason is driving it. I'm standing behind him with my arms around his waist. The weather is great. The sun is shining. There are puffy white clouds in the bright blue sky. A light breeze is blowing on our faces. The field is covered with little white daisies with yellow centers. We're laughing. I'm asking Aesop to go faster.

"When we get back home, our father yells at us. He's tall and muscular and has a very loud voice. We're not scared of him, though. We know he's a paper tiger. He likes to yell, but he's a softie. Our mother is in the corner of the room, laughing to herself.

"Our house looks like a Greek temple. It's white, rectangular, and has columns on the front and back. Our father is an army man. He's dressed in army clothes, leather breast plate, leather plates on his shins, and wears a helmet. He looks like a Roman soldier."

"Go to the next significant event," Janice instructed.

"Our father is leaving for war. He's done this before. We're kind of used to it, but we always wonder whether he'll come back. We're in Greece. I think the war is against the Persians. When Xerxes invaded. We're somber, we're not laughing or carrying on like that time we took the chariot. And Aesop is supposed to be the man of the house. This is a joke, of course. He always does what I tell him, although I'm younger. We're all standing there, looking at our father. Aesop is saying that he will obey. He'll do as he's told.

"A few days later, a messenger comes and says our father has been killed. We're sad. We realize we'll miss him a lot. Our mother is crying. She thinks she has nobody to protect her. Aesop is too young. Our grandfather comes to live with us. We need a head of household. He tells us we can no longer be naughty. We have to act responsible. The war ends in a couple of years. Greece won, so there are lots of celebrations. We're in a stadium. There's a victory celebration for the warriors. We're waving branches of laurel, shouting 'Hail to the Victors.'"

"Do you have a mate, a lover, or a close friend?"

"No, I don't. I'm closest to Aesop. We've continued to spend time together. I'm like a tomboy, strong willed and a trouble maker. And I don't like to be with other boys or girls. Aesop and I interact as if we're both boys. And we play games. We play a game like chess. And I beat him a lot. He thinks it's OK. He lets me do what I want. It's strange because he's older and he spends more time with me than with other boys.

"The next important event is Aesop's wedding. He's marrying a friend's daughter. Her name is Helen. I don't like her. I think she's dishonest. She plays games. I think she'll make Aesop unhappy. She cheats on him. I tell him to leave her. He's not happy, but thinks he should stay. I want her to leave, so we can be like old times. I told him what she's doing is dishonorable and that he's the laughing stock of the whole town. He says he doesn't want to know. He tells me to stop talking. He puts his hands over his ears. He's hurt. I don't want him to feel hurt. But I'm smart, so I'm going to think of a way to get rid of this evil woman. He doesn't really want her, but he doesn't have the strength to stand up to her. She's very wily, like a sorceress. She manipulates him. Every time he puts his foot down and tells her to shape up, she acts very seductively and he caves in. Then he hates himself for it."

"Look into his eyes and tell me what you see," Janice instructed.

"Pain. He wonders what he did to deserve this. I have to prove that Helen is conspiring with the enemy, so that she'll be ostracized. I go to the leaders and tell them that I saw her with an enemy soldier. They don't think it has anything to do with state matters. They think it's one of her trysts. I tell them I don't think so. I saw her pass him a roll of paper tied with a ribbon. I ask them to watch her to find the proof. After I give them the time and place where I saw them, they're watching her. I'm following her to get dirt I can use against her. She may be beautiful, but she's dumb. So she does it again. Same guy. Gives him a piece of paper. The security people see her and intervene. The piece of paper has a plan of the Treasury. Helen and the enemy soldier were conspiring to take the gold and run away. She got the plan from one of her lovers. They're both arrested, tried, and found guilty. My brother is in even more pain. He's sitting down with his head in his hands. I'm standing behind him with my hands on his shoulders. I tell him this is one way of getting rid of her. He thinks she brought shame to our family. How can he live after that? I'm afraid for him. I'm afraid he's going to kill himself. I don't want that. I just wanted her to leave."

"On the count of three, I want you to move to the next significant event in that lifetime," Janice instructed. "One, two, three. Tell me where you are and what is happening."

A picture of Aesop hanging from a beam in his room flashed through Kyllini/Janet's mind. She started sobbing uncontrollably.

"Don't hold the tears back," Janice said. "Let them come."

"He....he killed himself. I killed him," Kyllini/Janet wailed. She continued to sob, while Janice was passing her tissues.

"What happens next?" Janice asked softly.

"I'm at the funeral. I don't want to live, either," Kyllini/Janet said, dejected. "But I have to take care of my mother. She's really distraught. I don't think she's going to live long. She stops eating. She dies too. I wanted to do the same thing, but I didn't want to give her more grief. I talk to my teacher. I ask him, what I should do, whether I should be punished. He says 'no.' I meant well. It was his decision. I have to live."

"Now I want you to feel your body in that time and space and tell me where you feel the greatest discomfort," Janice interrupted.

"My left shoulder," Kyllini/Janet responded. "Somebody hit me with a cane. One of Aesop's friends. He said it was my fault he killed himself. I said no. I was trying to help him. I have to live to prove that he didn't die in vain. I have to build a memorial to him. He liked the sea. It has to be near the sea. I remembered the time we took the chariot. I will build a statue of us riding the chariot. I commission it to be built. The statue is finished and it's beautiful. It's bronze. I have it placed by the coast. I go and look at it every day at sunset. I remember we were happy once. I'm the only one left in the family. I don't want to have a family of my own. I read a lot of books. Everybody says I'm very strange. Women are not supposed to read books. But my teacher says it's OK. We should do what we feel like to reach our full potential. Those who say women aren't supposed to read books, pretty much ignore me. I think they're ignorant. My only friend, other than my teacher, is my nanny. She's old and kind. She always listens to me and takes care of me."

"I want you to go to the last day of your life in that lifetime," Janice instructed. "Tell me where you are and what is happening."

"I decided I've lived long enough," Kyllini/Janet responded. "I don't see any point in living any longer. I'm forty five years old. I'm home. My nanny has died. So, I drink hemlock, like Socrates."

"I want you to be aware of your last thoughts at the point of death," Janice said.

"I feel guilty," Kyllini/Janet responded. "I never forgave myself for what happened to Aesop."

"I want you to be aware of that guilt," Janice continued. "That's what you took with you at the point of death. Now, I want you to move beyond the death. Feel the lifting up, higher and higher, to higher levels of consciousness, to your Higher Self. Now from that perspective, I want you to overview that lifetime and tell me the effects of that lifetime upon you now."

"I shouldn't be possessive," I said. "I hate Greece. I have a lump on my left shoulder."

"I want you to look at the soul of your brother Aesop and tell me if it is anyone you recognize in this life."

"It's Marcus," I said wearily.

"Look at your mother and father and tell me if you recognize either one of them in this life."

"My ersatz parents, Jason Sr. and Beth."

"I want you to look at the person who hit you on the shoulder. Is it anyone that you recognize in this life?"

"No," I responded, disappointed.

"I want you to look at your teacher. Is it anyone you recognize in this life?"

"My uncle," I said softly, remembering my favorite uncle.

"There's one more person I would like to ask you about," Janice continued. "Please look at the soul, energy, and essence of the person who was your nanny in that lifetime. Do you recognize this person in this life?"

"My paternal grandmother," I responded.

"Continuing to overview that lifetime, are there any other effects that need to be brought to your conscious awareness?" Janice asked.

"I want to know who Helen is," I said, clenching my teeth.

"Please look at Helen's energy and essence," Janice instructed.

"I don't know her," I said, frustrated.

"You have just retrieved a very painful memory," Janice noted. "Before I bring you back into the room, I want to do a healing exercise."

I nodded my agreement.

"I want you to take a deep breath and relax," Janice continued. "Feel your body relax. Now I want you to visualize light in beautiful colors surround your body, moving around your body and starting to heal the pain from the past. And bring that healing energy into your mind/body system. Healing the guilt from the past, healing the pain. And as this energy begins to flow into your body/mind system, I want you to pay particular attention to your left shoulder. Visualize healing energy flowing through the cellular memory of your shoulder. Freeing the guilt and the pain that has been lodged in your body. I want you now to visualize, in any way that you can, Marcus in this life. See yourself and Marcus. I want you to be aware of any energy connection that may be a negative energy connection from that life. You may see it as a cord, as energy flowing, a rope, or chain. Anything that you may feel is tying you and Marcus."

"Yes. There is a link," I said softly. "It's a cord made out of white light. It connects our hearts."

"Now, I want you to visualize the cord between the two hearts," Janice went on, "and visualize more light freeing your own heart from the guilt of the past. Now look at Marcus and send him light and energy freeing his heart. Now allow the cords to begin to dissipate. And by that I don't mean that you're disconnecting the love. You're disconnecting the pain from the past. Try to see this in any way that you can. Visualize disconnecting the guilt and the pain from the past. And bringing more light and freedom and loving energy into the space between the two of you. And whenever you see something taking place, tell me about it."

I was silent for a long time. Then, I said, surprised, "I hear chimes. I don't know. Maybe like the spell is broken."

"OK," Janice said softly. "In just a few minutes, I'm going to bring you back into the room. But before I do, I want you to continue to feel healing light surrounding your body/mind system. In the space of loving energy between you and Marcus I want you to see more love and more freedom, freedom without attachment, love without attachment, that together you might support each other and be friends to each other in whatever way the relationship moves with loving attention and freedom between the two of you. Are you ready to come back into the room?"

"Yeah," I said.

"Before you do," Janice continued, "I would like for you to be receptive to seeing an image of a spiritual teacher or a spiritual guide or receiving a gift of a symbol that would speak to you of your own spiritual path. Tell me what happens."

"A harp," I exclaimed. "I don't understand."

"As you see the harp," Janice instructed, "I want you to listen for a message that will bring you more peace and more loving direction on your spiritual path. What does the harp mean?"

"Peace," I explained.

"Very good," Janice said. "I want you to stay with the image of the harp, as I bring you back into the room."

"Oh, boy," I sighed, as soon as I opened my eyes. "This was worse than the first one."

"You had a tough one this time," Janice agreed. "I think it was an important one though. I think part of the reason you have been responding to Marcus the way you have in this life has been out of guilt from that lifetime. In a desire to take care of him, you have been possessive. Remember what you said when you went up into spirit? 'I have to be less possessive.'"

"Yeah," I nodded. "What do I do next?"

"I want to do one more session before you go, to lift you up from the pain of this memory," Janice said. "You may want to go to a music store and buy a tape or

177

CD of harp music. It may be soothing to you. There may some other symbolism to the harp that neither you nor I are consciously aware of."

"I wish I knew what to do," I said pensively. "I want to do what's best for him."

"And for you also," Janice added. "It's interesting Janet. In this relationship, you often say things like that. 'I want to do what's best for him. I want to take care of him.' Now I know where it's coming from. What I would encourage you to do is let it settle in. Do nothing. You've reached a painful memory that has had an effect on the two of you now. You feel that you have to take care of him. And if there is any blame or hesitancy from him to trust you, it could come from that life."

"Yeah," I agreed. "He said he found it difficult to open up to me. I didn't think much of it, because he doesn't open up to anybody."

"Now I will tell you," Janice added. "When we do exercises, like the one we just did with the cord, there's a beneficial result for both people. I have seen this many times. If there's a tie or a cord that's pulling the people down or holding them back, in dissipating the cord and bringing more freedom and energy, I found it to be helpful to both people, whether one of them knows it or not. Marcus doesn't need to know any of this for it to be of benefit to him."

"This is really ironic," I observed. "I spontaneously remembered the pleasant thing and most everything else was unpleasant. And do you know what else is freaky? When I saw Marcus in Tashkent in December 1992, he told me, 'My life is a Greek tragedy.' I laughed and said, 'No it's not. I know about Greek tragedies.' He never adequately explained why he felt that way."

"For heaven's sake," Janice exclaimed. "What a thing to say. And you said you hated Greece?"

"Yes. I was born there and I've hated the place as long as I can remember. It was not only getting out. Every time I go back, I get tied up in knots. I knew there was something. My friends said it had to do with the present. They don't treat women well. But I knew there was something else. It was deeper than that. What did I know about women's lib when I was a kid? I did know, however, that the place gave me the creeps. Now I understand why I like Crete, but I hate Greece. In those days, they were not the same. So why did I choose to be born there? I guess to reconcile myself with the place. It was useful to remember this. It was awful, but it explains so much."

"It does explain a lot," Janice agreed. "And as long as the memory is hidden in your unconscious, it has more power over you. Regardless of where the relationship with Marcus goes in this life, as long as there are unconscious feelings on your part that you have to make up for something, it's not an equal and free relationship. You put yourself a notch below him. Do you understand?"

"Yeah, yeah," I said. "For instance, if he chose to hurt me, I wouldn't be able to defend myself. I know that. It would take a lot for me to put myself on an equal footing on this one. It was so weird when I got the first flashback. I sensed we were brother and sister. Then, I got the second one and we were making love and we were Chinese. I got really confused."

"So you sensed you were brother and sister?" Janice asked.

"Yes," I confirmed. "And this is how I felt about him, until I remembered Crete. Then it changed. It was so strange. He's a handsome man, and I never tried to sleep with him. Something held me back. We hugged and I felt I loved him, but I did not relate to him the way I normally do to men. And those dreams I had about him being in trouble and me trying to help him! The theme was always the same."

"You have to get rid of the unconscious triggers that make you feel as if you have to make up for something," Janice advised.

"But I do feel I have to make up for something," I protested. "How do I get rid of that feeling?"

"Whenever you drift off to sleep at night," Janice said. "Just ask for healing to take place to release the guilt from your unconscious. But there's another thing I have found helpful. Twice a day for the next two weeks, I suggest that you say mentally to yourself something along these lines: 'Marcus, I forgive you for any pain you may have caused me in this life or in any of our past lives together. Marcus, I ask you that you forgive me for any pain I may have caused you in this life or in any of our past lives together. I give thanks that we may give and receive forgiveness in this way.' And at the end of two weeks see if you feel differently. By your reaction to this session, I can see that you've been holding onto the guilt very, very strongly and it doesn't help either one of you. You really need to let it go. And I really need to see you again before you leave, a little happier and with more energy."

"I was pretty happy when I came in," I commented, "but after this, I took another nose dive. I feel another depression coming on. But I realize, you've got to know what it is to deal with it."

"It's absolutely true," Janice agreed. "It's not easy work, but it's powerfully healing work."

"And do you want to know something else weird?" I asked. "Have you heard of Eugene O'Neill's play _Mourning Becomes Electra?_"

Janice shook her head.

"It's a modern adaptation of Sophocles' Electra," I explained. "She was Orestes' sister. In the last scene, Electra, dressed in black, closes the shutters in the family's house. She's the only survivor. From the first time I heard about Electra, I felt I was like her. In high school, I did a comparison between Sophocles' Electra and O'Neill's Electra. I've wondered whether I'd be like her in this life."

"You know, people tell me: 'Janice, if reincarnation is real, why don't we remember?' I think we do remember. What you've mentioned here are memories."

"We do remember, we just don't know it," I agreed. "I've always liked mountains and hated Greece. Now I understand why. And the thing with the herbs. Now I know where it comes from."

I made another appointment with Janice for December 31. I thought it would be a good way to end the year.

"Will you be OK driving back?" Janice asked.

"Don't worry," I assured her, smiling faintly. "I'm not going to crash into a utility pole, or anything. I'm spiritually awake enough to know that suicide is no solution. I sensed right away that Marcus and I met in this life for a reason. The first three regressions didn't give me a clue. This one did. We definitely have unfinished business. If we don't finish it now, we'll have to finish it in one of our future lives. I want to settle the score now, but he seems to be terrified of me. If this doesn't change, we'll meet in a future life, for sure."

"Belief in reincarnation changes your perspective, doesn't it?" Janice observed, smiling.

"Belief is of the mind," I noted. "This is something I know in my heart and in my soul."

We walked out into the deserted parking lot. It was almost 10:00 p.m.

"Let me give you a hug," Janice said. "I'll see you on the 31st. Take care of yourself."

"I will," I assured her. "Like the song says: 'Pick yourself up, dust yourself off and start all over again.' I've done it before, I can do it again."

I got in my car. I took a deep breath and started the engine. I recalled additional incidents that didn't make sense to me before, but did now. In 1983, during my visit to Delphi, I had stared at the statue of the Charioteer for a long time. I'm the type who usually races through museums, never being able to stay more than a couple of hours. As soon as I saw the Charioteer, however, I stopped in my tracks and stared transfixed. When I got tired of standing, I sat down cross-legged in front of the statue and stared some more. And who did I go to Delphi with? Beth, my mother in Classical Greece. In 1993, I felt compelled to give Marcus a chess set. I hadn't asked him if he knew how to play. I had asked if he wanted to play, to which he had responded, "I haven't played in so long."

I thought of Jason Sr., my ersatz father, and got goose bumps. I often fell asleep on the couch during the 11:00 p.m. news. Jason used to wake me, shouting, "Wake up Athenians. The Spartans are at the gate."

The first time he said it, I had sleepily asked, "Oh yeah? Says who?"

"The King!" Jason had thundered.

After that, we called Jason, The King. His last present for Beth, his wife in ancient Greece and 20th Century Philadelphia, was a pair of earrings with the Greek key carved in them. Unconsciously, he too remembered.

One reason I had decided to undergo past life regression was to explore the flashbacks Marcus had triggered. I also hoped to find the root of Marcus's fear and resentment of women. I reasoned that if Marcus and I were soul mates, we would have spent many lives together. Perhaps by exploring my past lives, I would uncover the life during which Marcus had been traumatized. Dr. Weiss had stumbled upon past life regression while treating a patient who had not responded to talk therapy or hypnotic regression of her current life. Not knowing what else to do, he had hypnotized the patient and told her to go to the time when the problem had started. The woman had gone to ancient Egypt. After this last regression, I was convinced that Marcus's distrust of and hostility toward women went back to ancient Greece. Helen, his wife, had betrayed him and our city and brought shame to our family. Probably, Aesop also resented his sister, Kyllini, for helping uncover Helen's treason. In this life, he had chosen a mother who had also hurt him, but against whom he had not rebelled.

It was interesting that Janice had asked Kyllini to look into Aesop's eyes and tell her what she saw. "Pain," she had said. In this life, I had looked into Marcus's eyes as he was hugging me and saw pain mixed with fear. I had attributed it to events in this life. Now, I knew it went beyond this life. I was concerned that Marcus's mother in this life was Helen's reincarnation. That would make for very difficult karma. I wondered if I would have recognized her essence just by talking to her on the phone. Marcus had read Dr. Weiss's book and found it intriguing. He might be open to undergo past life regression himself, or at least current life regression. I was convinced that the retrieval of missing memories was key to his healing. His avoidant personality and reluctance to try new things, however, were hindering his recovery.

I wanted to let Marcus know immediately that I had uncovered something terribly significant for both of us. I did not feel up to calling, however. At the same time, I did not want to hit him with the entire transcript in a letter. A telegram! That would be the ticket. Something like:

"VIP brother/sister scenario. STOP Full text/tape to follow. STOP Janet. STOP."

I would call Western Union first thing in the morning. Marcus would have the cable as soon as he walked into his office. I slept fitfully that night, finally getting up at 6:00. I waited until 7:00 to call Western Union. I felt tired, but I quickly dismissed the thought of taking the day off. I needed to get to the office to get my mind off things. Besides, I did not want Leah to suspect something was wrong. The latter had moved in the previous Sunday and had enough problems of her own.

At home after work, I saw a message from Leah that almost made me faint.

"Western Union called. The telegram was delivered, but not received. Marcus no longer works there. Veeery interesting!"

A Washington D.C. address and phone number were included. I looked at the address: 2020 Pennsylvania Ave. N.W. That was not a residential address. I looked at the phone number. By the exchange, I realized the number belonged to someone in Georgetown. Marcus's friend, Bruce, lived in Arlington. There was that woman, Lisa Bayer, who had sent him the postcard in Tashkent. Maybe that was her number. I picked up the message and went upstairs. I lay on my bed and took a few deep breaths to calm down. Marcus had reacted to my hypnotic regressions, all right. Far more strongly than I had ever imagined. He had quit his plum assignment in San Francisco and had returned to Washington, while I was on my way to San Francisco. Whatever secret he was protecting, it was worth a whole lot to him. But what did he do with my books and tapes? Did he leave them in San Francisco the way he had left my skis in Tashkent? The worst went through my mind. Marcus was not acting like a rational person. Tomorrow, I would investigate, starting with the phone number and address. I had to get some sleep, first. I had to fortify myself for the face off with Marcus.

I woke up before dawn, shaken by another bad dream.

Marcus and I were in church at Christmas. The church was decorated with holly, poinsettias, and dozens of lit candles. The congregation was standing and singing Christmas carols. I felt euphoric. I turned to my left to look at Marcus. He was sitting sideways on the pew with his knees drawn to his chest, head on his knees, and arms around his legs. He was covered with a black tarp. My heart sank.

I woke up at that point. In interpreting the dream, I felt Marcus was at a place full of light and he had shut himself off from it. I waited until after eight to call the Georgetown number. The answering machine came on. The voice belonged to Sylvana Vargas! That scum bag was still jerking him around. I opened the Washington, D.C. phone book and located Vargas's listing. No address; just the phone number. Also, she was listed as Sylvan, giving the impression of being male. I walked out the door and headed for 2020 Pennsylvania Ave. Had Marcus quit the Foreign Service and gotten a job with the private sector? I would soon find out.

I knew exactly where 2000 Pennsylvania Ave was, but could not find 2020 Pennsylvania Ave. I asked one of the shopkeepers.

"I think it's where Mailboxes, Etc. is located," he responded.

I found Mailboxes, Etc. and asked if a Marcus Metamarro had a mailbox there.

"Yes, they do," I was told.

More bad news. If Marcus shared a mailbox with Vargas, his mail was not secure. Could I leave a message? No, I would have to mail it. I thanked the man and left. Next stop, the State Department's Office of Independent States and Commonwealth Affairs. I didn't even have to go that far. As soon as I went through the turnstile at the D Street entrance, I ran into Rob Howard, the head of the Central Asian Division in that office. He was coming up the escalator carrying a cup of coffee.

"Hi Rob. Do you happen to know the whereabouts of Marcus Metamarro?" I asked.

"I heard he's at the Korea Desk. He's going to the Japan Desk next. Great job. Bruce got a promotion out of it. San Francisco didn't work out. Tour guide job."

"So what?" I said, trying to keep my cool. "That's not why he was there. And he bailed out of the other thing too. But I'm going to be cool about it. I'm not going to blow my top."

"Oops," Rob said. "You and Marcus go way back, don't you?"

"Waaaay back," I emphasized. "Where's the Korea Desk?"

"Fifth floor, straight up," Rob informed me. "Come to my office. We'll call to make sure he's really there."

I didn't want to go to Marcus's office right away. I was afraid I would lose my temper and didn't want to make a scene in the Department. I headed to my friend Rajesh's office instead. He knew about my regressions and about Marcus. I wanted him to come with me to Marcus's office. I wanted a second opinion about Marcus's physical and psychological state. Rajesh and I walked up the four flights of stairs to Marcus's office. He wasn't there. I wrote on a piece of paper:

"So, this time you managed to curtail. I knew you would get the Japan job, as soon as I found out Bruce was in that office. Where's the box with my things? Please call. Janet."

The secretary didn't know where Marcus was or when he was coming back. We walked back down to Rajesh's office. He tried to console me.

"Forget about this guy. He's screwed up. Just take care of yourself."

"Raj, I can't forget him," I said. "He's a kindred spirit. I empathize with him. Could you call his number to see if he's back?"

Rajesh dialed the number and asked for Marcus. He nodded and gave me the receiver.

"I'm two floors below you," I said. "Do you have a few minutes?"

"Sure, come on up," Marcus sounded cordial.

I marched up the stairs to Marcus's office. He was typing with his back to the door.

"What's going on?" I asked calmly.

Marcus turned around to look at me.

"I called the forwarding number you left," I continued, "and got Vargas's voice mail."

Marcus shrugged. "That's where I'm staying."

"You're in love with HER?!!!" I exclaimed, incredulous.

"It's been wonderful," Marcus said, smiling. "I'm happy."

What you are, is full of shit, I thought. And this is not the answer to my question.

"Why did you curtail?" I continued.

"The job was boring. And now this," Marcus explained, smiling. "I drove all the way. I needed my car."

The way Marcus looked at me, as he uttered those words, sent shivers up my spine. He reminded me of Chester, my manic depressive former fiance, who drove thousands of miles to buy a lottery ticket. My God, he's insane, I thought.

"Where's the box with my things?" I asked calmly.

"It's with me, where I'm staying," Marcus explained.

"Did you listen to the tapes I sent you?" I continued.

"Why should I? Things are going well," Marcus shrugged again. He was trying to appear calm, but his eyes were full of fear. "I was up front with Sylvana about you," he continued. "She says the situation between us has to be resolved."

"We have unresolved issues," I said matter-of-factly. "I had a regression this past Tuesday that explained a lot. I visualized a cord linking us. Janice asked me to cut it and I couldn't."

"This stuff you're doing sounds very powerful," Marcus observed. "Is it helping you?"

"It's helped me a lot. It could help you too."

"Sylvana is skeptical about the soul mate stuff. I'm not so skeptical," he continued. "I read the book."

I don't give a fat rat's ass about that ugly dweeb's opinion, I thought. I want to know where you stand, but I doubt you'll spit it out any time soon.

Suddenly, I understood much more than Marcus could ever tell me. It made perfect sense for him to hook up with someone like Vargas. She took over where his exploitative, passive-aggressive mother had left off. I felt very sad. Marcus was in worse shape than I had imagined. I felt he was controlled by sinister forces, of which Vargas was a part. He had left San Francisco like a thief in the night three weeks before Christmas. He did not have the courtesy to tell me he was leaving and that he was taking my things with him. I did not feel I could have a rational discussion with someone, who, over a two-year period, had demonstrated that his thought processes were impaired. He needed professional help. Just at that moment, there was a knock on the door. The secretary opened it and stuck her head in.

"Your eleven o' clock is here," she said.

Marcus smiled at me and shrugged again.

"We're far from done," I said, as he got up to greet the visitor.

I left Marcus's office, trying to find the silver lining in this cloud. For one thing, with Marcus out of San Francisco, I could concentrate exclusively on myself. For another, Marcus could learn something useful from his involvement with Vargas, assuming he survived. People learn the most in relationship. I went out the D street entrance and got on the shuttle bus to Rosslyn. My office had moved to a State Department annex there. Probably nobody would miss me, if I didn't show up. I had already parceled out my portfolio, and it was Christmas party time. Hardly anybody was at work.

I called Janice Cummings from my office. I wanted a professional opinion on Marcus's behavior. I left an urgent message on the answering machine. Then, I called Sylvana Vargas. I wanted to hear her side of the story. Another answering machine. These machines work great, except when one needs to talk to a human being.

I returned a number of phone calls and answered questions for the colleagues who had taken over my portfolio. Before I knew it, the work day was over. I walked the two blocks to the metro station. During the ride home, I thought about my approach to Marcus. I would wait until I heard from Janice before I decided. The phone was ringing as I walked into the house. I ran to answer it. It was Janice. I explained the situation and my interpretation of it, leaving out my suspicions about Vargas's character.

"Marcus is putting physical distance between us. By moving into Vargas's house with my things and telling her about me, he's putting emotional distance between him and her. This way, nobody can touch him."

Janice agreed. "He needs help. Do you think he might want to see me?"

"I'll suggest it. He can have my slot on the 31st. In the meantime, can you call him up and tell him this?"

I gave Janice Marcus's office and home phone numbers. Janice promised to call.

"One thing is for sure," I told myself as soon as I hung up the phone. "My life is never boring. Let's see what comes next."

I copied the tape of the last regression. I planned to mail it to Marcus with a note explaining why he should listen to it. The following day, I stopped by the post office on my way to work and mailed the tape. I called Vargas again. I got an answering machine. It appeared that Vargas was screening her calls.

She must be the brains behind Operation Stonewall, I thought. Marcus is too rattled to think rationally. She figures I'll go to California in a couple of weeks and the whole thing will blow over. I think Ms. Vargas is ripe for a little consciousness raising. I called her alleged home number and left the following message:

"This is a message for Marcus: I love you unconditionally and pray that your tortured soul find peace. But how can you find peace when you run from place to place, and person to person? He knows who this is."

Then, I wrote Vargas a letter asking her not to break Marcus's heart because that would break mine, too. I wrote that I felt a strong connection to Marcus, which had been confirmed by four past-life regressions. I loved Marcus at the soul level, but his personality left a lot to be desired. For over two years, I had tried unsuccessfully to get him to talk about his feelings. I ended my letter by wishing Vargas good luck.

As much as I tried to see the silver lining in the situation, I was extremely upset at the turn of events. My body reminded me of that. My whole back became very stiff and painful. I found it difficult to bend over. I had to release that negative energy, but, somehow, I could not cry. I had to laugh, then. I visualized Marcus in the missionary position with Vargas and started to laugh hysterically. I laughed so hard, tears were streaming down my face. Marcus sleeping with Vargas seemed to me as improbable as the sun rising in the West. Their energies were too dissimilar. It would be the equivalent of a hummingbird mating with a hen. The first time I met Vargas, the picture of a hen had flashed through my mind.

I wiped my tears and started thinking about Marcus's behavior. Given the choice between work and play, he chose work. He curtailed an easy assignment at a fun place in favor of another hectic assignment. He had opined that sexy, blonde Diedre was out of his league and wanted me to believe that he was romantically involved with ugly, inhibited Vargas. I believed he was being brainwashed by someone with ulterior motives. Marcus's fear was palpable, as were his lack of freedom of movement and association. I also felt he was trying to protect me, but I still wanted to get to the bottom of his nutty behavior.

I took out the letter Marcus had sent me in October and copied it. On the copy, I circled the part about him feeling the need to find out who he was and how a year in San Francisco would help him in that effort. On the margin, I wrote: *"What happened to that plan?"*

On the back page, I wrote:

"You quit your job, left your family three weeks before Christmas, and drove cross-country like a lunatic. Were you consumed by passion for Sylvana? What are the WAC people going to think? Is this what your soul needs to progress? God sent me to you to pester you until you shape up. I promise I will do it. And if you ever get serious about looking for a wife, here's the recipe: 'One third Mother Teresa, one third Sigmund Freud, and one third Attila the Hun.' The last ingredient is necessary to keep you from acting like a jerk."

On a separate piece of paper, I wrote.

"I will be at the Silver Spring metro at 12:30 p.m. on 12/31. I will wait until 1:00 p.m. If you don't show up, I will go to the Department's chief shrink and say that you're unstable. I have written statements by you that are contradicted by your actions."

I stapled the latter piece of paper on one of Janice's cards. The date and time of the appointment I had made for him were written on the back of the card. I put everything into an envelope, sealed it, and wrote Marcus's name on the front. I sat on my bed and looked at the envelope. I can't give it to him, I thought. It's too harsh. But he really needs help. I think he's flipped out. I thought some more. I'll go to his office first thing Monday morning. If he looks happy and content, I will not give it to him. If he's on pins and needles, I'll give it to him.

Leah interrupted my thoughts. She called out from downstairs that she wanted to buy a Christmas tree. We got into her car and drove the half mile to the corner tree lot. We picked out a nice, full Douglas fir and brought it home.

I spent the weekend running errands. I would be away for Christmas. I had two more weekends after that before I left for California. Saturday, I made a run to the Eastern Shore to deliver my Christmas presents for the family. Sunday morning, I told Gerry about our unhappy life in ancient Crete.

"I think this is the main reason you're dead set against having children with me," I said. "In that life, I neglected our child. Memories of that are in your unconscious."

Gerry did not have any comments. He barely looked over the Sunday paper. I left him to his paper and went home. On Sunday afternoon, an express package arrived. It was the box of stuff I had mailed to Marcus in California. I looked at the sender's address and the date. It was the Mailboxes, Etc. address and the date was Friday, December 16. Marcus had mailed me the box the same day I had mailed him the tape of my last regression. I decided not to open it. There could be a message inside that would derail my plan.

Monday morning, I left my house one hour early. I wanted to be at the State Department at 8:30. Meetings usually started at 9:00, or later. Marcus would be just coming in then. My timing was perfect. I walked into Marcus's office as he was sitting down at his desk.

"Good morning," I said smiling.

One look at him and I knew this was not the picture of a happy, peaceful man.

"Hi, Janet," he said, looking at me sadly.

He did not seem surprised in the least to see me. I handed him the ultimatum.

"Goodbye," I said brightly, and walked out.

I felt so energized, I did not take the shuttle to Rosslyn. I walked over Memorial Bridge and through Arlington Cemetery. The cold air invigorated me and cooled my flushed face. I wondered if Marcus would call to comment on my note. I doubted it. I imagined his marching orders came from Vargas and they involved stonewalling. An immense feeling of sadness came over me as I thought of Marcus. He had chosen a hard life this time around. I hoped it would not end the way it had ended in ancient Greece. As for myself, I was certain that I would not opt for suicide, as I had then, regardless of what Marcus did.

I had to admit, however, that love without attachment was very difficult. I had gotten out of the picture when Marcus told me that he and Hilda were still in love. That was plausible. A love affair with Vargas was not. Instead, it pointed to Marcus's involvement in Vargas's nefarious activities. His refusal to face me and his rushed, cross-country drive in the middle of winter showed that something very big was at stake.

I knew that at the soul level Marcus and I loved each other. Our personalities, however, were entangled in this nerve wracking earth drama that caused us to lose sight of our true selves. I wanted the truth from Marcus. How could I give up on that? It was just as well he had left San Francisco before I had gotten there. He would not be any fun, anyway.

At the office, I waited until noon, took a deep breath, then called Marcus's mother in Oakland. I felt compelled to call the next of kin. Marcus needed help immediately.

"Mrs. Metamarro?" I asked, when a woman responded.

"Yes," a female voice answered tentatively.

"This is Janet Bradley. If you recall, I called a year and a half ago when Marcus was medevaced."

"Yes, yes, I remember," Eleanor Metamarro seemed to relax.

"Marcus did something crazy and I made an appointment for him with a therapist," I came right to the point.

"Marcus? My son, Marcus?" Mrs. Metamarro exclaimed.

"When was the last time you saw him?"

"Two weeks ago."

"Did he seem OK?"

"Well, yes," Mrs. Metamarro answered cautiously.

"Didn't you think it was strange for him to quit his job and drive cross country three weeks before Christmas? He had looked forward to that job and had not spent Christmas with you in at least two years."

"Well, no. He's an adult," Mrs. Metamarro said. "He said there was someone in Washington. We understand. I can give you his phone number, if you like."

"I have his phone number," I replied. "I saw him this morning and he seemed upset. I put pressure on him to get therapy. I have been consulting for two years with a psychologist friend, who believes he needs help."

"Were you lovers?" Mrs. Metamarro asked.

"No. He's afraid of intimacy. I can tell you much more about his behavior, if you like."

Mrs. Metamarro became defensive.

"He's been in therapy. Who hasn't? You can't make him go. Our children are adults, we don't interfere in their lives," she said abruptly.

I changed the subject.

"I lent Marcus a book entitled *Mothers, Sons, and Lovers*. Reading it upset him. Do you know why?"

"I know the book. He gave me a copy."

So that's how Marcus had confronted his mother. He gave her a copy of a book and skipped town. And his mother was keeping her mouth shut, as best she could.

"Someone in the family should talk to Marcus," I continued. "I don't think it should be you, though. Which one of his brothers gave him a set of tapes entitled Creating Love?"

"His oldest brother," Mrs. Metamarro replied.

"This brother should talk to him, then. Marcus is going through a difficult time right now. He needs all the support he can get."

"We will make a note of this. Marcus seems to want to distance himself from you," she added icily.

"And also from you," I remarked. "He does that every time a woman tries to get close to him. If he doesn't get help, he'll have a very lonely and unhappy life."

I concluded the conversation by giving Marcus's mother Janice's name and phone number. It was evident that I could not have a frank exchange of views with Marcus's mother. Maybe a letter would be the way to go. I prepared a packet for Mrs. Metamarro. I included some of Marcus's letters and cables that shed light on his character. I waited until the afternoon of the 22rd to mail it. I wanted to make sure that it would get there after Christmas. Then, I went home. Christmas Eve, I would drive to Upstate New York for my last Christmas with Gerry and his family, but my mind was already in California.

At home, I opened Marcus's package. It contained the books, tapes, and photographs I had mailed him the previous month. The Christmas presents had been opened. The two Chopra tapes were missing. Four other books I had lent him were also missing. I read his note. It was not as virulent as the one he had sent me in May. Icy and self-righteous was a better description. The underlying feeling, however, was unmistakably fear. In addition, he had lied again. How did I know? By analyzing his handwriting.

Marcus claimed to be happy and at peace, but his handwriting contradicted him. His baselines were fluctuating, indicating moodiness. His slant was all over the place. It went from slightly reclined, to vertical, to slightly inclined, showing emotional instability. The narrow, closely placed letters and angular connections showed someone who was extremely tense and closed to new ideas. The curl of concealment was present in the lower q and y zones, showing he was keeping secrets. I did not believe for a minute that he was in love with Vargas. If anything, she inspired fear. It would take intensive psychotherapy for him to get over the psychological damage she had caused. At the same time, I knew that everything happened for a reason and that I had to trust God's plan. I was sure that a lesson in patience for me was part of that plan.

"Why do I care if Marcus gets well or not?" I wondered. "I could still marry Gerry. Our friends and families, would like nothing better. We could announce our engagement over Christmas and have a June wedding. Gerry is reliable, predictable, and honest. I won't be wildly happy with him, but I won't be entirely miserable either. Why not marry Gerry?"

There was no other reason, other than the little voice inside me that screamed its objection and the knot in my stomach every time I visualized my wedding to Gerry. I had to honor that voice. That voice had told me there was something wrong with Chester before there were any symptoms of the bipolar disorder. That voice was telling me Marcus would be all right in the end and that we would be happy together. It seemed impossible at the moment, but the voice had never lied before.

I sighed, picked up the package, went upstairs, and stashed it in the closet with the wrapping paper. I took out my ski bag and started packing it with ski clothes and other warm clothing. I would miss the White Christmases in Upstate New York. Gerry's family went all out for the occasion. The pile of presents was almost as big as the tree. There were enough cookies and fruitcakes to feed an army. To me, however, the most attractive thing was the white stuff outside the door. It was heaven to roll out of bed in the morning and go for a ski tour before breakfast. Ice skating was also possible, either on lake Ontario, or in the rink in town.

Having finished packing, I inspected my Christmas presents. Because of the aborted Bosnia trip, I had finished shopping in November, but had not wrapped everything. I finished wrapping the last presents and put them in a big shopping bag. I debated whether I should go to work the next day, or not. Nothing was really going on and according to tradition, everyone would be dismissed at noon. It almost wasn't worth the metro fare. I would see how I felt in the morning. I read a bit, did a meditation, and went to bed.

At 3:30 a.m., I woke up from a sound sleep to the most bizarre and exhilarating experience of my life. I felt the presence of an energy field enveloping my body. The feeling was electric. And there was no mistake as to whose energy that was. It was Marcus's. The cool, reserved Marcus was all over me, and it felt divine. I felt the energy move from my face to my breasts and hips all the way down to my toes. Then, I felt it moving up my legs and into my vagina. I must be dreaming, I thought. But how can I be dreaming with my eyes wide open?

Then, I felt the thrusting. It was the most exhilarating lovemaking I had ever experienced, in this life. I had multiple orgasms, and felt like I had died and gone to heaven. When I felt the energy dissipate, I looked at the clock: 4:00 a.m. The experience had lasted half an hour.

After my head had stopped spinning, I looked for a logical explanation for this astounding experience. Why not? I thought to myself. I feel Marcus's energy around me all the time. This is how I know how he feels and can detect his lies. He was probably dreaming about making love to me, so he projected his energy here, and it did what his waking personality is terrified of doing. Since the personality was asleep, there were no inhibitions and he was fantastic. The question is will he remember any of this when he wakes up?

Just in case, I got up, changed the sheets, put on my silk night shirt, and straightened out the room. I went back to bed, but sleep was out of the question. I recalled the time I had first sensed a struggle going on inside Marcus. I had thought, at the time, that maybe he was trying to decide whether he was gay or straight. After this experience, however, I opted for another explanation. Marcus was torn between his attraction to me and something fear-producing. Was it fear of sex? Had he been molested as a child and had repressed the memory? The repressed memory was only one of the problems. The other problems were his fear of uncovering the memory and dealing with it and the Vargas mind and movement control. Damn that woman. By choosing to associate with her, Marcus was delaying his healing process. What were her motives, though? Did she want a green card so she could bring her mother to the States, or was she after something much bigger? I fumed at the thought of her using Marcus. Then I calmed down.

"Hey. He's a smart guy and he's pushing forty. At some point, he should be able to make his own decisions and quit being a puppet on somebody's string."

A smile spread across my face.

I hope he has more dreams like this, I thought. I wonder if there is anything I can do to help the process along. One thing I can do is learn how to induce out of body experiences at will. Then, I can return the favor he did me tonight. I have to learn more about dreams, anyway.

One thing was for sure. I would skip work today. I would bask in the afterglow of this fantastic experience, then try to catch some more sleep. I waited until 9:00, then called Rita. As I had expected, everyone was going home at noon. I asked Rita to charge me three hours annual leave and wished her Happy Holidays. Then I called Janice. The latter was more advanced in metaphysics, so she might be able to explain my paranormal experience. Fortunately, Janice was at the office.

"Am I glad you're in!" I gushed. "You won't believe what happened to me this morning!" I described my experience as best I could. "What do you make of this?" I asked Janice.

"It may be the Kundalini energy rising," Janice suggested.

"From what I've read, the Kundalini goes from the bottom of the spine up," I said. "This felt like something enveloping me, then like a ghost making love to me. I have never heard of people having orgasms from the Kundalini energy. Have you?"

Janice had not heard of anything like that either.

"It's my karma to blaze trails," I laughed. "So far, I have done this in the physical sphere. Now I'm branching out into metaphysics. I can't wait to find out what's next."

"By the way," Janice said. "I called Marcus at both the numbers you gave me, but he never returned my calls."

"That's Marcus for you," I observed. "King of Stonewall. I didn't really expect anything different. Maybe a miracle will happen next week, and he will show up for the appointment. I'll be there, though."

Christmas Eve arrived. I was not ready to walk out the door as soon as Gerry arrived, which met with his disapproval, but the drive was not as bad as I had feared. I was looking forward to California, so I was in a good mood. Once in a while, I would visualize Marcus in bed with Vargas and would burst out laughing. If his waking self only knew what his sleeping self could do, Marcus would be easily cured. Gerry was looking at me, wondering what was going on.

"I just thought of something funny," I explained.

We arrived in Watertown just before dinner. Christmas Eve dinner would be at Gerry's parents and Christmas dinner at his sister's Tracy's house down the road. Gerry's family knew that I was headed for California, although I had made it clear that this was not a permanent assignment. I felt, though, that at some point I should let them know that I had no intention of marrying Gerry. He and I had started dating when Tracy's children were in High School. Now both of them had graduated from college and were married. The eldest even had a child. And Gerry and I were still dating. My decision not to marry Gerry was confirmed as we were sitting down to Christmas dinner.

"You sit here, Tammy," Tracy told me.

Tammy was Gerry's ex-wife. They had been divorced for fifteen years. Tracy immediately apologized, but I thought, that does it. I'm out of here. I would save my announcement for some time after Christmas.

The time came the following day. I told Gerry's mother that I was looking for a foot locker to ship some things to California. Rose said that she was going downtown anyway and offered to drive me to the army surplus store. On the way over, she sought investment advice from me. Her husband was awfully conservative and kept their money in a savings account. That got me going.

"Like father like son. Furthermore, after fifteen years, Gerry still has Tammy's name on his account. If she wanted to, she could clean him out."

Rose was shocked. "No!" she gasped.

"Yes. Gerry's risk aversion is driving me crazy. He's a smart man, but he's losing thousands of dollars every year by keeping his money in a bank account. This is only one of the things we fight about. Another is that he doesn't talk. I'm supposed to read his mind, and if I don't read it right, he gives me the cold shoulder. I could never marry him. We would fight constantly."

Rose understood. "The Haases don't talk," she confirmed.

I was relieved that announcing my intentions had been so easy. At the army store, I found something better than a foot locker: soft trunks. They were like huge duffel bags made of canvas. I bought three of them. I could take them on the plane. The charge for excess baggage should be cheaper than shipping separately. With this chore out of the way and a few ski tours under my belt, I flew back to Washington on the 28th. Gerry would drive back on the 31st.

Marcus's appointment with Janice was at 1:30, on the 31st. As I had written in my note, I showed up at the Silver Spring metro at 12:30. I waited for half an hour, reading the paper. Marcus did not show up. I drove to Janice's by myself. The latter was opening the door to the building, as I drove up.

"It's only you," she remarked.

"You didn't really expect Mr. Avoider to show up, did you?" I said.

"You never know what the Universe might bring you," Janice observed.

We walked to Janice's office.

"How do you feel?" Janice asked as soon as I sat down in the recliner.

"Considering all the stuff that's happened in the last two weeks, I feel pretty good," I said. "I sure hope what you try out on me today will not change things."

"Only for the better," Janice assured me.

She turned out the lights, lit the candle, and put me through the relaxation routine.

"As you feel deeply relaxed, I want you to imagine a white light coming down from above your head, surrounding and protecting your body and mind. This is the universal light energy, the light of the Buddha and the Christ consciousness, and the Ascended Masters. Sense and feel the light protecting you and bringing you to a higher level of understanding. Allow yourself to relax and go deeper, and deeper. Now I want you to sense, feel, imagine, or picture in any way that you can, Marcus standing before you. And as you sense and feel him, I want you to be aware of energy connections between the two of you. You may view them as lines, cords, or ropes. And whenever you have this image, I want you to tell me what you sense."

"It's like a spider web," I said. "There are many, many lines around us and between us. They seem to be made of gold thread."

"Good, good. Now, I want you to begin to view where the strongest connection of this web is to your and Marcus's body."

"The middle of my forehead and Marcus's heart," I replied.

"OK. Good," Janice said. "Now as you view this, I want you to allow yourself to go deeper and deeper. Relax. I want you to bring to you a light, a transmuting flame, or an energy that will assist in disconnecting from the webbing that ties the two of you together. And I want you to understand that you are not disconnecting from the soul of the person, you are not disconnecting from the loving energy between the two of you, but you are disconnecting from the compulsive energetic connection that can result in excessive thinking or overemotional ties to the other person. Are you ready to do that?"

"Uh huh," I agreed.

"Now start disconnecting the webbing around you, particularly in the area around your forehead. If that is accomplished, let me know."

"The flame is not strong enough," I said after a long pause.

"OK. Then, I want you to begin to ask for assistance," Janice said. "I want you to allow a spiritual teacher, or spirit guide, or someone from that dimension to come to you to assist. And whenever that happens, let me know."

Another long silence.

"Yeah. There is someone," I whispered. "He's an old man, wearing a white robe. He has a long, white beard and carries a sword. He says his name is Theodore. I don't know any Theodore."

"OK. Good. Now I want you to feel the loving energy of Theodore's sword as he is disconnecting the ties that link you psychically to Marcus, particularly around the area of the forehead. And I want you to feel the loving energy moving into your forehead. And when that is completed, let me know."

"He doesn't have the strength to cut the cord," I said.

"OK. Recognize that you need to assist him by letting go," Janice instructed. "Just let go to greater freedom and greater love for your own spirit."

"I can't visualize it," I said, frustrated.

"Give yourself more time," Janice persisted. "A lot of the problem here is in your letting go and your willingness to allow the loving energy to flow freely between you, without cords, ties, or webbing. Without the energy pull that is inhibiting you."

I was silent for a few minutes.

"What is happening now?" Janice wanted to know.

"Nothing much," I replied. "The cord bounces back like elastic."

"OK. I want you to listen for a message from Theodore. Ask him why you keep drawing the web back to you," Janice instructed.

Quite a few minutes passed before I responded.

"I guess it's because I feel he's part of me."

"Yes," Janice concurred. "I want you to recognize that in disconnecting the ties, you're not disconnecting the soul connection you have to this person. You are only disconnecting the psychic energy that ties you to him, so that both of you can be freer. He must be free to have his own experience, so that he can grow. As long as you're carrying the energy for him, it's not benefitting either one of you. It's OK to let it go."

After a long silence, I said: "OK. I think I've done it."

"I want you to take a moment to surround yourself with healing light, especially in the area of your forehead, the third eye. Allowing greater love of yourself, and your own needs, and your own growth. Before I bring you back into the room, I want you to ask Theodore if he has a message for you."

It took me a long time to reply. Finally, I said, "He says there has to be free will. I can't force anything."

"Good, good," Janice sounded pleased. "Please thank him for coming. I want you to know that when you need guidance, you can meditate and ask Theodore to assist you and remind you that there must be free will."

"I don't understand why the cords were different today," I said, as soon as I opened my eyes. "Two weeks ago, I just saw one cord made of light. It felt kind of nice. It was not constricting. This web was something else. It felt like we had gotten tangled up even more."

"A lot of things happened in the last two weeks," Janice observed.

"Yes," I said. "It's as if the more Marcus tries to get away, the stronger the ties between us get. I didn't like the web. It felt suffocating. I couldn't move. Maybe I needed to feel that way to let go. But I don't know how long this will last. A day has not passed since I met him that I haven't thought of him. I think the pull goes both ways, I'm not the only one doing it, especially after last week's experience. And who's Theodore? He has a fitting name though. Do you know what it means?"

"No," Janice said.

"It's Greek for gift of God."

Janice recommended some books that would assist in my growth. I wrote down the titles and authors. I knew I would find many more such books in California.

"Stay in touch," Janice said as we got up to leave. "Your story is very interesting. This is the first time I have come across two souls who have been together for so long. And I've been in this business for a long time."

"I certainly will," I assured her. "I don't know if I will do any more of this in California. I'm taking a pay cut, so I won't have that much money. I'll probably do more when I get back. You will still be here, won't you?"

"I don't have any plans to move," Janice said.

"Then I'll call you when I get back," I said.

We walked into the parking lot and hugged each other. I got into my car and gathered my thoughts. I felt much calmer than I had felt in the past two weeks. I had been programmed by my father to be possessive. Marcus was helping me reprogram myself. The web gave me a sense for how suffocating possessiveness feels. I wanted to feel free and independent. I had to allow others to feel the same way, especially the one I loved the most. I also had to learn to be patient. This was the other lesson Marcus was teaching me. I felt an outpouring of love toward him. I started the engine.

"If I told anyone that the man I love moved in with the female equivalent of Darth Vader and I love him even more for it, they would think I'm nuts. It goes to show you that everything is in our heads. We can choose to react one way or another. A less enlightened soul could have cursed Marcus out or physically assaulted him. I love him even more. I think I'm getting the hang of unconditional love. Not that it's easy, mind you."

In a few hours, a New Year would arrive. I looked forward to my California assignment. I felt blessed and full of joy. All was well with the world. I drove off singing my favorite Christmas carol: "Rudolph the red-nosed reindeer, had a very shiny nose....."

EPILOGUE
Healing and Speaking Out

I had a wonderful time in California, managing to extend my stay by six weeks. I taught three days a week. The rest of the time, I spent doing sports, studying psychology and alternative medicine, and going to personal growth workshops. The focus of my studies was the effect of childhood trauma on adult behavior and the mind/body connection. In addition to treating myself, I wanted to understand my parents and Marcus. I lived in a house adjacent to the Golden Gate National Recreation Area with its many hiking trails. The ocean was a mile away. I became fast friends with the owner, Grace, who also came from a dysfunctional family. I went hiking almost daily. My most eager hiking buddy was Nikko-San, the neighbors' Akita. Watching the sun set in the Pacific became one of my regular activities. Most weekends, I went skiing. In *1995*, the Sierras got the most snow they had gotten in forty years. I did the best skiing of my life until late May. I also got my SCUBA certification.

Being away from Gerry confirmed my decision that I did not want to marry him. I had to decide, however, whether I wanted to drive cross country with him. Gerry planned to arrive on July 3, but gave me the option to cancel. By July 1, the thought of driving cross country with fussy Gerry, became intolerable for me. I could barely stand driving 400 miles with him, how could I survive driving 3,000 miles? I called and asked him not to come.

"What the hell do you mean?" he exploded.

"I mean," I explained calmly "that I don't want to drive cross-country with you. Furthermore, I don't think we should continue as before when I get back. Things between us didn't work during the past ten years. It's unlikely they'll work in the future."

"You never loved me," Gerry said bitterly. "You played me for a fool. I was convenient and then became inconvenient."

"I loved you the only way I knew how," I said. "Why did you stick around for ten years, if you thought I didn't love you? Why didn't you say or do something?"

"I was hoping you'd love me some day," Gerry responded.

I was stunned.

"You love that other fellow, don't you?" Gerry continued.

"I do," I admitted, "but it's nothing physical. He's chronically ill and has no will to heal. He's afraid to relive his childhood trauma like I did. He lives with another woman now."

"I don't give a damn about the physical. It's the emotional tie that counts," Gerry shouted. "Are you going to drive with him?"

"No. I'm going to drive by myself."

"It's irresponsible for a woman to drive cross country alone," Gerry shouted. "Ship the car and fly."

I felt the blood rush to my head.

"This conversation has lasted long enough," I said calmly. "Goodbye."

I sat on my bed fuming. That male chauvinist! He had finally shown his true colors. For ten years, he had tried to mold me into his ideal woman, a cross between Peggy Fleming and Martha Stewart. He was blind to, and totally unaccepting of my wild, masculine side. I refused to disown part of my soul, so Gerry would feel content and safe.

"Do you know what your problem is?" a classmate, a bearded bear of a man had told me when I was an undergraduate. "You've got balls as big as your boobs."

I had laughed. "I don't consider that a problem," I had replied. "I consider it a compliment. Thank you very much."

Back then, my motto had been: "Mrs. after Ph.D." I didn't want to be like all those women who had quit the program to keep their families together. Now my motto is: "Will only marry someone who's worked on himself and is beyond gender roles.' In his book *I Don't Want to Talk About It*, Terrence Real calls the model of the breadwinner male and the comforting, compliant female traditional emotional pornography. He writes: "most pornography does play out in the arena of sexuality a broader male fantasy—a fantasy of women's boundless, joyful compliance." My feelings exactly. I would take this one step further and say that any system in which power is disproportionately concentrated in the hands of one person undermines the mental health of all members of the system.

After my return from California, I spent many weekends at the National Library of Medicine in Bethesda, MD studying personality development and disorders, childhood trauma, post traumatic stress syndrome, and addictions. I attended lectures and workshops by Brad Blanton, John Bradshaw, and Wayne Dyer and read books by Otto Kernberg, Jan Dirksen, Donald Dutton, Mic Hunter, Susan Forward, Patricia Love, Alice Miller and other mental health professionals. The first item on my agenda was to discover the nature of my father's psychological trauma. The second item was understanding Marcus, whose behavior closely matched that of my father. Then came understanding myself, relatives, friends, and colleagues.

My mother, who had lived and suffered with my father for 33 years, didn't know what caused her husband's suffering. His sisters were either unaware or unwilling to talk. Finally, after refusing to answer the questions in two of my letters, my uncle revealed the horror of my father's life. As a three-month-old, he had almost died of heat exhaustion when his mother left him, wrapped up in swaddling clothes, in the field she worked. His abuse and deprivation continued through WWII and Greece's post WWII Civil War. He never talked about what had happened to him, but spent a lifetime medicating his body and abusing his family. Usually, his ailments had no physical cause. My mother's inability to confront him, prolonged the suffering of the whole family and led to his early death.

My new found joy and happiness contrasts with the condition of most of my friends, who continue to suffer greatly. I'm still looking for someone who has had a happy childhood. Below is a partial list of my friends and acquaintances, all victims of childhood trauma. Their names have been changed to protect their privacy.

<u>Chester</u>: First of six children, born out of wedlock. He found out as an adult when his mother left a copy of her marriage certificate on the TV set. He and four siblings were diagnosed with bipolar illness in their thirties and forties and were

prescribed lithium. The sixth sibling refused to be tested.

Dick: Emotionally abandoned as an infant by depressed mother; repeatedly molested by female teacher at age fourteen. Two divorces. Addicted to alcohol, nicotine, spending. Dropped out of counseling, divorced wife no. 2, and married a compliant foreigner who spoke little English. Overdosed on antidepressants in early 1997.

Gerry: Distant father, smothering mother. Spent a lot of time alone with the farm animals. His first grade teacher told him he was slow. He still believes this, although he almost has a Ph.D. in engineering. An early marriage ended in divorce. He refuses treatment.

Jack: Emotionally abandoned by mother, verbally abused by father. Accident prone, suffered near death experience after an accident. Has abused drugs and sex, suffers from many physical ailments. Emotionally and verbally abused by Grace (repetition compulsion, folie a deux). Medicates body and has had some counseling.

Paul: Almost starved as an infant. Probably molested by sex addict father. Diagnosed with borderline personality and dissociative (multiple personality) disorder. Like his father, he's a sex addict. Has had some counseling, but refuses medication. In horrific marriage with Dorothy, which may end soon.

Roy: Estranged parents, smothered by mother. After decades of therapy, he overcame his fear of engulfment enough to get married for the first time at age 55. He's one of my heroes.

Warren: His father died when he was an infant. His mother left him with the grandparents, so she could get a job in another town. The grandfather beat him and a group of older girls molested him at age seven. Covertly depressed, cannot let anyone get close to him. Marriage ended in divorce. Refuses treatment.

Claire: Father died before she was born. Enmeshed with a resentful mother who told her she smoked heavily when she was pregnant with her, hoping to miscarry. Currently, in unhappy marriage. Treats physical ailments.

Connie: Grew up in emotionally and physically abusive home. Dropped out of prestigious college after suffering nervous breakdown. Originally diagnosed with bipolar illness; recently self-diagnosed borderline personality disorder. Has had decades of counseling and medication. Kidney function has been impaired as a result.

Dorothy: Parents divorced, has an emotionally and verbally abusive mother, was molested by store keeper at age nine. Dropped out of pre-med program to marry Paul. Suffers from various physical ailments and is frequently depressed. She has had counseling and has started process of divorcing Paul.

Grace: Daughter of violent, alcoholic, child molester father and emotionally abusive mother. Parents divorced when she was twelve, mother enlisted her to help raise younger siblings. Chronically depressed, addicted to work and spending, has abused alcohol and sex, suffers from mood swings and uncontrollable anger. Has been in a series of intense and unstable relationships. Never married. Has used geographic treatment (moved 2,000 miles away from home) and has had some counseling. Currently, refuses counseling and medication. Unaware of her fears of abandonment and intimacy, blames Jack for problems in the relationship.

<u>Kitty</u>: Frequently absent abusive father, physically and emotionally abusive mother. One brother died of alcoholism another dropped out of detox treatment. Briefly married to Dick. Chronically depressed, suffers from chronic pain. Medicates her body and is currently in counseling.

<u>Tara</u>: Incest victim. Suffers from depression, eating disorder, high blood pressure. Currently in counseling.

I've shared with some of the above my healing experience, my books and bibliography, and listen when they feel like talking. I treat the children in my life with the love and respect I did not experience from my parents and protect them from potential trauma. My reward is to hear them say: "It's so much fun when Janet is here."

I am enormously grateful to my aunt, maternal grandparents, and a neighbor who nurtured me when I needed it most: between birth and three years of age. I credit them and my strong spirit with my clean bill of mental health. Even as a small child I knew I was more than a little battered body, because I could leave my body (dissociate) to avoid feeling the pain.

And what of Marcus? He's again in a hectic overseas post after having had four hectic jobs in Washington in less than four years. This is my clue that he still uses addiction to work as a way of dealing with his trauma. Sylvana Vargas became Marcus's de jure spouse in a secret ceremony whose likely primary objective was to grant her permanent residence in the United States. Judging by her behavior since December 1994, she and the nefarious interests she represents continue to exploit Marcus's illness.

I pray daily that Marcus find the courage to heal and, in my heart, I know he will. I've sent him a lot of love over the past five years. All he has to do is let go of the fear, so he can take in the love. Fear and love cannot live in the same house. I miss his smile, laugh, and quick step, but I'm grateful that I no longer have to watch his suffering. This is one of the gifts he has given me. After our incarnation in ancient Crete, our spirits agreed to be joined. In subsequent incarnations, some of Marcus's spirit has been in me and some of my spirit has been in him. We are one. Those whom God has joined together no man can put asunder.

Silver Spring, MD, September 1998